BOARDWALK PLAYGROUND

THE MAKING, UNMAKING, & REMAKING OF ATLANTIC CITY

DAVID G. SCHWARTZ

WINCHESTER

Winchester Books
Las Vegas, Nevada

Boardwalk Playground:
The Making, Unmaking, & Remaking of Atlantic City

Paperback edition ISBN 978-0-9900016-2-1

Library of Congress call number F144.A8 S38 2015

Layout by David G. Schwartz
Cover refinement courtesy 15-North Inc.

Proudly designed and printed in the United States of America

Text set in Adobe Caslon Pro
Titles set in LT Nutshell and Champagne & Limousines

http://boardwalkplayground.com

For the people of Atlantic City—keep on dreaming.

And in memory of John Cianfoni, Chris Columbo, Skinny D'Amato, and Hank Tyner—Atlantic City originals, each of whom taught me so much.

"The Great Fire of 1902," "High Flyers," "A Civil Reunion," "The Great War and the Shore," "Speaking Easy," "Nucky's Alley, "Old Creepy Checks In," "Dimouts and Camp Boardwalk," "A Mighty Storm," "Gambling Takes a Dice," "Storm of the Century," "Convention Controversy," "The First Shot," "One More Time," "Jersey Hustle," "First in Line." "The Survivor," "Lord of the Boards," "The Wooden Way," "Home of the Punch," "Boardwalk Heavyweight," "A Central Attraction," "Showplace of the Nation," "Pier Pressure," "The Concrete Palace," "Garden Spot," "A Good Dining Deed," "Million Dollar Address," "The World's Meeting Place," "Organic History," "Seaside Skyscraper," "Kentucky and the Curb," "At the Five," "Eat Where They are Caught," "Diamond Dining," "In the Neighborhood," "First Family," "Making History, "The Dandy Mayor," "Field of Dreams," "Time Keeper," "'Pop' Quiz," "The Star Maker," "City Painter," "Boardwalk Emperor," "Political Juggernaut," "Lighting the Way," "The Sweetest Storm," "Dream of a Million Girls," "Rolling Merrily Along," "Trolleying Around," "An Atlantic City Original," "Curtain Up!," "Honor Guard," "The Easter Parade," "I'll Remember April," "Starting the Season," "'Twas the Season," "Spreading Enlightenment," "The City's Hospital," "Pride of the Vikings," "Fire Pirates," "Watching the Waves," "Ocean Marathon," "Hitting the Boards," "The Sport of Kings," "Flight Path," "The Shore's Lifeline," "From the Heart," "A Popular Pachyderm," "The City of Ventnor City," "A Resort Reborn," "Hail, Caesar," "Landing on Park Place," "Sand Blasted," "Touch of Gold," "Boardwalk Bunny," "Tropical Retreat," "Trump's Tower," "By the Bay," "Showboating by the Sea," "The Crown Jewel," and "Roads Not Taken" originally published in *Casino Connection* magazine.

"Another Ebb Tide" and "Coming Back Again" originally published in *Vegas Seven* magazine.

Contents

Two
Classic Hospitality

Three
Personalities

Acknowledgements

No one can write and publish a book without a great deal of help from others. Since this effort was compiled from work I did going back twelve years, I very well may have omitted some people who were enormously helpful; I apologize for any such lapses.

My gratitude begins with Roger Gros, publisher of *Casino Connection*, who had the vision to believe that his readers would be interested in a monthly slice of Atlantic City history. If it weren't for Roger hiring me to write a monthly column, I would never have found the time to do the research for this book, as close to my heart as Atlantic City history is. Roger also encouraged me to revise, extend, and publish my writings on Atlantic City as a book.

The Atlantic City Heritage Collections of the Atlantic City Free Public Library are an indispensable resource for Atlantic City history, and my thanks go out to the entire staff there, particularly Pat Rothenberg and Heather Halperin.

I was lucky to have Svetlana and Greg Blake Miller (who originally edited the *Vegas Seven* columns) of Olympian Creative edit my manuscript for me, Meg Daniel expertly index it, and ace photo editor Robert Rossiello help me with photographs. Atlantic City historian Allen "Boo" Pergament was incredibly generous with his great photo archive and his time.

This is as good a place as any to formally say thank you to everyone I worked with in Atlantic City—whether it was at the City of Ventnor City Beach Crew, the Peanut Shoppe, the Trump Taj Mahal, the Monaco Motel, or any of the other places that paid me to show up over the years. I learned more from some of you than I did in any school, and your heart, wisdom, and persistence inspires me every day.

I'd also like to thank all of my teachers at Atlantic City High School, particularly Peter Murphy, who got me started down the writing road. One of the real pleasures of writing this book was the chance to talk about people and places that have shaped me—thank you all for helping me get there.

To get the book into production, I ran a Kickstarter campaign. I'd like to thank everyone who contributed, particularly Adam Bauer, Mike Esfahani, Becky McBreen, Rob Taylor, Joseph Seliga, Bradley Tecktiel, Ricardo Rodriguez, Guy Humpage, Linda Weisenstein, Chris Resor, Bogan Painter, Jim Grasso, Ian Jay, Bob Glickman, Loren Kaiser, Peter Erickson, Harvey T. Enokida, Dave Smith, Roy Parpart, Kurt Rickhoff, Doug Montgomery, Andy Hoffman, Mark Wojtowicz, William Pittock, Brian Chevrier, Bill Palmer, William Gillingham, Tim & Michelle Dressen, Bo Bernhard, João Ramos Graça, Brandon Griffiths, Chris Davis, John & Ute Lowery, Dr. Taylor Joo, Joe Koltunowicz, Oliver Lovat, Jim Solyntjes, Peter A. Machon, Han Choi, Richard Greenberg, Daniel Kruszka, Chris Lynn, Jennifer Dunleavy, Danielle Mallek, and Mike Prescott.

Extra special thanks go out to Connor Knight, Barton Kroeger, Matthew Stanford, Jefferey W. Compton, Aaron J. Byram, Hunter Hillegas, Christian Carroll, Gordon Clark, Eric Rosenthal, and Don & Kiley Rawlins. Thanks everyone! You helped make this book happen.

And of course, my family has been there for me all the time. You are more important to me than anything else, and I love you forever.

Finally, my most acute gratitude at this unique moment is for you, my reader. Thanks for picking my book up and letting me into your head for a little while. I hope you like it.

Introduction

Growing up on the beach teaches you two things: change is a constant, but things come back. Nothing—the weather, the crowds, the shoreline—is stable. Some mornings you see dolphins sporting just past the breakers; others, the ocean just spits up seaweed and rotting clams. One day paradise, the next a pit. But if you miss your perfect wave, don't worry; another will roll in soon enough.

I grew up in Atlantic City, just like my parents. My grandparents moved there looking for opportunity and, since they all stayed, I suppose they found it. Born in 1973, I can vaguely remember what life was like before legal gambling came (some of my earliest memories are the implosions of old buildings like the Marlborough Blenheim to make way for new construction). But I came of age alongside the casinos.

Those were the years when Atlantic City seemed to have beaten the odds. New Jersey beach resorts were on their way out; nothing could bring back the visitors, the money, the jobs, the good life. Or could it? By turning to casinos, the city had defied the decline that reached from Cape May to Asbury Park. With enough hustle and enough money, even a beaten-down town could break the cycle and laugh in the face of history.

I first left Atlantic City for school, and left for good (for now, at least) in 2001 when I took the job I have now at the University of Nevada, Las Vegas. Because my work revolves around gambling and casinos, I found myself chronicling, at a distance, the goings-on in my birthplace: the rise of The Borgata, the challenges of competition, a new wave of development that broke too early.

Watching the present unfold, I was haunted by the city's past. As a kid I always had the sense of living in a city of shrunken grandeur. My grandparents and parents, surely, had been there for the glory days. The Boardwalk used to be more crowded, the people better dressed, the streets cleaner. There was still excitement—what kid doesn't like implosions and video game arcades—but everything that gave the city character, from the diving horse to the Easter Parade—was gone. Living with the ghost of a better past probably shaped my decision to get a degree in history and contributed to my appreciation of bygone days. So it was probably a given, once I'd decided to become a historian, that I'd write about Atlantic City.

I've talked about Atlantic City in a few of my books about gambling history, but that didn't satisfy my need to write more about my hometown. Luckily, I had a great outlet to do that kind of writing. I originally wrote many of these stories for *Casino Connection*, a magazine catering primarily to casino employees, a group I'm proud to have once belonged to. The question I asked myself before I wrote anything was: if I had ten minutes to sit next to someone in the employee cafeteria and tell them something they might want to know about the city's past, what would it be?

That pretty much sets the tone for this book.

Atlantic City has always been a fantastic place in the truest sense: yes, it was built from bricks and wood and reinforced concrete, but it was given life by, as they used to say, "ocean, emotion, and constant promotion." In other words, there was a lot of fantasy mixed in with the plain facts. Like my current home, Las Vegas, Atlantic City has always been something more than the sum of its parts.

For me the big discovery was that, born when I was, I hadn't "just missed" the golden age. Atlantic City had been sinking since before my parents were born, and even my grandparents had caught the tail end, if that, of the really good times. That's three generations living through a receding tide, mistaking the last wave for an increasingly-distant high water line.

So maybe in retrospect no one should be surprised that the big news in Atlantic City today is the decline of its casino industry. In 2014, four casinos (Atlantic Club, Showboat, Revel, Trump Plaza) closed, leaving just eight properties open. Some of them seem relatively secure, but most people think that more will be closing soon. There simply isn't enough gambling business to go around, thanks to newer and closer casinos opening around the region. In 2006, the city's casinos won $5.2 billion from gamblers; in 2014, that figure fell to $2.7 billion, a 47 percent drop. Midway through 2015, it looks to be falling even further. With that kind of shrink, it's a little surprising that it took so long for casinos to close. The surface cause of the decline—increased competition—did not come suddenly or without warning. Yet, in retrospect, those entrusted with the leadership of the city, the state of New Jersey, and the companies that own casinos were caught unaware, surprised that the tide had ebbed, although all the signs had been there.

While I'm not sure just what shape the casino business will take in Atlantic City in the future, I have no doubt that the city itself, notwithstanding media reports to the contrary, will survive. It's easy to look at shuttered gambling halls and into the faces of those who have been left not just unemployed but completely unmoored and conclude that the city has reached the end. But Atlantic City has faced adversity before and bounced back. Sometimes, it took longer than it should have (the first major proposal to legalize casinos came in 1936; voters ultimately okayed them forty years later), but—and this is the important thing—it always happened. It isn't always quick or painless, but people find a way.

In a few chapters, you'll get a sense of why I think Atlantic City will change and survive, and as you're reading, you might want to look at how some seemingly-crazy ideas in the past not only worked, but became iconic (a diving horse?). What seemingly implausible ideas can work in the 21st century? Once again, I'm not sure, but the people of Atlantic City have shown themselves to be so resilient and creative—and you're holding a book with the stories that proves this—that I can't believe they aren't out there.

What I'm trying to say is that, in addition to celebrating the past of Atlantic City, this book, I hope, might give us some cheer in the present and help inspire some ideas for the future. Our ancestors were much more clever and enterprising than we seem to give them credit for; I think they still have something to teach us all.

This book compiles the columns I originally wrote for *Casino Connection*, along with two articles I wrote for *Vegas Seven* and over a dozen new chapters that fill in a few blank spaces. The columns were originally written for an audience of casino employees and those around them; this isn't an academic book, and I have not footnoted or cited my sources. I have, however, included some notes on sources and a bibliography at the end of the book.

I have organized the book into five parts. The first part, "Rise, Fall, Rise, Fall," gives a brief tour of about two dozen major events and eras in Atlantic City's history. I start by telling the story of the city's founding, and end with a chapter considering its current state. This isn't a comprehensive history, but rather a look at selected events, with some chapters focusing on extended periods like the Great Depression and the exuberance of the 1980s, with others looking at a single occasion, like the catastrophic 1902 fire and the Abscam investigation, which threatened the integrity of Atlantic City's casino industry in its earliest years.

Part Two, "Classic Hospitality," looks at twenty institutions that defined Atlantic City for visitors in the pre-casino days. Here I talk about the history of the Boardwalk and the hotels, restaurants, and nightclubs that made Atlantic City the World's Playground, starting with the United States Hotel and all the way through White House Subs.

The third part, "Personalities," examines ten residents of Atlantic City that made a mark on the city. It isn't necessarily the ten most famous or influential local figures, but it is a selection of people who I thought readers would want to learn more about, people like Mayor Franklin Stoy (a major figure in turn-of-the-century Atlantic City) and legendary drummer Chris Columbo, who played with everyone from Fletcher Henderson to Louis Jordan in a career that spanned more than seven decades.

The fourth section, "The Community," is about local organizations—like the Beach Patrol and fire department—and institutions (jitneys, the Around-the-Island swim, Miss America). In the middle is a series of columns I wrote chronicling the major holidays during Atlantic City's classic era. It closes with an in-depth look at the history of Ventnor, Atlantic City's nearest neighbor.

The fifth and final part, "The Casino Capital of the East," has a short history of each of the city's fifteen casinos. Most of these originally appeared in *Casino Connection*, but I was missing a few, which appear here for the first time. In all cases, I have updated the history through today. Yhe Trump Plaza piece, for example, which originally appeared in the January 2010 magazine, focused mostly on the property's first years. Needless to say, I've updated it to reflect its closing; I've given most of the casino chapters, even those about places that didn't close, similar treatments.

The final chapter, "Coming Back Again," is based on a *Vegas Seven* piece that I wrote after a visit back home in 2013. I've revised it a little, taking advantage of the lack of space constraints to tell a little more of the story and to bring it up to date. I'll tell you this: it's the most unabashedly personal thing I've written about Atlantic City, and I can't think of a better note to end on. Whenever you read this book, I hope that chapter helps you understand the Atlantic City I've known all my life.

One last note: I chose the book's title, *Boardwalk Playground: The Making, Unmaking, and Remaking of Atlantic City*, for a few reasons. The most obvious is that it is a riff on the well-known HBO series based on Nelson Johnson's book *Boardwalk Empire*. It's reacting to the usual depiction of Atlantic City as an exotic setting with picturesque corruption. I guess that's a good story to tell, but it's not the one I want to share: I want to tell the story of the city that my family lived in, focusing maybe a little more on the highlights than the low points. I want someone who lives or visits there to read this book and walk away with a better appreciation of the city's past. That might be as simple as knowing that a place called the Ambassador used to be where the Tropicana is today or learning just who Bader Field is named for.

The title's also a reminder that, at its core, Atlantic City is a place where people came—and still come—to play. Is that splashing around in the surf while wearing bloomers? Betting on horses in a backroom? Promenading down the Boardwalk dressed in your Sunday finest? Sneaking a highball in a speakeasy controlled by Nucky Johnson? Having a family vacation at a classic hotel? Shooting craps? Grooving to live music on the city's newest pier? It doesn't really matter—it's all the same. People come to enjoy themselves. There's a reason why the place got away with calling itself the World's Playground for many years—because it really was.

Also, people raise their kids in and around Atlantic City, and that it doesn't have to be as adult-focused as it has been since the advent of casinos to really be itself. This tourist and gambler destination was the place where a lot of us grew up.

Finally, the subtitle summarizes everything I've learned about the city: it's been built up and torn down more than once, so it's not surprising to see it happen again.

I hope that this collection of Atlantic City stories conveys the scale and sweep of the city's past and everything about it that I find so fascinating. Whether you are reliving old memories or learning about the city for the first time, I hope these tales fascinate you, too.

One

Rise, Fall, Rise, Fall

The Doctor's Dream

A barrier island is probably not the best place to build a city, but something about Absecon Island—maybe those cool ocean breezes—has been luring visitors for hundreds of years. Eventually, that lure became so strong that a few visionary souls decided to live there permanently.

Who was the first person to visit Absecon Island? No one knows. The Lennai Lenape Indians didn't record what year they first set foot on the island, but at the time of European contact groups had been spending summers there for some time. British colonists showed no interest in settling the area, with few visits beyond the occasional whaling vessel stopping on what was then called Cedar or Absecon Beach to replenish its stocks. The island was first mapped in 1691, and various speculators had bought large portions of it, but there were no permanent settlers until 1783, just after the American Revolution had ended, when mustered-out lieutenant Jeremiah Leeds bought title to land on Absecon Beach.

Two years later, he moved there, clearing land and developing a small farmstead around what is now Arkansas and Arctic Avenues. Where shoppers now come to buy Adidas sneakers and Gap jeans, Leeds built the first permanent settlement on the island.

At the time, Absecon Beach was mostly, as its name suggests, beach: the area's famous fine sand was everywhere, punctuated by stands of oak, cedar, and holly trees and ponds, hills, and valleys. It seemed a wild, untamable land.

But Jeremiah Leeds found he liked Absecon Beach, buying as much of it as he could. By the time of his death in 1838, he owned more than a thousand acres, most of it bought at 40 cents an acre.

He didn't have many neighbors, which suited him fine, though he let mainlanders graze their cattle on his land.

Jeremiah Leeds's children and grandchildren formed the nucleus of a village on the island, which in 1842 celebrated its first wedding. Farms and pastures dominated the settlement, with those from the mainland irregularly rowing over to fish. Leeds' wife Millicent opened a tavern, Aunt Millie's Boarding House, which was the humble start of the tourist business on the island.

In 1850, Doctor Jonathan Pitney, an Absecon resident, began publicizing the merits of Absecon Beach as a health resort. In a series of letters to Philadelphia newspapers, he expounded his belief that salt air and fresh breezes could heal a variety of ailments. The problem was that there was no easy way to get to the island from Philadelphia—travel by stagecoach was slow and bumpy, as well as expensive. Anyone who could afford a trip to the shore would instead visit the established resort of Cape May, which could only be reached by boat or stagecoach.

Pitney wanted a railroad carved out of the Pine Barrens, running from Philadelphia to his little seaside paradise. He didn't sway public opinion, but he convinced glass and iron magnate Samuel Richards that a railroad certainly wouldn't hurt his Hammonton-area industrial works and might raise the value of his sizable land holdings. Through his influence in the New Jersey legislature, Richards was able to secure a charter for the Camden and Atlantic Railroad Company in 1852.

The company hired Richard Osborne to survey the route and construct the railway. As he was extending the tracks, changes began to sweep the small village on the island. In 1853, residents accepted Osborne's recommendation that the settlement be renamed Atlantic City. At the time, it was an act of wishful thinking—this was no metropolis, but it was a modern name that made perfectly clear what the main attraction was: the ocean waters.

In addition to surveying the railroad, Osborne lent his talents to the layout of Atlantic City. He designed the grid of streets and avenues that blanketed a flattened and filled-in island. With its avenues named for famous oceans and seas (Pacific, Atlantic, Arctic, Baltic, Mediterranean, Adriatic, Caspian) and states, Atlantic City promised a cosmopolitan appeal.

Atlantic City was officially incorporated on March 3, 1854; it extended only as far west as Iowa Avenue. The city was in the midst of a building boom that would see the construction of several hotels, including the United States, which, at its maximum size of 600 rooms, was the largest hotel in the nation for a time and was, at the start, the most significant building in the city. On May 1, Chalkey Leeds, son of Jeremiah, was chosen mayor in a meeting held in the United States Hotel; he was elected by 18 men, who dropped their ballots into a cigar box with a hole cut into its top.

The city was ready for the railroad. On July 1, 1854, the first train steamed out of Cooper's Ferry terminal in Camden. Two and a half hours later, it arrived at its destination—a makeshift terminal just across the bay from Absecon Island. Rowboats carried the 600 pioneers over the bay, where they boarded a second train, which took them to the United States, at Maryland and Atlantic Avenues. They were encouraged to enjoy the pleasures of the cool seaside on a warm summer day and given dinner in the hotel.

Getting visitors to the "city" was one thing; developing it was another. The Camden and Atlantic Land Company, an adjunct to the railroad, bought all of the land still owned by Jeremiah Leeds's heirs for $17.50 an acre—a decent return on Leeds' original investment, but a fraction of what the land would eventually be worth.

Atlantic City's first years were lean—Pitney's dreamed-of tidal wave of health-seeking visitors wouldn't materialize until first one, then two competing railroads led to a reduction in fares. Eventually, however, Jeremiah Leeds, Jonathan Pitney, and Samuel Richards were vindicated; Atlantic City became not just a regional seaside resort, but the "world's playground."

Free and Easy

In 1854, things moved quickly for Atlantic City. In the space of a few months in the spring and early summer, the tiny seaside town was incorporated, elected its first mayor, and, most importantly, was linked to Philadelphia via the Camden and Atlantic railroad. New hotels and a range of new businesses opened to cater to the throngs of visitors that would surely come.

Dr. Jonathan Pitney, who had been fighting for years to establish Atlantic City as a health resort, had been sure that, once the railroad was running, there wouldn't be enough rooms for all of the health-seeking vacationers. But, in the early years, he seemed to have been wrong. Those with the time and money to spend a week or more down the shore preferred the more-established Cape May. The truly well-off didn't think much of the newcomer, and with the cheapest fare on the Camden and Atlantic at $3 for a round trip, the masses of weary working-class Philadelphians couldn't afford the journey.

What's more, the city, despite its picturesque sand dunes and breakers, wasn't all that healthy. The salt marshes that bordered the island and the ponds that still dotted it bred mosquitoes and greenhead flies. The latter were a particular menace. Clouds of female flies darkened the skies, biting tourists and locals alike, and making the summer, at times, miserable for every warm-blooded creature on the island.

The city didn't take the insect problem lying down. In 1856, it embarked on a campaign to fill the ponds, level the hills, and extend the streets of the city, which in addition to expanding the city, would eliminate breeding grounds for summertime pests. This was a definite public good, but, as would be the case in the city's future, someone had an angle. Reportedly, the city simultaneously hired one man to flatten a hill and a second to fill in a pond. The first man simply got in touch with the second, giving him a ready source for clean fill and pocketing a nice paycheck for his own hard work. This might have been the first hustle in Atlantic City's government, but it certainly wasn't the last, and it set the tone for much of what followed: there was easy money to be made, if you had the right angle.

The process of evening out Absecon Island was slow. The summer of 1858 was particularly bad: horses, bleeding from greenhead bites, lay down in the street and refused to continue; cattle, driven mad by the stings, threw themselves into the surf; and people burned bonfires around and sometimes inside their homes to drive the insects out. Eventually, though, Atlantic City got the upper hand, and greenheads became a nuisance rather than a menace.

The outbreak of the Civil War in 1861 robbed the city of any traction it might have been gaining; the area's resources were diverted to meet the needs of the Union, and the fighting, though it remained far from the shore, didn't exactly stoke tourism. After the war's 1865 end, Atlantic City resumed its modest growth, ready to establish itself as a summertime destination in a newly reunified and growing country.

By the end of the 1860s, the city could boast four "first class" and eleven "second-class" hotels which, together with 15 boarding houses, took in the summer visitors. Business remained seasonal, with not just businesses but even two of the city's three churches closing during the winter months.

Part of what held the city back was what had created it: the railroad. It took more than two hours to get from Philadelphia to Atlantic City, and the cars, which lacked sealed windows, were overwhelmed by dust and soot. Some took to wearing oversized dusters over their clothes to remain somewhat pristine, but in the early years it took a hardy soul to ride the rails.

Yet, by the late 1860s, Atlantic City was catching on. A correspondent for the *New York Tribune*, writing in 1867, described the joy with which locals greeted his train when it arrived at nightfall: bands played, landlords, clerks, and waiters smiled expectantly, and a host of well-dressed men and women welcomed the visitors. "It is worth a trip here," he wrote, "to see how thoroughly happy human beings can be under favorable circumstances.... What a free and easy, devil may care look they all have!"

With that welcoming attitude, Atlantic City slowly emerged as a summer resort, with the beach its major attraction. At this point, the crowds became something of a problem; shopkeepers and hotel owners, annoyed by visitors' tendency to track beach sand inside their businesses, wasted little time in devising a solution: the world's first boardwalk, which debuted in 1870.

By 1871, the city was popular enough that a regatta, pitting thirty boats against each other in three days of racing, was held—the first major special event successfully conducted in the city. Culminating in a "grand masquerade ball," the regatta might have been the moment that Atlantic City finally arrived as a legitimate seaside destination.

The railroad, though, held the key. Improvements from the Camden and Atlantic, chief among them glass windows, made the trip much more comfortable. In 1877, a second line—the Philadelphia and Atlantic City—started operations after a 90-day track-laying blitz. This narrow gauge road had considerably fewer creature comforts than the Camden and Atlantic, but fares were half the cost. The $1 daily excursion fare, well within the reach of working-class Philadelphians, made a trip to the shore a reality for thousands of new tourists. When, in 1880, a direct route to New York City opened courtesy of the West Jersey Division of the Pennsylvania Railroad, Atlantic City was well on its way.

Atlantic City wasn't an overnight success; for its first 15 years, the city barely scraped by. But thanks to the contributions of local businesses and far-sighted railroaders, Atlantic City put itself on the map.

Queen of the Coast

With two, then three, railroads competing for fares in the 1870s, Atlantic City started to attract more visitors. For the most part, they were not drawn to the city as an exclusive health resort, which had been Jonathan Pitney's original vision, but because it was easy to get to and not overly expensive (perhaps a good lesson for 21st century Atlantic City).

In 1874, a *New York Tribune* writer described Atlantic City's advantages as "cheap and easy access; comfortable living at moderate prices; and a particularly dry and healthful atmosphere." Day excursions from Philadelphia cost only $1.50, with group discounts for churches, Sunday schools, and other organizations. Furthermore, trains ran the length of the city, letting overnight visitors get off right in front of their hotels.

By that year, there were three "major" hotels, with well over 100 rooms each: Congress Hall, the United States, and the Surf House, supplemented by dozens of smaller hotels and boarding houses and an amazing 500 cottages. Some of the hotels that later dominated Atlantic City, like the Chalfonte, Traymore, and Dennis, started in these years as cottages or small rooming houses.

Some of the city's early progress would today be taken for granted. The first brick building on the island was constructed in 1878—it was Reed's drug store at the corner of Atlantic and Delaware Avenues. With fire a common hazard, brick was a wise investment, and it soon spread.

Yet there remained much to be done. Before the 1870 construction of the Boardwalk, there was no definite division between city and beach—the cottages and boarding houses simply petered out a few hundred yards from the ocean, with crudely-built "bathing shanties" blocking the view of the waves. As the tourist business picked up, though, hotel operators refined the beach-going experience; the shanties disappeared, and, while the mosquitoes could still be troublesome, the city established itself as a true popular resort.

By 1880, it was undisputable that Atlantic City had made the big time. The year-round population was more than 5,000—a huge increase from the 1,000 residents ten years earlier, to say nothing of the handful at the city's incorporation in 1854.

This was just the start. The next decade would see Atlantic City's population double and double again before the end of the 19th century. These were the city's first boom years.

The major problem that remained was how to extend the summer season. At the time, it started not in May, but in early July, and lasted until early September. As early as 1882, promoters organized a mid-September musical festival, held on the lawn of the United States Hotel, to attract post-Labor Day visitors. By that year, many of the city's hotels had enough business to remain open through the winter, although several still closed their doors for the cold months.

In 1885 the city enjoyed its best summer yet, with dignitaries including Vice President Thomas Hendricks, who stayed at the Traymore with his wife, and the man who Hendricks had beaten in the 1884 election, Republican vice presidential candidate John A. Logan. Logan, a Union general during the Civil War and senator from Illinois, stayed at the Ashland hotel on Atlantic Avenue.

Guests that summer enjoyed a number of amusements. Dances (or "hops," as they were called then) were popular and plentiful, as were performances in the many opera houses that dotted the city. Outdoors, bathing in the sea and horseback riding were the preferred diversions, though many contented themselves with promenading on the Boardwalk and watching the throngs doing the same. They also began enjoying exhibitions, performances, and games on the city's piers, which offered relatively inexpensive entertainment to the masses.

In these years, Atlantic City began to appeal to a national audience. Working and middle-class Philadelphians remained its bread-and-butter, but visitors from New York, Maryland, and Washington, D.C., became common, and dignitaries from as far as Kentucky were known to visit.

The summer of 1887 saw another triumph. By the end of July,

the city was so crowded that, despite an abundance of new hotel construction (which, detractors had earlier warned, was far out of proportion to demand and would lead to an inevitable collapse), some visitors found themselves sleeping on staircases or retuning home for the evening for lack of accommodations. Filling the gap, scores of new cottages were built, and some visitors who had stayed for a few days in hotels extended their time in Atlantic City, booking a cottage for a week or more. The following summer, there was even more business, with nearly every room in the city booked at the height of the season.

In these years the city expanded, pushing down the island to Jackson Avenue. Longport, by the 1880s, was being promoted as a satellite resort, and the entire length of Atlantic Avenue was graded and paved with gravel and seashells. A punishing 1889 hurricane was, it seemed, little more than an excuse to rebuild everything on a larger scale.

By 1890, the hotels had succeeded in establishing a winter season, beginning in January and running through March. Railroads promoted a trip to the shore as a way to "escape the disagreeable weather." While Atlantic City wasn't immune to the cold, it was considerably balmier than Philadelphia or New York, and much more convenient than warmer resorts further south.

With visitation rising and business booming, money poured into the city, with a host of new hotels, piers, theaters, and attractions rising from the sand. By 1900, nearly 30,000 residents called Atlantic City home, and more growth was seen as not only possible, but logical. Jonathan Pitney may not have approved of the sometimes unhealthy attractions, but no one could deny that Absecon Island had become, as boosters liked to say, "the queen of the coast."

The Great Fire of 1902

Mrs. O'Leary's cow is famous for kicking over the lantern that started the great Chicago Fire of 1871. Even if the cow wasn't to blame (it's rumored that an over-excited craps-shooter actually started the blaze), most schoolchildren learn the story. But few know the tale of how an Atlantic City dog—allegedly—started a 1902 blaze that destroyed a large swath of valuable Boardwalk real estate.

The exact cause of the terrible fire was never officially determined, though initial reports indicated that sometime before 9 a.m. on April 3, 1902, an unnamed black dog in Brady's Bathhouse knocked over a lamp while frolicking. The flames quickly engulfed the bathhouse's combustible curtains and woodwork before spreading to the adjoining Tarlton Hotel.

Whipped by the wind, the fire raged along the beachfront from Illinois (today's Martin Luther King Boulevard) to New York Avenues, destroying or damaging over 30 buildings, including 10 hotels, 18 stores, four bathhouses, the city's largest theatre, and two private residences.

Guests in the burning hotels fled them in panic, sometimes gathering their belongings, often not. Streaming onto the already-crowded Boardwalk, they turned what had been a bright spring morning into pandemonium.

The city's volunteer fire departments fought tenaciously but were quickly overwhelmed by the blaze, and sent out a call for help. Three companies of Philadelphia firefighters gathered their equipment, crossed the Delaware via ferry and raced for the shore on special trains, getting there at about half past noon. Two companies from Camden joined them.

Seeing smoke billowing from the Mervine and Rio Grande hotels on New York Avenue, Philadelphia's Engine Company 43 made their stand there, bravely remaining in the buildings until their upper floors began to collapse. Regrouping outside with the 21, they dug in and turned the tide.

Meanwhile, Company 48 faced the fire on a different front: the Boardwalk. The Wooden Way burned down to its iron pilings nearly to Captain John Young's Ocean Pier at Tennessee Avenue. As firefighters doused the flames on the boards, the wind swept a burning ember onto the center of the pier and started a blaze that would engulf Marine hall, cutting the pier in two. Young and several others who found themselves trapped on the pier were only saved by the energetic efforts of the 48 and quick work of volunteers manning rescue boats that saved them.

By 5:15 p.m. the combined forces of the Atlantic City, Camden, and Philadelphia firefighters had triumphed over the flames. Without their joint effort, it is likely that the fire would have been far worse, perhaps jumping Illinois Avenue and reaching the Traymore, Brighton, Shelburne, and Dennis. Miraculously, no one was killed in the fire, though several police officers and fire fighters were injured while battling the blaze.

The flames still caused chaos. Several hotel safes lay among the smoking ruins, packed with jewels, cash, and other valuables. To prevent looting, city authorities called on the Company L of the Third Regiment of the National Guard, which was supplemented by the Morris Guards. They formed a cordon around the area, allowing access only to firefighters and, later, construction workers. Thousands of dollars worth of valuables were thus saved.

By the time it was over, though, the fire cut a swath through the beachfront. Between an unburned part of the Windsor Hotel, on Illinois, and the burned ruins of the Rio Grande Hotel, was a scene of total ruin: there wasn't enough remaining to even identify where the burned hotels had been. A heap of tables, beds, rugs, and kitchen utensils, rescued from the flames, sprawled on the beach, while a grand piano sat, in a foot of mud, on New York Avenue.

The city reacted quickly, with an eye on the short and long term. It wouldn't do to have a large section of the city's main attraction burned out on the eve of the summer tourist season. At 3 p.m. on April 5, City Council voted to replace and enlarge the burned section of Boardwalk, ordering lumber and hiring workers.

Rebuilding the Boardwalk took only 10 hours. By the following afternoon, the work was done, and thousands of visitors flocked to the newly-laid boards, seeing for themselves the smoking 700 by 300-foot crater that had once been prime beachfront property.

Yet there was also an eye on the future. At the same meeting that authorized the hasty rebuild of the Boardwalk, the council ordered three new fire engines and an additional 4,000 feet of hose, to knock down future conflagrations more quickly. To lessen the chances of a catastrophic fire in the first place, it set into motion an amendment of the City Charter which would allow the council to restrict any buildings constructed along the beach to brick and stone.

Tellingly, no one was surprised by the speedy turnaround and rebuild, attributing it to the "characteristic energy" of the city. The never-say-die which attitude allowed the city to rebound from this tragedy perhaps provides a lesson for today's leaders.

Golden Jubilee

The year 1904 was a good one for Atlantic City. Over the previous quarter-century the city's population had grown by 1,000 percent. Dreamers imagined that, by 1929, 200,000 residents would call the city home. The future looked bright.

With the city on the upswing, local newspaperman and historian Alfred Heston suggested that the year be a celebration of the 50th anniversary of the city's founding, complete with a carnival. Heston initially suggested that a committee of 50 be formed to organize the commemoration, with each member responsible for a single year of history.

Mayor Franklin Stoy did not put that plan into action, but he did appoint a board of directors to mount a respectable celebration of his city's history. The group agreed that while the city technically turned 50 years old on May 1, it would be better for everyone if the official celebration was held in the middle of June. The weather would be better, the flowers in fuller bloom, and, most importantly, there would be more people in attendance; this was three weeks after the Memorial Day start of the summer season.

The committee finally settled on Wednesday, June 15, through Saturday, June 18, as the dates of the official Golden Jubilee Semi-Centennial celebration.

To mark the occasion, the committee built a "court of honor" between South Carolina and Tennessee Avenues on Atlantic Avenue. The Court's centerpiece was a 56 foot high rival to Paris's Arc de Triomphe. Designed by Philadelphia architect Joseph M. Huston free of charge (Huston was a friend of decorating committee chairman Colonel Thomas Potter), the memorial arch depicted a gigantic Neptune in a seashell chariot being pulled by six immense seahorses.

The committee also erected a "founder's column" at Indiana and Park Place Avenue. The column featured the names of several men who had been influential in the city's founding: Samuel Richards, Dr. Jonathan Pitney, Enoch Doughty, Andrew K. Hay, John C. DaCosta, Walter D. Bell, Stephen Colwell, Joseph Porter, William Coffin, William W. Fleming and Richard B. Osborne. There had been some uncertainty as to just who constituted a founder, and the list, drafted by Heston and approved by the rest of the committee, has one notable omission: no one from the Leeds family appears on it. Neither Jeremiah Leeds, the island's first permanent resident, nor Chalkey Leeds, its first mayor, nor any of the men and women who helped establish the settlement on Absecon Beach in the early 19th century, were honored.

On Wednesday, June 15, the Jubilee celebration officially began with the dedication of the court of honor and founder's column. After an opening prayer, prominent local citizens offered reminiscences of the city's founding and hopes for its future. Dr. T. K. Reed's sentiments reflected the accomplishments of the past half-century and a boundless faith in the future: "Many an impecunious youth has acquired wealth and prominence here: and in the light of the wonders they have performed, it seems as if the men of Atlantic City must have imbibed the spirit of the might and majesty of the ocean. The numerous knotty problems presented for their solution were mastered with sound Judgment and a courage that knew no surrender. Let us inscribe their names in our hall of fame and carve them on shafts more lasting than Egyptian obelisks.

"The future of Atlantic City is assured. Here is the lure of the sea and a climate of unsurpassed excellence. Its great staple is the ocean and it will never be a drug on the market. It will never go out of fashion. The multitude will seek its shores so long as human beings inhabit the earth."

That night, 326 invited guests attended a gala banquet at the Hotel Windsor, at which toasts were made and congratulations were shared among all. There were evening activities for those without dinner clothes as well: for three nights, the city offered a fireworks show called "The Last Days of Pompeii" on the beach at North Carolina Avenue.

On June 16, Louis Kuehnle, commodore of the Atlantic City Yacht Club, presided over a marine parade. Participants included his own group, the Ventnor Yacht club, the Philadelphia Yacht Club, the Corinthian Yacht Club of Philadelphia and assorted, unaffiliated boat owners from other cities. Trailing behind official entrants was an impromptu armada of small sailboats and other craft. Thousands of people lined the Boardwalk to watch the brightly-decorated yachts sail past.

The following day, Friday, saw the floral parade, in which almost 100 chairs, each decorated with displays of flowers, were pushed from the Lighthouse to Florida Avenue and back, with thousands of onlookers enjoying the show.

On Saturday, June 18, the city held a "civic and military" parade, in which community leaders shared the spotlight with several organizations, including the New Jersey National Guard's Third Regiment, which incorporated its annual field day into the parade. Other participants included Chalkey Leeds, the city's first mayor, and Franklin Stoy, its current chief executive; two passengers from the first scheduled train to the city, which ran on July 4, 1854; and George Farish, who had worked as superintendent of construction on the railroad.

The Jubilee officially ended the night of the 18th, but the court of honor and its surrounding electrical displays remained in operation under after Labor Day. It was a time for Atlantic City to imagine what the next 50, or even 100, years would bring. Heston himself waxed poetic.

"With these facts as matters of history," he wrote, "with the knowledge of the wonderful progress and achievements during the hundred years which made up the nineteenth century, what more wonderful progress, what incomprehensible achievements will mark the close of the twentieth century? What will be the relative greatness of Atlantic City in the year 2000? As a resort, of course, she will be pre-eminent— far in the lead of any other city in the world to which people resort for health, rest or pleasure."

Heston could not have foreseen the decay of the 1960s, the struggle of the 1970s, the bonanza of the 1980s, or the current decline. While few share his optimism that Atlantic City will be the world's leading resort in a hundred years, his writing reminds us that history takes many paths, often unexpected, and that Atlantic City has seen many good and bad turns.

High Flyers

Today, Atlantic City is working to re-invent itself as a destination. The Atlantic City Airshow, "Thunder Over the Boardwalk," has become a city tradition. Since 2003, the spectacle of U.S. Air Force Thunderbirds and scores of other military aircraft buzzing over the Atlantic Ocean has drawn hundreds of thousands of spectators to the city each year. The 2010 edition marked the 100th anniversary of the extravaganza that put Atlantic City on the aeronautical map.

In the summer of 1910, powered flight was still quite new. A scant four years earlier, Orville and Wilbur Wright had patented their "flying machine." Inventors, engineers and daredevils were making aviation history. That year, air shows from Los Angeles to New York showed Americans just what was going on over their heads.

As the world's playground, Atlantic City couldn't miss out on the excitement. The city's Aero Club organized an "airship week" to give the community and its visitors "the greatest experience" they had ever had. Planning began late—the July 4 event was first announced in late June—but club members quickly built a $20,000 war chest (about $450,000 today) and began soliciting the most famous aviators of the era to appear. Anticipation was high.

The city was perfect for aviation, supporters argued, because of its flatness—there were no hills and certainly no mountains to create topographic challenges for aviators, who were already pushing the envelope of aeronautical technology. With steady winds and easy access from several metropolitan areas, it was the perfect place for up-and-coming flyers to strut their stuff.

"A new science, weird and strange and yet in its experimental stage, is to be tried out at the shore in such a way that every single inhabitant can view the spectacle," trumpeted the *Atlantic City Daily Press* on July 3. Best of all, said the *Press*, "Everything is as free as the air."

Club president John J. White and secretary Albert T. Bell put the show together, hoping to increase public appreciation of flying and deliver "wholesome publicity" for Atlantic City.

White and Bell lured one of the biggest names in aviation, Glenn Hammond Curtiss, to the exhibition. This was one of the true standouts of the new science of flying. With only an eighth-grade formal education, 32-year-old Curtiss combined an inventive spirit with a keen interest in mechanics. He parlayed a job as a Western Union bicycle messenger into a racing career, then opened a bicycle shop. From there, he began experimenting with internal combustion engines and motorcycles. Curtiss set a land speed record of over 136 miles per hour in 1907, leading the press to dub him "the fastest man in the world." Soon he was building and flying his own airplanes and setting records in the air.

In May 1910, Curtiss became the first man to fly between Albany and New York City. He pocketed $100,000 for the feat, then sent his plane to Atlantic City by train, broken up in sections, for Aero Week.

On July 4, 1910, the carnival finally began, with 100,000 people in attendance. Curtiss was the star, flying a mile from Ocean Pier to Million Dollar Pier, less than 30 feet over the heads of spectators. As a dangerous land breeze buffeted his fragile craft, the pilot approached a landing strip on the sand. Suddenly, a little girl dashed from her parents' side and into the path of his plane. The crowd gasped as Curtiss quickly pulled up and circled for another pass. That time, a bather ran out of the ocean and into his path. The third time was the charm, as Curtiss landed without a hitch. He called it the most dangerous flight of his career.

The following day, he flew the entire length of the city, taking eight and a half minutes. On the third day, he did it again, achieving a speed of 80 miles per hour.

Thursday was a bit of a dud. Two of the Wright Brothers' planes arrived, but dark skies and windy conditions made flying impossible. Still, crowds marveled at a massive Wright biplane exhibited at Ocean Pier.

On Friday, however, Walter Brookins piloted the Wright craft through a series of dips and turns in a thrilling display. Not to be outdone, Curtiss took a surprise flight to Ventnor Heights. The crowds were thrilled by the aeronautic derring-do.

To demonstrate the military applications of flight, Curtiss also dropped oranges (acting as proxies for bombs) around several yachts. A more elaborate "mock battle" between a decommissioned gunship and a squadron of planes had been canceled, lest foreign powers discover American military secrets. As it was, Curtiss's demonstration suggested the complexities that aircraft would bring to modern war.

The best was yet to come. As the show came to an end, Brookins shattered his previous world altitude record, reaching a height of 6,175 feet. Curtiss set another record, flying 50 miles over the Atlantic and staying in the air for one hour, 14 minutes, 59 seconds. Attendees left satisfied, happy that they'd seen history made.

It was a great moment for flight and a triumph for the Aero Club, but for the hotels of Atlantic City, it was just another big event in a summer of them, and before the last plane had left town, they were focusing on the next set of arrivals.

A Civil Reunion

In 2010, one of the most interesting gatherings the city has ever seen celebrated its 100th anniversary: the National Encampment of the Grand Army of the Republic, a group dedicated to remembering the sacrifices made by members of the Union Army during the Civil War, America's deadliest conflict.

In September 1910, Atlantic City was the site of the 44th meeting of the GAR, an organization of Civil War veterans who fought for the Union from 1861 to 1865.

In the aftermath of that struggle, returning servicemen sought the company of their former brothers-in-arms for both social and political reasons. Organized into state-level departments and local posts, the GAR met for the first time in Indianapolis in November 1866. The massive assemblies became an annual tradition.

The GAR moved around the country, avoiding the South (though Washington, D.C. hosted several conventions). By 1910, it was Atlantic City's turn.

In Reconstruction years, interest in the group was keen, and the GAR was influential in both electing Republican candidates and promoting civil rights for black Americans, particularly veterans. In the 1880s, the group began advocating for federal veteran's pensions, and membership soared. In 1890, the GAR boasted more than 409,000 members, making it a political force.

By the time the group got to Atlantic City twenty years later, though, the group had less than 214,000 members. It had been 45 years since the end of hostilities, and most veterans were in their 60s or older. In an age when the average life expectancy for men was less than 50, the GAR's ranks were losing an increasing amount of members each year.

Even so, the arrival of the GAR was viewed as a coup for the city. Hotels competed to host the veterans as the city rolled out a patriotic welcome for the war heroes.

On Sunday, September 18, 85-year-old General Daniel Sickles, the last surviving corps commander from the conflict, welcomed the soldiers from the stage of Steeplechase Pier. Sickles, who had lost his leg at Gettysburg, declared that the reunions were "the breath of life" to him (he would die four years later), and spoke about the continuing reconciliation between North and South.

By Monday, more than 10,000 former soldiers had filled the city's hotels, which echoed with reminiscences of long-ago battles. That evening, the Morris Guards, glittering in blue and gold uniforms, stood watch as Commander in Chief Samuel R. Van Sant of Minnesota was fêted in an elaborate reception in Steel Pier's Music Hall.

The National Encampment officially opened on Tuesday night at Million Dollar Pier. New Jersey Governor John Franklin Fort, Atlantic City Mayor Franklin Stoy and others looked on as Colonel F. M. Sterrett officially called the group to order under a canopy of glowing lights and American flags. Van Sant, a former Minnesota governor, was given a diamond-studded badge to honor his commitment to the organization and the Union Army. To cheers, the one-legged General Sickles was carried to the stage on the shoulders of his former soldiers.

The following day brought the greatest spectacle of the week, as 10,000-plus veterans, dressed in Union blue and carrying frayed regimental flags, paraded through the streets of the city, joined by the Women's Relief Corp (nurses who supported the Union effort), Ladies of the GAR (wives of the soldiers), and the Sons and Daughters of Veterans. Seventy-five Atlantic City veterans took part in the parade and received particularly enthusiastic applause. According to GAR Adjutant General George O. Eddy, it was the group's most successful parade ever, due in large part to the hospitality of Atlantic City's residents.

President William Howard Taft did not come to the Encampment, causing some ill will among the veterans. It was customary for presidents, particularly Republican ones, to attend, at least briefly. But Vice President John Sherman did attend, as did perpetual Democratic presidential candidate William Jennings Bryan.

On Friday, the Encampment adjourned, and the veterans began to head back to their homes. When the Lincoln Post of Newark, New

Jersey, left on the 6 p.m. train, the meeting was officially in the record books.

Atlantic City had acquitted itself well over the week's festivities. Though the GAR didn't return, the message was clear: Atlantic City could handle any meeting, no matter how large. The following decade saw the city's convention business soar.

The GAR continued to meet for another 39 years. At its final meeting in Indianapolis, only 16 members remained. The last Union veteran, a former drummer boy, died in 1956, closing a sad chapter in American history in which Atlantic City played a role.

The Great War and the Shore

In the years after its 1914 outbreak, the war in Europe seemed distant in Atlantic City. Yes, there was the threat of submarine war, but in general life continued along the Boardwalk as before.

That ended when the United States joined World War I in April 1917. After three years of hostilities between the Allies (principally Great Britain, France, and Russia) and the Central powers (Germany and Austria-Hungary), the United States entered on the side of the Allies. Although all fighting took place in Europe, reminders of the impact of "the Great War" on Atlantic City remain to this day.

Congress authorized a draft; by June, nearly 10 million men had registered for the draft. Atlantic City contributed more than its share, as Atlantic County stood seventh in the number of enlistments for New Jersey. In addition to sending men to join the American Expeditionary Force, which fought in France, residents of Atlantic City organized a home guard to maintain the peace at home. Notably, Atlantic City's black community proudly supported the effort, contributing two complete companies.

By 1917, Atlantic City was well established as a convention town, and it hosted the first major meeting of businessmen during the war. At this meeting, held that September, the attendees discussed how they could better coordinate domestic business to help the war effort. Herbert Hoover, then Federal Food Administrator but later president, spoke forcefully at the conference about the dangers of socialism, should the businessmen not voluntarily aid the government. Hoover's "volunteerism" would become a watchword of government/business relations in the 1920s.

During the war, Atlantic City remained a favored destination, though much of the happy-go-lucky mood of the vacation town was obscured by wartime exigencies. Women—and even men—who summered at the shore no longer lazed around on beaches or in hotels: they knitted to help "the boys over there."

Though the Central Powers launched no attacks on the New Jersey mainland, submarine and naval warfare remained an important part of hostilities, and with the official entrance of the United States into the war, gained in intensity. Germans actually laid mines near Lewes, Delaware, in an attempt to incapacitate the port of Philadelphia. The specter of naval combat came even closer to Atlantic City in June 1918, when a fleet of fishing boats based in the town was thought to have fallen prey to a German warship. Fortunately, the ships evaded sinking and returned safely home.

Atlantic City sent men to fight, conserved materials needed by the military, and hosted a number of national conventions to discuss the war, ranging from brewers to military engineers. All told, the city admirably assisted the rest of the nation during a time of national crisis, from the initial call to combat until the war-ending armistice silenced the guns on November 11, 1918.

Five years after the armistice, Atlantic City unveiled a monument to those who served during the First World War. Located at Albany and Ventnor Avenues, it still welcomes those who use the nearby bridge; for years, it watched over Atlantic City High School, which opened in 1923, just as the monument was completed.

Originally, the war memorial was at the center of a traffic circle, bane to many a young or unconfident driver, but in 1988 the city realigned the streets to eliminate the circle; the monument now stands in Captain John A. O'Donnell Memorial Park.

The monument was modeled after a Greek temple (hence the 16 Doric columns along its perimeter); the statue inside is called "Liberty in Distress," a fitting tribute to the soldiers of a war to make the world safe for democracy. Atop a mangled heap of bodies, a female figure, her robe stripped, looks skyward.

Around the outside of the monument the names of World War I battles are carved into the marble. Though memories of the war are fading (Frank Buckles, the last U.S. veteran of the conflict, died in 2011), the monument serves as a constant reminder that, when asked, Atlantic City has always served its country.

A Roaring Empire

With the Great War over, Atlantic City returned to the good times. Over the previous 20 years, it had become a leading destination for conventions, and it continued to host gatherings of everyone from schoolteachers and shoe salesmen to labor unionists and evangelists. Throughout the 1920s, conventions would remain a tremendous draw for the city, with meetings held in hotels and on piers. The rise in convention bookings suggested that the city's amazing growth as both a tourist destination and a metropolitan area would continue in the new decade.

The city also solidified its position as a proving ground for Broadway. Shows that aimed to make the big time in Manhattan frequently staged productions in Atlantic City first; if they could please audiences and critics there, they would move up to the Great White way. As a result, Atlantic City was a center for drama and show business.

There was change coming, though. The passage of the Eighteenth Amendment and the Volstead Act led to the federal Prohibition of the production, importation, and distribution of alcohol, which threatened to crimp Atlantic City's style. Although the city was promoted as a wholesome family resort, a large amount of its appeal was owed to the numerous saloons that lined the Boardwalk and major streets. As January 17, 1920, the date when Prohibition would take effect, approached, there was some trepidation. New Year's celebrations were somewhat muted, with more dancing and less drinking than in years past. Most restaurants had already started paring down their beverage selections and they discovered, to their surprise, that plenty of visitors still came to have fun.

By early February, it was reported that, although the city's saloons had closed, there was a sudden boom in candy shops, drug stores, and soda fountains. It appeared, on the surface at least, that those who had been indulging in drink had suddenly developed a craving for sweets.

In reality, many of those establishments were likely fronts for not-so-discreet speakeasies. Under the aegis of Enoch "Nucky" Johnson, Atlantic City ran full throttle throughout Prohibition, and bootleggers had a significant presence in Atlantic City.

The change in tastes (or, at least, change in how those tastes were met) did not slow new construction. In January 1920, work on the $4.5 million, 15-story Ritz-Carlton hotel started. It was the first of a string of new hotels slated for construction that spring whose total cost was $20 million. Once the Ritz-Carlton was finished, Nucky Johnson wasted no time in making it his personal showplace; his parties there were the stuff of legend, and he did business with politicos and rumrunners alike in his suite.

Gambling, for which the city had long been known, flourished as well, with plenty of places to bet on horse races, thanks to the city's numerous horse rooms, and gambling dens where vacationers could shoot craps and play poker.

For a while, it looked good for Atlantic City. The drys could boast that they'd closed the saloons, the wets could still get liquor, and everyone, it seemed, could gamble. Some, however, were not pleased with the wide-open nature of the town. In July 1921, Mayor Edward Bader announced a plan to eliminate undesirables from Atlantic City forever. According to the *New York Times*, a special squad of detectives from the Burns Agency, working at the behest of major hotel owners and armed with a list of "every gambler, crook, booze seller, or other undesirable" in town, was making a clean sweep. The paper reported an immediate decline in betting activity in the major resorts, as well as fewer cappers and steerers soliciting gamblers for dice and cards.

Rumors of gambling's death, however, were greatly exaggerated. Once the heat was off, the cards, dice, and betting forms resumed their flight, and, despite periodic raids, crackdowns, and vice nets, both gambling and liquor would remain in easy supply throughout the decade. Illegal gambling wouldn't be rooted out of Atlantic City until the 1950s, following a hearing conducted by the Kefauver Committee (though not Kefauver himself) at the Traymore hotel.

With illicit gambling and drinking as well as the advertised family pleasures drawing visitors throughout the year, several new hotels and expansions followed the Ritz-Carlton. With more conventions and attractions like the Miss America pageant, business boomed like never before. Further underlining the growth of the city, in 1923 a spacious, modern high school opened at Atlantic and Albany Avenues, and a new convention hall opened on the Boardwalk in 1929.

Not all of the projects went off without a hitch, though. In 1921, a hotel named for President Warren G. Harding was announced; it was to be named for the leader and to have a special suite reserved for him. By the time it finally opened in 1926, the resort was called the President, as Harding died in 1923. The hotel struggled, being sold in early 1929 for $2.3 million, far less than its $4 million construction cost.

Despite the President's struggles, at the end of the decade conditions seemed better than they had at the decade's start. The summer of 1929 was, according to hotel operators, the best in history, with proprietors of both the major Boardwalk hotels and the smaller establishments farther from the beach struggling to find room for arrivals. Even with every vacant piece of land being used as a lot, there was no room for cars to park. "Unusual prosperity" a *New York Times* headline called it, and in hindsight it was. The Wall Street crash of October 1929 signaled the start of the Great Depression, which put a definite end on the high rolling 1920s.

Betting the Ponies

Atlantic City got its start as a quick getaway, accessible from Philadelphia by train in two hours; within a few years, transit times had been cut to just over an hour. A visit to the shore might not seem like such a big deal now, but in the long years before the invention of air conditioning, paying a few dollars to get out of the inner city heat and bask in the ocean breeze was about as good as it got for middle- and working-class Philadelphians.

Of course, buying a ticket wasn't supposed to be the visitors' only expense. Atlantic City residents hoped to make a living from them, but it didn't always work out that way. The local term "shoobie" for out-of-towners comes from a time when day-trippers brought their lunches from home in shoeboxes, thus earning the scorn of local merchants.

Still, everyone has money to spend, and if they didn't want to spend it on food or souvenirs, they might be willing to risk it. So it isn't surprising that, in the early 20th century, Atlantic City hosted a thriving—though illegal—gaming business that catered to many of these day-trippers.

As early as the 1890s, railroads brought on average 10,000 visitors a day to the shore during the season, sometimes many more. While most of them came for the "family" attractions the city was noted for, such as the beach and Boardwalk, there were, inevitably, those who wanted something a bit more adult. They often found it in the horse rooms of Atlantic City.

Because gambling was technically illegal (though it continued with the tacit cooperation of politicians and police alike), horse rooms did not advertise, nor were they available to an unwary public: most horse rooms were in the backs of bars or cigar stores. Within the horse rooms, players could place bets on horse racing from around the nation. In an age before simulcasting, these were the race books.

Operators of horse rooms obtained information about races and race results from a race wire service, which sent out race information over the telegraph or telephone. Large blackboards displayed odds and results, and an announcer would narrate a description of the race as results came in—this dramatic effort helped greatly to increase excitement and therefore betting. With the aid of the *Daily Racing Form* and the updated information provided by the horse room, bettors placed their wagers and hoped for the best.

While most horse rooms were simple, with wooden benches and no amenities, some bordered on lavish, with complementary coffee and sandwiches and separate rooms for female and high-action bettors. The more upscale horse rooms could be mistaken for a stockbroker's office.

Horse rooms actively courted day-trippers from Philadelphia, often paying train fare and sometimes arranging automobile service from the city, much as Atlantic City's legal casinos later relied on buses to bring prospective gamblers into town. Horse rooms had, even by today's standards, aggressive marketing campaigns; though they didn't advertise in papers, they employed touts to bring bettors in. On the streets of Atlantic City and in the train stations of Philadelphia, eager touts steered bettors to the horse rooms.

Though they often offered bettors a craps game, horse rooms were distinct from illegal casinos in Atlantic City, which usually operated from the back room of a nightclub. Horse rooms captured the sizable market for race betting, which steadily increased during the first decades of the 20th century before booming during the Great Depression.

Because the rooms were illegal, there was plenty of room for cheating and outright theft. In 1921, Englishman H. H. Thomas reportedly lost $100,000 to scammers who had promised that, by tapping into the race wire and receiving results early, they could defraud local horse rooms. Thomas had already lost $200,000 betting with the same operators on Havana races, but wised up and went to the authorities after losing even more in Atlantic City. A cursory investigation revealed that, in a scam reminiscent of *The Sting*, the horse rooms had been set up only to defraud Mr. Thomas. Yet most of the rooms were on the level (more or less), and they remained popular into the 1940s.

So where have the horse rooms gone? Horse rooms in Atlantic City declined for the same reason as horse rooms in other cities: a change in how Americans gambled.

After World War II, betting on team sports began to displace betting on horse races. Since sports news and results were widely published in newspapers and broadcast over radio and later television, bettors did not need to go to a special place for access to the latest information. Bookies no longer needed the race wire to inform them of changing race or track conditions; they now only needed to determine the odds for each game, accept bets, pay the winners, and collect from the losers. As a result, bookmaking became a far less organized and centralized business, and the horse rooms went the way of the Diving Horse. The crackdown on illegal gambling in the wake of the Kefauver Committee's hearing in town was the final nail in the coffin.

The advent of race simulcast rooms in legal casinos in the 1990s returned horse rooms, after a fashion, to Atlantic City, showing that there are still those who like to bet the ponies while down the shore. Despite operating on the wrong side of the law, the horse rooms of old Atlantic City have a place in history as an early daytripper-based gaming and tourism industry on Absecon Island.

Speaking Easy

Atlantic City today earns much of its livelihood from a legal casino industry that caters to the desires of Americans to gamble, earning it a solid reputation as the casino capital of the East. But in the not-too-distant past, Atlantic City was known as a hotbed of rumrunners and bootleggers who profited from the public's willingness to flout the official ban on the sale, manufacture, and transportation of alcoholic beverages.

These years saw a fair amount of drama, as viewers of HBO's hit series *Boardwalk Empire* know. The real story of Prohibition in Atlantic City has just as much excitement.

When the 18th Amendment became law on January 16, 1920, the Prohibition Party finally achieved its aims—by federal law, the manufacture, purchase, transportation, import, export, and sale of alcoholic beverages became illegal. Yet Americans found they could not set aside their fondness for spirits so easily. To fill the sudden need for illegal intoxicants, an army of rumrunners, moonshiners, and bootleggers appeared throughout the United States. Distributing clandestinely-brewed spirits and smuggling bootleg rum from Mexico and Cuba and whiskey from Canada, criminal syndicates found that Americans' appetites for illegal alcohol made for lucrative business.

With some history as an anything-goes resort town, it isn't surprising that Atlantic City became a favored haunt of bootleggers. It is somewhat ironic, though, that the city that hosted the 1912 Prohibition Party national conference became notorious as a trans-shipping point for bootlegged alcohol. Just as the city recently attempted to court families while promoting itself as "always turned on," Atlantic City residents found no conflict in hosting family-

friendly events like the Easter Parade (a fixture since 1860) or the
Miss America Pageant (a Prohibition-era innovation in 1921) while
bootleggers used Smuggler's Cove in the Inlet or other rendezvous
points as gateways for their traffic in illicit liquor.

Some of the most notorious bootleggers in the country boasted
Atlantic City connections. In freewheeling Atlantic County,
dominated by political boss Enoch "Nucky" Johnson, rumrunners
found that political and police protection was readily available for a
fair price. Some rumrunners, in fact, employed Atlantic City police to
escort their shipments of illegal alcohol. Such an escort ensured that
the cargo would reach its destination without harassment by federal
Prohibition agents or hijacking by rival bootleggers, a very real threat
in the lawless world of the bootleggers.

Though Atlantic City had many natural advantages that
recommended it as a haven for bootleggers, most researchers point to
a 1923 bargain allegedly struck between Johnson and reported crime
syndicate boss Salvatore Lucania, better known as Charles "Lucky"
Luciano. Reportedly, in that year Johnson guaranteed exclusive
landing rights in Atlantic City and protection for the cargo of Luciano
and his associates—who at that time included such notables as Frank
Costello, Joe Adonis, Meyer Lansky, and Ben Siegel—in exchange
for ten percent of all profits from the syndicate's illegal operations,
including but not limited to rumrunning and illegal gambling.

So while Atlantic City prospered as a convention town, hosting
about 400 conventions a year during the 1920s, it gained another
kind of fame as a center for bootlegging. As much as 40 percent of
all alcohol illegally imported into the United States from 1926 to
1933 reportedly came through the Atlantic City area. While some
law-abiding citizens may have chafed at the knowledge that the
federal laws against alcohol were being broken with impunity and
few consequences, none questioned the prosperity that the 1920s
brought to Atlantic City. A combination of bootlegging money and
legitimate travel and tourism made the 1920s a roaring decade on
Absecon Island.

Perhaps the high point of Atlantic City's notoriety as a friendly
spot for bootleggers came in 1929, with a reputed "Mafia syndicate
convention" attended by the usual suspects from the New York area—
Luciano, Lansky, Adonis, Costello, Dutch Schultz, and others—as
well as visiting dignitaries like Al Capone of Chicago. The legend
of this moment, which combined Atlantic City's reputation as a

premier convention center with its whispered repute as a haven for well-connected lawbreakers, stands as a high point in the history of Atlantic City, months before the onset of the Great Depression signalled the end of the prosperous twenties.

Just as the coming of the Depression ended the convention and tourism boom and optimism of the 1920s, the ratification of the 21st Amendment in 1933, which canceled the 18th Amendment and ended the curious experiment in national Prohibition, brought an end to Atlantic City's days as a bootlegging capital. While few would argue that the rackets or organized crime abandoned Atlantic City with the demise of Prohibition rumrunning, little remains of that era outside of occasional reminders that, before it was the casino capital of the East, Atlantic City could lay claim to the title of bootlegging capital of the nation.

Nucky's Alley

Visitors to Atlantic City, like many resort towns, have always come for many reasons: relaxation, excitement, family run, nightlife, and escape from the ordinary. For some, a trip to the beach suffices; others find an afternoon in front of the penny slots is enough. Yet others crave excitement of a more physical nature.

Certainly not seeking romance, they were nevertheless intent on experiencing, at least, physical intimacy. While prostitution has always been illegal in the state of New Jersey, at times it was tolerated—and even sponsored—by the powers that be in Atlantic City.

As early as the 1880s, newspapers commented on the proliferation of brothels across the city in locations like Chalfonte Avenue and Westminster Place, a small side street also known as "Snake Alley." In 1890, it was estimated that as many as 100 pleasure dens could be found in Atlantic City, then a town with barely 13,000 inhabitants. As Atlantic City continued to attract visitors, brothels remained a barely-hidden offering. In the 1920s, Atlantic City was in the midst of an unprecedented boom. Thousands of visitors arrived each day. Though Prohibition had forced the closure of many nightclubs, speakeasies, where liquor flowed freely with only the smallest pretense toward stealth, were easy to find. At the same time, prostitution flourished as well. Although both prostitution and alcohol were illegal, police gave little thought to enforcing the laws, as purveyors of both vices enjoyed the protection of Enoch L. "Nucky" Johnson, the reigning political power in all of Atlantic County.

Johnson not only allowed speakeasies to flourish as "good for business," but he actually owned the Silver Slipper Supper Club in the early 1920s, and collected a share of the profits from all illicit enterprises as protection money. He did not draw the line at liquor and gambling. He permitted houses of prostitution to continue doing business on a section of South Chalfonte Avenue known as "Prostitute's Alley," where, similar to red light districts across the country, working girls stood in the windows and doorways of houses of ill repute, tempting their customers with their considerable charms. The going rate for an encounter, usually 50 cents, could escalate to as high as one dollar if the working girl was especially skilled or attractive.

Many of the denizens of Prostitute's Alley had originally come to Atlantic City with high hopes. As a major entertainment center, with nightclubs, theaters, and lavish entertainment spectacles on its famous piers, Atlantic City was a place where a talented young performer could be discovered. At least, many young women hoped, that was the case. But many of them, finding no luck gaining employment as a singer or chorus line dancer, ended up joining the ranks of the city's prostitutes.

Under Nucky Johnson's regime, houses of ill repute flourished, but they were subject to a modicum of regulation. All women working in the city had to be free from disease, and a Johnson employee named "Dr. Ducky" made weekly rounds of the city's cathouses, inspecting prostitutes for disease and performing abortions. While these safeguards certainly did not diminish the chances for prostitutes to contract sexually transmitted diseases, apparently Johnson and others felt they extended sufficient protection to the men who frequented them, and were therefore adequate.

Under the reform regime of Mayor Thomas "Two-gun" Taggart in the early 1940s, official toleration of both gambling and prostitution (alcohol consumption had been re-legalized in 1933, and the taps flowed freely since) diminished, though the crusading reform mayor could not completely drive either vice out of town. Even after Taggart left power, prostitution, while still present, did not return to its previously public stature.

Eventually, prostitution dispersed throughout the city, as bordellos gave way to streetwalkers. Until successful police efforts to "clean up" Pacific Avenue, sections of that thoroughfare were notorious haunts for ladies of the evening. While prostitution still exists today, it is no more openly tolerated than any other crime. Atlantic City has come a long way, indeed, from its early heyday as a vice capital and adult playground.

Old Creepy Checks In

During the Great Depression, America was transfixed by a series of colorful bank robbers who bedeviled law enforcement. Characters like John Dillinger, "Machine Gun" Kelly, Baby Face Nelson, and Bonnie and Clyde traded bullets with police while robbing banks, evading capture, and breaking out of jails across the Midwest.

One of the most famous groups was the Barker-Karpis gang. Though Federal Bureau of Investigation director J. Edgar Hoover told the public that Fred and Dock Barker's mother, Kate "Ma" Barker, was the criminal mastermind behind the gang, she was never involved in planning or carrying out any of the gang's crimes. The actual brain behind the gang was Alvin Karpis, born to Lithuanian immigrants in Montreal, Quebec, Canada, in 1907.

Karpis, alleged to have a near-photographic memory, was usually known by the alias Ray, though he garnered the nickname "Old Creepy" for his perpetually dour expression. He was reportedly a dead ringer for horror actor Boris Karloff.

After Karpis began collaborating with Freddie Barker in 1931, the gang robbed banks, kidnapped rich citizens, and hijacked mail deliveries with remarkable efficiency. From 1931 to 1933, the gang picked its targets at will.

But in 1934, the tide began to turn against the "public enemies," as John Dillinger, Pretty Boy Floyd, Baby Face Nelson, and Bonnie and Clyde were all killed by police or federal agents, and several others were apprehended. On January 16, Fred Barker and his mother were killed after a shootout with FBI agents in Florida, and G-men were hot on the trail of Karpis.

With the death or capture of many of the most notorious outlaws, Karpis officially became "Public Enemy Number One" and the focus of an intensive manhunt. Fleeing Miami after the deaths of the Barkers, Karpis was the subject of a national police bulletin.

Just after midnight on January 19, Karpis arrived at the Dan-Mor Hotel, three blocks off the Boardwalk on Kentucky Avenue. This was not the Traymore or Marlborough-Blenheim—the Dan-Mor was more of a glorified rooming house. Karpis, together with his partner in crime Harry Campbell, checked into the hotel after having driven all night.

Karpis's eight-months pregnant girlfriend, Delores Delaney, was already checked into room 400 of the Dan-Mor (Karpis received room 403). That afternoon, Karpis arranged for a doctor (Carl Surran, who was coincidentally the Atlantic City Police Department's official surgeon) examine Delaney. He, Delaney, Campbell, and another woman spent much of the day shopping for winter clothes. Spooked after seeing a man and women they believed were following them several times, Karpis and Campbell agreed to leave Atlantic City the next day.

Walking his beat around 3:30 a.m. (now the morning of the 20th), Officer Elias Saab learned of the bulletin for Karpis. Saab was shocked to discover that one of the cars parked in the Coast Garage on Kentucky Avenue matched the description of the Karpis getaway car. He called the station, and three detectives immediately arrived at the Dan-Mor.

The hotel's manager was at first uncooperative. While he dickered with the police, his wife went upstairs and awoke Karpis (dressed only in his long underwear), taking him to another room and pleading with him to surrender himself, though she did not know who he was or the nature of the charges he faced.

Suddenly, a detective entered the room and grabbed Karpis, who helpfully agreed to enter room 403 and persuade "the men" in there to surrender. Instead, once inside, he dressed. He and Campbell then flung open the door and opened fire. As the police fled (one was shot in the face) Karpis grabbed the women in room 400 and ran to a back alley. While the women waited there (Delaney had been shot in the leg and could only move slowly), Karpis and Campbell blasted their way across the street and into the garage.

Unable to find their car, they drove off in a Pontiac, driving down Kentucky Avenue in search of their woman friends. Instead, they hit the dead-end at the Boardwalk. Trading gunshots with police, they wheeled around, searching desperately for the women. Unable to find them, they decided to flee. Shooting at a group of police, they were able to get off Absecon Island; the pair did not stop driving until they reached Toledo, Ohio.

After escaping from Atlantic City, Karpis continued robbing banks until the FBI cornered him in New Orleans. On April 30, 1936, federal agents captured Karpis, as FBI Director Hoover flew in personally to arrest the fugitive. Karpis would serve 33 years in Alcatraz (he was that prison's longest-serving inmate) and was deported after his release in 1969, dying in Spain 10 years later. Though his time in Atlantic City was brief, it was one of the city's most notorious criminal episodes.

The First Slowdown

There had been slowdowns in Atlantic City before—World War I had somewhat reduced the tourist trade—but the Great Depression was the city's first real, sustained economic challenge. With unemployment as high as 25 percent, vacationing in a summer resort was the least of many working people's concerns.

Despite the worsening conditions, vacationers and business travelers continued to come to Atlantic City at first. In the summer of 1930, 15,000 members of the Benevolent and Protective Order of the Elks gathered in the city, taking over several hotels. President Herbert Hoover, in a message sent by automobile, urged the group's members to resume building, as new construction projects would employ Americans and pump money into the economy.

There was not, however, ample business for all, and some hoteliers got desperate as traffic declined. As early as March 1930, George Stoess, owner of the Breslin Hotel, was convicted of violating anti-narcotics laws. Stoess had, apparently, converted the entire fourth floor of his hotel into an opium den. Other hotels turned to the open sale of alcohol; later that year, the Hotel Brennan and Georgette Hotel were threatened with closure for letting liquor flow freely. Hotels faced a dilemma: their customers wanted to drink, and with bootlegging flourishing in the city, booze was easy to get. There was always the chance, however, that honest law enforcement could spoil the party. Those who made sure to maintain a solid friendship with political boss Nucky Johnson rarely suffered this fate. Sometimes, the raids were comic; in 1929 and again in 1932, police shuttered the ironically-named "Extra Dry Café" for violations of the Volstead Act. In the latter year, police discovered two barrels of beer and an assortment of other illicit beverages during their roust. The cat-and-mouse of Prohibition ended in 1933, but the return of legal drinking did not appreciably help Atlantic City's prospects.

Still, the city soldiered on. Construction started prior to the crash continued. In June 1930, the 16-story, 230-room Ludy hotel opened at South Carolina and the Boardwalk. The last of the major Boardwalk hotels of the classic era opened in December of that year. The $5 million Claridge stood at 24 stories—the tallest hotel in the city and the tallest structure in the state—and boasted a five-story tower from which guests could enjoy unimpeded views of the island. It did well enough that some builders saw room in the market for growth—a group announced plans for a 40-story hotel at Maryland and the Boardwalk in 1932—but none were able to attract investors.

Atlantic City business owners met the challenge of the Depression head on. In December 1930, they announced an agreement to create a voluntary form of unemployment insurance: each company would deduct ten cents from every worker's paycheck and, matching it with a 10-cent contribution from the business, create a $50,000 fund that would provide relief for the city's unemployed, at least through the spring. The measure wasn't sufficient to solve the problem of unemployment in the city, but it demonstrated the community spirit of its people.

That spirit, though, was often not enough. Newspapers reported a rash of suicides throughout the decade; a variety of men and women, unable to adjust to hard times, ended their lives by jumping from Boardwalk hotels. Many of those hotels had their own problems; a rash of foreclosures hit storied resorts from the Ambassador to the Ritz-Carlton to the Knickerbocker. Local banks, like the Chelsea Second National, failed as well, contributing to the sense of malaise.

There were attempts to stem the tide. The 1934 Easter Parade drew 350,000 celebrants, the biggest crowd to visit Atlantic City since the crash. Government programs helped: the Civil Works Administration spent $75,000 and employed 450 men in a beautification program that saw the redecking of the Boardwalk and the painting of public buildings. The following year, the city successfully revived the Miss America, giving the city an annual event to remind potential visitors that yes, it was still open for business. That same summer, the city continued its Boardwalk revitalization plan, replanking and painting its 1,500 benches a "relaxing green" and adding 300 more.

There was another big change in 1935: in April of that year, following a special ribbon-cutting ceremony and fashion show, the city opened the Boardwalk from Iowa to Jackson Avenues to bicycles for the first time. Bicycles are still permitted, during certain hours, today.

All of these changes, big and small, helped to attract more visitors. In 1935, a record 500,000 visitors thronged the town for the Easter Parade. Despite a light rain, the parade itself was a triumph for the city, and throughout that summer business was brisk. That fall, the *Christian Science Monitor* proclaimed Atlantic City "the greatest convention city in the world," citing its thousand hotels (many of them small boarding houses), "active Chamber of Commerce and Convention Bureau," its massive new convention hall, unparalleled ease of access from many major cities, and a variety of attractions. The beach was the main draw, but a host of events throughout the year, ranging from the annual Atlantic City Horse Show in the spring to a festival of lights in December, kept visitors interested.

Those efforts paid off. In 1937, despite the country's ongoing financial woes and a rainy August, the city had a record year, with visitation up 20 percent from the previous year. And yet there were signs that the city was not through the worst of it. In 1936, Mayor Charles White spoke of the need for a master plan to adequately prepare the city for growth. He laid out an ambitious proposal that was ahead of its time, catering simultaneously to the masses, the wealthy, and, incredibly enough, gamblers. One section of the beachfront would be devoted to cabanas and clubs for the super-rich, while another would cater to the less well-off with amusement parks and other attractions; this would rival Coney Island. It's telling that the area around Convention Hall was already dilapidated enough that it was suggested as the best site for this urban renewal.

The final element of White's plan was to open a gambling casino "rivalling that of Monte Carlo" and a racetrack, pending legalization by the state. It would take another forty years of urban decline for voters to approve the former, while the horseracing returned to the Atlantic City area in 1946. White knew then what it took many people four decades to realize: that, properly controlled, legal gambling could be one element in the appeal of Atlantic City. For the time being, though, his "all things to all people" plans were not acted on; had they been, the city's history may have been quite different.

In a sense, the economic stress of the Depression never really ended; the crowds returned in the 1930s, but the city never recaptured the all-out prosperity of the 1920s. Instead, it adapted, sometimes successfully, sometimes not, to its declining position as a great American resort. In the city's next chapter, however, it would prove its service to its country during wartime.

Dimouts and Camp Boardwalk

World War Two was the largest military conflict of the 20th century; it reshaped the world. Even in Atlantic City, thousands of miles from the battlefields of Europe, Africa, Asia, and the Pacific, the war had a tremendous impact.

The rising tensions of the late 1930s, as it became apparent that Nazi Germany would stop at nothing to achieve its goals, were reflected in Atlantic City. The Great War had featured submarine warfare and even the mining of the Delaware Bay. What would the potential impact of hostilities be on the city, which was still suffering through the Depression?

After the Pearl Harbor attack of December 7, 1941, all Americans found out firsthand the sacrifices wartime demanded. Atlantic City was not alone, but it was impacted more than others.

The first casualty of the war for Absecon Island was the bright lights of Atlantic City and its Boardwalk. Concerned about U-boats, the United States Army demanded that citizens and businesses reduce the glow of lights from the city. They were not worried about a bombing raid on the city itself, but that the illumination thrown up by the lights would silhouette Allied ships, making them easy targets for German U-boats.

For that reason, starting in March 1942, civil defense authorities took drastic steps. Even though they didn't order a complete blackout, they promulgated a "dimout" that impacted virtually every aspect of life after dark on the island. Over 5,000 neon signs were turned off, automobile headlights were muted by special baffles, and streetlights selectively blacked out. Lights on the Boardwalk, for example, were painted nearly all black, with only a small triangle of light allowed out.

In addition, the fronts of all Boardwalk shops and restaurants were dimmed by blue cellophane, blue fluorescent lights, or awnings. All hotel, apartment, and home windows facing the sea were ordered curtained after dark. Some hotels reminded their guests of the need for care with cards that read: "Help save the lives of men at sea. Pull window shades down all the way when lights are on. Turn off all lights on leaving room. By order of the United States Navy."

As a result of the dimout, Atlantic City entered a strange new world of blue light and shadow after dark, with silhouetted figures stumbling over curbs and loose boards. To enforce the darkening, the regular police were supplemented by several hundred wardens.

Atlantic City's dimout was viewed as a success, and was imitated up and down the Atlantic coast. It lasted until midnight of October 31, 1943, when the U-boat threat had apparently been eliminated from the coastal waters.

The city was most famous, though, for Camp Boardwalk, which transformed Atlantic City into a basic training and later recuperation center.

The effort started in 1942, when the army took over Convention Hall, which became the headquarters of Army Air Forces Basic Training Center Number Seven. Forty-five of the city's hotels were commandeered by the military as temporary barracks, who leased them at the rate of a dollar per room per day, far before the market rate. Convention Hall itself housed offices and training facilities.

Under the leadership of Colonel Robert P. Glassburn, the center trained more than 250,000 new soldiers. Glassburn felt that, with time of the essence, Atlantic City was the ideal place for the massive program. But in July 1943, training facilities were shifted to Greensboro, North Carolina, and Camp Boardwalk entered its next phase: medical center.

At first, Haddon Hall was the station hospital for the training center. In August 1943, the Army Air Force announced the creation of Thomas England General Hospital, which included, in addition to Haddon Hall, the Chalfonte, Cedarcraft, Keystone, New England, Rydal, and Warwick Hotels. In the fall, the Colton Manor, Dennis and Traymore Hotels were added to the organization. The hospital provided recovery and rehabilitation services for soliders who had been wounded in the conflict.

The 1944 hurricane damaged but did not incapacitate the General Hospital, and thousands of wounded soldiers recuperated in Atlantic

City, up to and after the war's end in August 1945. By January of 1946, activities at Thomas England General Hospital began to wind down, and hotels were gradually returned to civilian use. By June 30, the hospital was only a memory.

In recognition of its efforts, Atlantic City had a B-29 Superfortress named in its honor, and, in the last weeks of the war, the Navy launched a Victory ship named the *S.S. Atlantic City Victory*. These ships, used to carry supplies, were an important part of the Allied strategy in the war, and one was named for the city to commemorate its contribution to the war effort.

The world was a different place when World War II ended, and Atlantic City would be profoundly changed as well. For the moment, however, its citizens could rest knowing that they had helped to turn the tide against the forces of evil that threatened democracy and peace worldwide.

A Mighty Storm

Many longtime Atlantic City area residents still remember the "Great Nor'easter" of March 1962 that pounded Absecon Island as a storm for the ages, but those who were around recall a 1944 hurricane that was nearly as destructive. Like the 1962 storm, this meteorological blitzkrieg left a trail of destruction but did not break the spirit of the people of Atlantic City.

From July to October of 1944, there were a total of 11 tropical storms and hurricanes formed in the Atlantic Ocean. Since this was before the advent of named storms, the storm was simply known as "hurricane number 7" to meteorologists; the media and public simply called it a destructive storm. Having formed around September 9 east of the Caribbean, the hurricane churned its way up the Eastern Seaboard of the United States, leaving a 500-mile path of havoc that began at Cape Hatteras and ended in Massachusetts.

Locally, the hurricane created calamity of the greatest magnitude when it ravaged the South Jersey coast on September 14. Absecon Island was entirely cut off from the rest of the world: highways were under as much as five feet of water and train tracks were obstructed by fallen trees. Rumors circulated in New York City that Atlantic City was all but wiped out, with hundreds homeless, the Boardwalk completely destroyed, and millions of dollars in damages. In response, the City of Philadelphia sent hundreds of policemen, ambulances, and rescue workers to the area.

The actual damage was not so severe; much of the Boardwalk was salvaged, and thankfully casualties were light, with only two dead and 40 injured. Yet the hurricane, striking a town already transformed by World War II, was still catastrophic. Under the storm's onslaught, the electricity failed at 5:25 p.m., and the city was plunged into darkness. Military police stood vigil on the Boardwalk (the city was a major military recuperation center), and all of the city's restaurants, bars, and stores closed.

There was little comfort in knowing that the city wasn't suffering in solitude. Cape May, Wildwood, and Ocean City were similarly stricken, with the last city under several feet of water.

Though the summer season had officially closed earlier in the month, the city was still full of residents, recuperating soldiers, veterans, and officers on leave, many of them with their wives. As the situation deteriorated, hundreds flocked to the city's train station, hoping to catch a train off the island. With the tracks effectively blocked, however, none were able to leave. By the evening, though, the worst had passed; the winds started to subside around 9:30 and by 10, weather conditions were normal. The worst had passed.

Still, area towns faced the daunting task of cleaning up the disaster. New Jersey Governor Walter Edge called for immediate federal aid, noting the need to provide facilities for convalescing members of the armed forces. Their health was, indeed, in jeopardy: the patients of Thomas England General Hospital, the military care center that had taken over Chalfonte-Haddon Hall, were evacuated all the way to Fort Dix and Staten Island.

The wind and water had caused severe damage to many structures, including the Boardwalk. The total cost of the storm's onslaught on Absecon Island was estimated at $4 million.

But the city was remarkably resilient. Steel Pier was damaged but open again for business even before the hurricane had completely dissolved in the North Atlantic. Two weeks later, a semblance of normalcy had returned. Horseback season opened as scheduled on the beach on October 1, while the beachfront hotels were filled with conference-goers discussing the looming postwar industrial transition to a peacetime economy. Within a month, all military patients had been transferred back to Atlantic City, and, for many, life continued as before.

But the hurricane did leave a lasting mark on Atlantic City. Heinz Pier, formerly known as the Iron Pier, was so badly damaged that it was later demolished. Garden Pier remained closed for nearly a decade.

The strongest imprint, however, was left on the Boardwalk. The Ventnor, Margate, and Longport Boardwalks were severely thrashed, and in many places completely washed out. Ventnor rebuilt its stretch of the Wooden Way (though later replaced sections with aluminum), while Margate and Longport never rebuilt theirs. T.S. Eliot aficionados could now sit on Margate's sands and truly connect nothing with nothing.

To this day, if you are out for a run, ride, or stroll and are forced to turn around at Fredricksburg Avenue, you can thank the September 1944 hurricane for the Boardwalk's sudden end. This, perhaps, was the storm's greatest legacy.

Gambling Takes a Dive

Today Americans take it for granted that there is such a thing as organized crime, but in 1950 and 1951 it took a special committee of the United States Senate to determine that such a nefarious threat existed. Though the committee's major revelations unfolded in New York, Illinois, and Chicago, a two-day stop-off in Atlantic City provided some insights into the state of vice in the city.

Tennessee Democrat Estes Kefauver (rhymes with "keep off her") chaired the committee from its May 1950 inception to May of 1951. After that, Democrat Herbert O'Conor of Maryland ran the show. And it was a show, with televised hearings in cities around the country. Kefauver became a national television star based on his committee's investigations in Miami, Tampa, New Orleans, Kansas City, Cleveland, St. Louis, Detroit, Los Angeles, San Francisco, Las Vegas, Philadelphia, Washington, Chicago, and New York City.

By the time Kefauver stepped down from the committee, it had interviewed more than 800 witnesses, and focused national attention on organized crime as never before. During the March 1951 New York hearings, the sight of gangsters bristling at the questions of committee counsel Rudolph Halley became familiar, as did the stock response "I refuse to answer on the ground that it may tend to incriminate or degrade me." The hearings were a television landmark and garnered the committee mountains of publicity.

It was only a few months later, but the committee was already past its prime when in arrived in Atlantic City on July 6, 1951. The bloom was off the rose: testimony as televised theater was played out, and Kefauver himself had left the committee, though he did stop in town on June 27 to speak to the annual convention of Lions International. He confined his remarks to the need for cooperation among the world's democracy's to meet the Soviet threat, and did not comment on local crime.

Still, the committee had made such an impact that any attention from the body—even when the cameras were switched off—was notable.

Atlantic City wasn't one of the committee's marquee targets—those were New York City, Florida, and Chicago—but it was important enough to be included in the committee's August 31, 1951 *Final Report* as one of three "medium-sized" cities spotlighted for their vice.

The committee met in executive session on July 6 and 7th in Atlantic City, forgoing dramatic public hearings for a more intimate experience in rooms 325 and 326 of the Traymore Hotel. That's right—the "executive session" took place in a regular hotel room.

Lester Hunt of Wyoming, the only actual senator who had made the trip to Atlantic City, presided over the sessions and special counsel Samuel Lane asked most of the questions.

The hearings started promptly at 10 a.m. with the testimony of Jack Portock, one of the "Four Horsemen," a group of five or more policemen who had been ostracized for attempting to enforce anti-gambling statutes. His fellow Horseman Frank Gribben followed him. They painted a picture of a police department in the thrall of criminals.

Other witnesses included Robert Warke, a retired judge, Harry Saunders, the chief of police, and an assortment of public officials and former gambling operators.

The committee finished their work by 1:40 Thursday afternoon and quickly returned to Washington D.C. to share their findings. They were not, on the whole, satisfied that authorities on Absecon Island were doing their best to end the menace of organized gambling.

The committee's final report, issued August 31, 1951, concluded that Atlantic City was "riddled with rackets, including nearly every known type of gambling" from bingo to the numbers (illegal lottery). Nearly every cigar store, the report alleged, was a front for a bookmaker, and the police deliberately refused to enforce anti-gambling statutes.

The committee found the area under the stranglehold of a two-headed monster: state senator Frank S. "Hap" Farley controlled the county's politics, while Herman "Stumpy" Orman ran the "rackets," chiefly gambling.

The committee invited Orman to testify, and he did, though he evinced a peculiarly helpful amnesia. "His knowledge of local government and personalities was excellent," the final report deadpanned, but "with regard to financial matters, he was unable to remember transactions that had occurred only a few months before." Orman took the fifth when asked why, in recent years, he'd deposited about $16,000 more in his bank account than, according to his taxes, he'd made in gross income.

Two weeks later, the committee met in Washington and heard a reprise of the Horsemen's testimony as well as other witnesses.

When speaking before the committee, most public officials maintained that cracking down on the "rackets" would be bad for business. History may have proven them right: after most of the city's illegal gambling closed down in the 1950s thanks in part to the attention focused on it by the committee, Atlantic City entered a tailspin that only ended with the legalization of gambling in 1976.

One man's vice, it seems, is another's redevelopment.

Things Fall Apart

A tlantic City survived the Great Depression and, with the federal largesse of Camp Boardwalk, made it through World War II. But a greater foe would prove too much—almost—for the city in the years after the war.

Looking back, there is no single root cause of Atlantic City's decline, which became apparent in the 1960s but which had, in truth, started decades earlier. There was no one incident that made potential visitors stay away, no one decision that, if undone, would have kept the city on top. If, perhaps, business and government leaders had been more visionary in the 1930s and 1940s—if, for example, they had embraced Mayor Charles White's 1936 revitalization plan, which included legalized gambling—the decline might have been prevented, but no one, it seemed was in a position to make the changes that needed to be made.

In any event, it was large-scale social and economic shifts that ended the good times in Atlantic City, some external and some internal. The advent of cheap air travel opened up Florida and the Caribbean to less-than-affluent residents of the Eastern seaboard cities; these destinations were warmer, more exotic, and more novel than Atlantic City, and, once they were within reach, got the lion's share of those residents' travel dollars.

Gambling prohibition probably contributed to the decline. After the Kefauver report, local authorities finally achieved the reform goal of shuttering the city's illegal gambling dens. It's possible that those who were coming to Atlantic City to gamble instead took their money to Las Vegas, whose casinos boomed as the Boardwalk declined. Though the gambling spots were illegal, they were undoubtedly popular; if they weren't they would not have been so difficult to suppress.

The decline in tourist numbers led to a drop in investment, which fed into a vicious cycle: with deteriorating facilities and not much new, there were fewer reasons to visit Atlantic City, but unless more people were visiting and new projects could promise a return on investment, no one wanted to spend money building. After the Claridge's 1930 opening, there were no new major hotels built until the Brighton/Sands, which opened in 1980. That's a half-century between openings—as significant a commentary on the slowdown as can be imagined.

At first, city officials assumed that, as after the First World War, Atlantic City would quickly return to prosperity after demobilization. And, initially, things looked bright.

In 1954, Atlantic City celebrated its centennial, which was also hailed as the 75th anniversary of the introduction of electric light. The Absecon Lighthouse was restored and opened to visitors, and Garden Pier, which had been demolished in the 1944 hurricane, was finally rebuilt and reopened as a community center. It would host free concerts all that summer, a complement to the lighted parade of ten floats depicting the city's history that progressed down the Boardwalk each night.

In contrast to the semi-centennial's celebration dinner, which featured an exclusive list of invited guests, the Centennial Birthday Dinner was open to anyone who could afford the five dollar per plate charge. It was a popular event; the 5,600 guests packed Convention Hall, where they saw tributes to stars of the past like Guy Lombardo and Paul Whiteman. After a year of celebrations, the city closed the centennial in December with a two-mile display of red-and-green lighted Christmas trees running from Albany Avenue to Garden Pier.

Compared to the semi-centennial, the 100-year celebration was backward-looking. While, at the 50-year mark, Alfred Heston could boast that his city was on a trajectory that would vault it into the top ranks of world vacation cities, the centennial seemed more about celebrating a vanishing past than planning for the future—another sign that the city was on a downward slope.

There remained excitement in the city, mostly around entertainment. The 500 Club was one of the greatest showrooms in the nation, and Frank Sinatra's haunt through the worst of the bad times. Into the 1970s, jazz artists like Johnny Hodges, Wild Bill Davis, and Lonnie Smith released albums recorded at Atlantic City venues like Grace's Little Belmont and Club Harlem.

But underneath the exuberance was decay. An attempt in the 1950s to revive the Broadway theatrical try-out circuit in Atlantic City, which had come to an abrupt halt with the 1929 crash, failed. By the late 1950s, city could hope, at best, for 250,000 attendees at its annual Easter Parade; that was half of the 500,000 who turned out in 1937, during the gloom of the Depression.

By the 1970 centennial of the Boardwalk, there was little doubt something was wrong. Atlantic City was the poorest city in New Jersey, with endemic unemployment, and aging housing stock, and sky-high crime rates. Although the Marlborough-Blenheim remained busy thanks to the loyalty of its aging clientele, other hotels were not as lucky. The Ritz-Carlton was converted to apartments, as was the President. The 700-room Ambassador, the city's largest hotel, had simply closed its doors in 1966. Within a few years, the Traymore would be demolished. While the city somewhat made up the loss in rooms by adding motels—like Howard Johnson's and Holiday Inn—it had clearly lost much of its glamor.

Facing unprecedented competition and suffering from a lack of investment, Atlantic City seemed to be in a death spiral. It would have been a wild dreamer, indeed, who could imagine that, in just a decade, the city would host the world's most profitable casinos.

Yet there remained life, and hope. The city's convention bookings remained strong (despite the fiasco of the 1964 Democratic National Convention), and calls to legalize gambling became louder and more strident.

The decline of Atlantic City after World War II was slower than the one it is facing today, but it offers valuable lessons. While the bulk of the grand hotels remained opened, many leaders insisted nothing was wrong; sure, business was slower, but it was bound to bounce back. But the old business never returned. It took a step in an entirely different direction—casino gambling—to bring crowds and investment back.

Casino gambling gave Atlantic City a new lease on life for about 30 years. The conditions that led to that revival—namely, a regional monopoly on gambling—were never guaranteed to last. Now they are gone, if not forever, certainly for the foreseeable future. The time has come for bold, reckless visionaries to imagine a different future for Atlantic City, one where quarter slot players are as important as regatta participants or Easter Parade attendees.

The Big Decline proved that nothing is owed to Atlantic City: when other vacation spots offer greater appeal and better value, sentiment won't keep most visitors returning to the shore. The casino revival proved that the city could reinvent itself. Now, as the city slides into another trough, it needs, more than ever, another rebirth.

Storm of the Century

Perched precariously on a barrier island—a glorified sandbar, really—Atlantic City has been battered by its share of storms. Deadly squalls, and the tidal surge they bring, have caused much destruction over the years, but residents and businesses have coped with them, and even profited from them. Salt-water taffy, for example, reportedly received its name after an 1883 summer storm doused a boardwalk merchant's stock of taffy; turning a negative into a positive, he renamed it salt-water taffy. Most other storms, though, left little more than damage in their wakes. One of the most fearsome to strike the area, the nor'easter of 1962, is still remembered today.

A 1944 hurricane had devastated much of the city and destroyed Heinz Pier, which had never been that successful anyway. But the "perfect storm" of March 6, 1962 is reckoned as an even more fearsome deluge. This storm was not just a local phenomenon; it was part of an immense, multi-centered system that soaked the East Coast from New England to Virginia with snow, rain, gale-force winds, and high tides. Throughout the region, the storm was responsible for as many as 15 deaths, and it left 85,000 homes without power in its wake.

Locally, two deadly incidents showed the storm's fury and the danger to both rescuers and residents. Angelo Leonetti, the police chief of Beach Haven Inlet, and Robert Osborne, of the town's rescue squad, perished when waves struck and overturned their truck while they were attempting to evacuate stranded residents. Later that night, also in Beach Haven Inlet, a Coast Guard amphibious vehicle carrying seven people overturned. Although the Coast Guard crewmen and the residents they were ferrying to safety linked hands and attempted to make their way to the Coast Guard station, four of the residents were swept away by the pounding waves.

The storm began before dawn as a steadily increasing snowfall. In some areas, the snow continued. New York City accumulated about an inch of snow, which soon turned to slush as it mixed with rain. Northern Virginia received 22 inches of snow, and it fell in areas as far south as Huntsville, Alabama. At the Jersey shore, though, the snow quickly turned to a driving rain.

Yet rain was the least of the area's problems. The storm's gale-force winds whipped the tides dangerously high. The storm surge was so intense that the ocean and bay actually met—Atlantic City was essentially underwater. Two thousand homes lost electric power, and dozens of train passengers, inexplicably on their way to the shore in the middle of one of the worst storms of the century, were stranded in Absecon, waiting hours before a bus could make its way into Atlantic City.

Still, city residents tried to function as best they could. Staffers at the *Atlantic City Press*, then headquartered on Virginia Avenue on Atlantic City's north side, continued to work at putting out their paper even after the high tide had covered much of the building's first floor with water. Police, fire, and rescue employees also valiantly labored to protect the lives of local residents and visitors.

Other barrier islands had just as bad luck. Monmouth County officials evacuated residents of low-lying areas before high tide inundated low-lying areas, doubtless saving lives. Asbury Park's convention center was flooded, and sections of its boardwalk were damaged when a surge of sand, pushed by the tide, forced it to buckle. Water four to five feet high reportedly covered every house in Sea Isle City, and beach towns as far north as Long Island were similarly inundated; three luxurious summer homes were smashed by waves in the exclusive town of Westhampton Beach.

The storm ultimately caused in excess of $1 million in damage in the Atlantic City area. It smashed two sections of the city's boardwalk, washing out two hundred feet of the wooden way in the Inlet and a 65-foot approach at Maine Avenue. In addition, the storm washed away a 50-foot section at the end of Steel Pier used for a water circus and destroyed thirty feet of the pier's middle section, thus cutting it in half. The pier, which opened in 1898, was rebuilt, but after a devastating fire in 1982, closed until it was rebuilt in 1993 by the Trump Taj Mahal.

The destruction left in the storm's wake likely advanced the decline of the city, one that would be painfully obvious during the 1964 Democratic Convention. After that nadir, the city's fortunes would only revive with the legalization of casino gaming in 1976. Had the situation not been so desperate, New Jersey voters might not have passed the pro-casino referendum. The terrible nor'easter of March 1962, may have indirectly set into motion the forces that would one day see the city's rebirth as the casino capital of the East.

Convention Controversy

A tlantic City's had several turning points: the moment that Dr. Jonathan Pitney realized a beach resort could be a hit; the arrival of the first railroad car in 1854; the construction of the first Boardwalk in 1870; and the start of casino gaming May 26, 1978. Those dates all heralded positive changes. But one less happy turning point happened August 24-27, 1964, when the Democratic National Convention focused national attention on the city—to its detriment.

Paradoxically, the big meeting of Democrats had been lured to the shore by Republican state Senator Frank S. "Hap" Farley. The 1964 convention was part of Farley's master plan to attract both parties' 1968 conventions to town and to solidify Atlantic City as a convention hub in an attempt to stave off its ongoing decline.

The spring was a hopeful time for the city. Construction on the Atlantic City Expressway was nearly finished, and resort officials believed that the convention might augur a new age for the city. Convention Hall was outfitted with a nearly $2 million air conditioning system. With new motels ready to open in Atlantic City and surrounding towns, city boosters hoped the convention would re-introduce the beach resort to thousands of visitors. Those who came for political business, it was hoped would stay for pleasure.

"Everything possible," a news report from June stated, "will be done to encourage lengthy visits, including politeness on the part of waiters, waitresses, chambermaids, bellhops, taxicab drivers, and other service employees."

But there were doubts elsewhere. A *New York Times* restaurant review which ran immediately before the convention dismissed

Atlantic City as "Coney Island with illusions of grandeur" and declared to be its food "conventional" at best.

Long before the convention, there was no doubt as to who would be nominated. Lyndon Baines Johnson had been elected as Vice President in 1960 and, following the November 1963 assassination of John F. Kennedy, had been leading the nation for less than a year. Though Johnson would dominate the convention's politics, Kennedy's presence was never far away; a week before the meeting, New Jersey governor Richard Hughes unveiled a bronze bust of Kennedy, sculpted by Evangelos Frudakis of Ventnor, on the Boardwalk in front of Convention Hall.

The convention got off to good start, as more than 80 volunteers greeted arriving delegates at the region's airports, bus stations, and train depots. Throughout the town, hawkers sold LBJ cowboy hats, candy jars, and cufflinks, and spirits were running high.

The convention's greatest drama involved the selection of the vice president (ultimately, it was Senator Hubert H. Humphrey of Minnesota) and a battle over seating the Mississippi delegation. The latter has earned the convention a place in American history textbooks, typically the only mention of Atlantic City in those tomes.

In 1964, the Mississippi Democratic Party was strictly segregated. Denied a place in the party's primaries, black Mississippians formed the core of the Mississippi Freedom Democratic Party. This integrated political group selected delegates to the national convention, sending 64 members by bus to Atlantic City. But after the national party refused to unseat the "regular" Mississippi delegation, the MFDP delegates remained to draw attention to the party's racial inequities.

Though the delegation was not officially seated, their appearance at the convention was a pivotal moment in the civil rights movement, and soon the Voting Rights Act—championed by President Johnson—would open the door to greater black participation in politics, which in turn fostered the integration of political parties throughout the South.

One of the convention's most notable moments was a film tribute to the slain leader. His brother, Attorney General Robert F. Kennedy, gave a short speech lionizing the fallen president's commitment to the Democratic Party, helping those less fortunate, and a strong national defense. Before allowing him to say a word, the audience gave RFK more than 20 minutes of uninterrupted applause. It was the convention's emotional high point, and a moment that local residents remembered decades later.

But soon after, it became apparent that the convention had not been an economic success. One local shopkeeper said that business had "dropped like an elevator," and the week's business was down by as much as 50 percent compared to a usual August. For years, service people complained about what bad tippers delegates had been.

Worse yet, the national media was just as disenchanted with Atlantic City as the city was with the convention. Poor accommodations, worse service, and high prices infuriated many delegates and irritated reporters. One California delegate reported that her hotel was "just dirty and falling apart." Newspaper and magazine coverage of the convention sent the message that the city itself was similarly worn.

In a sense, the 1964 convention was a necessary step before Atlantic City's revival. It demonstrated, without question, that the city had deteriorated, and that it needed to chart a new path. Within a decade, most residents would agree that casino gaming alone could save the resort.

But before the city could rise, it had to reach bottom. So the 1964 Democratic National Convention deserves a place in Atlantic City history beside those other, happier landmarks.

The First Shot

Casino gaming has been an Atlantic City reality for over 30 years now. It seems impossible to imagine an Absecon Island without casinos, but the first attempt to legalize gambling—and create the casino gaming industry in Atlantic City—actually went down in defeat.

The debate over legal casinos in Atlantic City was already old in the 1970s. Back in the wide-open days of Nucky Johnson, gambling was technically illegal, though proprietors who greased the right palms had few problems. But by the 1950s stricter enforcement drove gambling underground. The city's decades-long association with gambling, it appeared, was over.

But there were always those who wanted another way. The first calls to legalize gambling for the benefit of Atlatnic City went unheeded, but as the decline continued, many sensible residents began to argue that allowing legally what had once been an illicit lure—gambling—might trigger an economic turnaround. By early 1972, advocates of expanded legal gambling—from off track betting to casinos—were beating the drums in the Statehouse. New Jersey's lottery, new in 1970, was apparently a success, and further gambling legalization seemed a fair bet. Though the sitting governor, William Cahill, was adamantly against any such expansion, the 1973 election proved auspicious: Cahill was knocked out of the Republican Party, and new governor Brendan Byrne had already expressed support for Atlantic City casinos. After his election, he proposed a constitutional amendment that, followed by a local referendum, would allow casinos to open in Atlantic City.

But all was not smooth sailing. Even as Atlantic City casino proponents were trying to get a resolution before the legislature, a group of Newark residents began arguing that their city, too, should get casinos. Those in favor of Atlantic City casinos had ideas that weren't, in retrospect, much better. Some foresaw state-owned casinos co-existing with privately-built hotels. One proponent suggested that requiring patrons to don formal attire and levying steep admissions charges would be the best way to keep those who "couldn't afford" to gamble out of the casinos.

These were not the most unrealistic ideas floating around. One businessman predicted that the tourist traffic generated by gambling would justify an unprecedented change to the city: the Boardwalk would be glassed in from end to end, and visitors would stroll down boards covered by a red carpet, beneath dangling chandeliers.

By April 1974, when the constitutional amendment was being drafted in the Legislature, a political rift opened between the governor, who favored casinos in only Atlantic City, and the Assembly, which passed a bill allowing casinos anywhere in the state. Byrne eventually dropped his opposition, and the Senate approved the measure by exactly the three-fifths needed. The amendment was placed on the November 5, 1974 ballot.

As it was written, the amendment required that a local referendum approve state-run casinos for any area, and Governor Byrne suggested that Atlantic City would be the first to get casinos; if successful there, other cities might choose to have them. This appeared to give Atlantic City a chance.

But opposition to the casinos, scattered at first, had coalesced by August, and the lack of any coherent pro-casino strategy or champion (Byrne declared himself neutral on the modified amendment) bolstered the "no" forces. Though religious organizations were the most vocal opponents, it is likely that they received at least tacit support from those involved in the horseracing industry in both New Jersey and New York. Opponents argued that the costs of regulation would be prohibitive, that there was no way of preventing organized crime from dominating the gaming business, and that casinos were both morally and fiscally irresponsible.

The pro-casino forces, with a vastly larger campaign war chest, seemed so far ahead that they got complacent. As they vaguely suggested that Atlantic City would become "Monte Carlo USA" rather than "Las Vegas East," support for the measure dwindled. The possibility of casinos popping up anywhere in the state, not just Atlantic City, further alienated the electorate.

In the run-up to the referendum, supporters like Atlantic City Mayor Joseph Bradway argued strenuously in favor of casinos and damned the hypocrisy of churches who ran bingo games opposing casinos on moral grounds. But on the Sunday before the election, church pulpits around the state resonated with sermons on the evils of gambling. Nevada Attorney General Bob List didn't help matters when he warned that it took a massive amount of governmental power and financial resources to keep the Silver State's gaming industry honest, and that any other state that rolled the dice on legal casinos, including New Jersey, would be hard-pressed to keep "undesirables" out.

It was not surprising then, when on Election Day, casino backers' worst fears came true: voters overwhelmingly opposed the referendum, and the dream of reviving Atlantic City seemed doom to failure. But those who imagined a better tomorrow for Absecon Island refused to admit defeat and, in a historic reverse, succeeded in winning passage of a casino referendum only two years later.

One More Time

In 1976, the nation's Bicentennial year, New Jersey voters gave Atlantic City a second chance at glory. The city had fallen far from its former standing as the "world's playground." Jobs had disappeared, infrastructure was decaying, and tourism had dwindled.

In 1968, at a testimonial for 500 Club owner Paul "Skinny" D'Amato, city power brokers first discussed casino gambling as a cure for the city's ills. Within six years, they managed to get a measure on the New Jersey ballot. The 1974 referendum would have allowed casinos to open anywhere in the state after a local vote.

But gambling opponents, including clergymen, advised their constituents to vote no, and the referendum failed. These were dark days, but some didn't give up hope. A small citizen contingent pressed for casinos. Without gambling, they argued, the city could not reverse its decline. Some considered them impractical dreamers, but they refused to take no for an answer.

In retrospect, the casino boosters should have been taken more seriously. Gambling was in the middle of a long winning streak. After New Hampshire began the nation's first modern lottery in 1964, several states, including New Jersey, legalized them. Horse racing had been growing for decades. On the other side of the country, Nevada had proven that casino gaming could be regulated, and Las Vegas had become a neon metropolis on the strength of its tourist economy.

In April 1976, the New Jersey State Senate, on 24-9 vote, the bare minimum required, approved putting a measure allowing casinos in Atlantic City only before the voters. Governor Brendan Byrne, who believed that gambling expansion on the East Coast was inevitable and wanted to maximize the benefit to his state, was an enthusiastic supporter.

This time, the pro-casino campaign was far better organized and more persuasive. Casino supporters were able to swing most of the state's clergy, including leaders in the powerful Catholic community, and undercut the moral argument against gambling. The new referendum, specifying that casinos be restricted to Atlantic City, quelled fears of rampant statewide casino-building.

In a shrewd political move, advocates had a portion of gaming taxes earmarked for senior citizen programs, thus securing the support of a large voting bloc. Law enforcement and business leaders also spoke in favor of the measure, and the increasing economic desperation of Atlantic City was eloquent testimony to its necessity.

But the city still faced an uphill fight. Anti-casino crusaders declared that gambling would be followed by organized crime, corruption and mass bankruptcies, giving the Garden State a foretaste of Armageddon.

State Senator Anne Martindell, in her unsuccessful fight to kill the referendum in the statehouse, even summoned the ghost of Estes Kefauver, quoting his warnings that, when given the "cloak of respectability," gamblers' money would quickly dominate politics.

But those who wanted casinos had arguments of their own. State Senator William Musto pointed out, in the debate in the statehouse, that legalized horseracing and lotteries had "turned out all right."

Casino advocates hired political consultant Sanford Weiner to assist the Committee to Rebuild Atlantic City, the central pro-casino group. Weiner was put in charge of a $1 million campaign fund, an incredible amount of money at the time. The anti-casino groups only raised $21,000.

Weiner's marketing blitz focused on several themes: "Help Yourself," reminding voters that casinos could enrich more than their owners; "Atlantic City Only," which eased fears of a casino in every backyard; and "Casinos Yes," just in case anyone was in doubt about which way to vote.

The vote came in an election season that was at once cynical and expectant. The Bicentennial stirred patriotic pride, but the Vietnam war and the Watergate scandal had left Americans skeptical about the nation's leaders. The presidential election pitted Democrat Jimmy Carter against Richard Nixon's hand-picked vice president Gerald Ford, who had pardoned his scandal-plagued former boss.

In this environment, it made sense to vote for casinos. After all, the prohibition of gambling hadn't stopped games of chance, and Atlantic City couldn't be worse off. For senior citizens, the financial assistance promised by the measure was a godsend, and enough reason to let Atlantic City deal with casinos.

Weiner did more than tout the potential benefits of gambling; he met the critics head on, demanding that Senator Martindell provide some proof of her allegations that gangsters would dominate legal casinos. She didn't.

Finally, after months of debate, discussion and persuasion, New Jersey voters went to the polls. On November 2, 1976, more than 1.2 million people voted in favor of the referendum—the exact same number who had voted against it two years before. By a margin of 200,000 votes, the measure passed.

The impact on the city was immediate; following the vote, Convention Hall recorded its best two months of bookings in its history up to that point. Groups like the United Auto Workers, which had stayed away for years, announced their return thanks to the prospect of new hotel rooms. Property values rose as prospective casino owners began (or continued) buying up real estate. More importantly, hope returned to the city.

With this victory, Atlantic City opened the door to its future. Without the trials and triumph of 1976, the city's history—and many of our lives—would have turned out quite differently.

Jersey Hustle

Popularized in the movie *American Hustle*, the Abscam inquiry was a black eye for the state of New Jersey and its fledgling casino industry, but one from which it quickly recovered, though with some regulatory changes.

The investigation—in which FBI agents posed as the henchman of a fictitious Arab sheik, Kambir Abdul Rahman, to uncover a corrupt congressman—took its name from Abdul Enterprises, the sheik's alleged company. Though Atlantic City wasn't a primary target of the sting, repercussions here led to big changes in the way New Jersey regulates casinos.

News of the investigation broke like a thunderbolt on February 2, 1980. The FBI announced it had snared numerous public officials, including New Jersey Senator Harrison Williams and seven members of Congress, in a two-year undercover investigation. The probe also included a member of the Casino Control Commission.

It was a critical time for Atlantic City's gaming industry. Over the objections of the Division of Gaming Enforcement, the first casino, Resorts International, had just received its permanent license. Though Caesars Boardwalk Regency and Bally's Park Place operated under temporary licenses, key figures at both casinos had been forced to step aside due to concerns about organized crime and corruption.

Allegations that a Casino Control Commissioner was tainted by malfeasance called the entire regulatory structure into question.

"It's scary because it creates such an aura of wrongdoing," said an anonymous casino executive at the time. "One has to ask, who else is involved?" Commission Chairman Joseph P. Lordi admitted that the regulatory body's reputation was at stake.

Ironically, the casino industry wasn't even a target of the FBI. Abscam had begun as a simple investigation into the theft of two pieces of artwork from a New York apartment building. It broadened into a more general investigation of organized crime and political corruption. In 1980, casino gambling was the hottest thing going in New Jersey, so it was only a matter of time before it became part of the inquiry.

Abscam started with FBI agents posing as Sheik Rahman's assistants approaching public officials seeking political asylum and help with purported investments in port facilities and a titanium mine. It wasn't hard work. Once they offered money in exchange for favors, the agents heard from officials who weren't even on their radar. Congressmen lined up to sell their offices, and unwittingly incriminated themselves.

The investigation wound its way to Atlantic City when Camden Mayor and New Jersey state Senator Angelo Errichetti reportedly told undercover agents that, in exchange for $400,000, he could help the sheik secure land, build a casino, and get a gaming license. Errichetti reportedly boasted that he could deliver three of five Casino Control Commission votes. He suggested a $100,000 bribe for Vice Chairman Kenneth MacDonald, and claimed that MacDonald "controlled" Lordi.

MacDonald resigned immediately. Lordi denied any wrongdoing. As many as 60 public officials had been implicated. Licensing hearings for Caesars and Bally's ground to a halt, and some wondered whether the entire regulatory structure needed an overhaul.

Abscam had another Absecon Island connection. To impress sting targets, the FBI had rented fancy digs including a townhouse in Washington's upscale Georgetown area and a lavish Florida yacht. Locally, the accomodations were a little less flashy—a rented eighth-floor condo in Ventnor's Regency Towers.

Despite the Abscam furor, not all legislators sold out. New Jersey Congressmen William Hughes, James Florio and James Howard not only spurned the undercover agents, they reported them to the FBI.

In the end, Abscam led to bribery and conspiracy convictions for Senators Williams and Errichetti as well as New Jersey Congressman Frank Thompson. Others caught in the snare were Congressmen Raymond Lederer and Michael "Ozzie" Myers (both of Pennsylvania), John Jenrette (South Carolina), and Richard Kelly (Florida).

The investigation forced changes in New Jersey gaming. The Casino Control Commission went from a part-time to a full-time body, and the Casino Control Act was amended to prohibit temporary permits. With the commission's regulatory mandate more clearly defined, state officials hoped to avoid another ugly episode. One Abscam, they decided, was enough.

Though it ended careers and threatened reputations, the Abscam scandal did not slow down the growth of the gaming industry, though it did provide regulators with a cautionary tale: while they were watching the gaming industry for malfeasance, those in government were just as susceptible to corruption as those working in casinos.

Second Life

The success of Resorts International guaranteed two things: that more operators would invest in Atlantic City and that, eventually, other states would experiment with legalizing casino gambling. In the 1980s, Atlantic City enjoyed the benefits of the former; it was a good fifteen years until the impact of the latter was realized.

Even before Resorts opened, skeptics feared that, if casino gambling was such a good thing, someone else would get in on the action. A Florida referendum to legalize casinos failed in November 1978, but Southern Florida and New York's Catskills were considered potential casino competitors before the first bet was even made in Atlantic City.

That might be why, after Resorts' opening, there was such a scramble to get properties open. Caesars World opened its Boardwalk Regency in a hastily-converted Howard Johnson's in June 1979, and in December of that year Bally's Park Place, using the historic Dennis Hotel's rooms, opened.

In 1980, the Brighton, Harrah's Marina, and Golden Nugget set out to carve their own piece of the expanding casino pie and, in the following year, the Playboy, Claridge, and Tropicana took their first bets.

By the early 1980s, Atlantic City's casino market was booming, with each casino making millions a week—an unprecedented amount.

Today, it is hard to remember just how successful Atlantic City casinos were in their early years. In 1982, the city's nine casinos earned more gaming revenue than the more-than-40 casinos of the Las Vegas Strip, the nation's established casino leader. Atlantic City casinos earned more from gambling than any other casinos in the world. With one-sixth the guest rooms of Las Vegas, Atlantic City in 1984 had more than double the visitors.

There was stiff competition for the Strip's high rollers, but Atlantic City prospered in dealing with a new kind of customer: the day-tripper. With public transit not as good as it might be and Atlantic City International Airport not offering many direct or convenient flights, the majority of visitors to Atlantic City casinos have always come by car. That, in and of itself, wasn't so different from Nevada, where a substantial portion of guests typically drove up from California. Atlantic City's visitors, though, rarely spent the night.

In addition, casino buses, which ferried gamblers from surrounding areas daily, were a major source of visitors. Bus people, who typically played slot machines and generally tried to maximize their comp offers, represented more than two-fifths of all Atlantic City visitors from 1983 to 1988—a huge number.

Yet the prevalence of bus people wasn't necessarily good for the casinos. By the late 1980s, "bus wars," in which casinos upped their promotional offers in a bid to win play from these fickle guests, had led many casinos to bankruptcy. Relying on players who, for an extra $5 in coin, would switch properties, was not sustainable. In the early 1990s, the proportion of bus visitors fell to a more manageable but still-significant 28 percent.

Despite the seemingly easy money and a monopoly outside Nevada, casinos faced barriers to profitability. Early Casino Control Commission regulations were byzantine and, it sometimes seemed, designed to frustrate operators and players alike rather than provide sensible oversight. Casinos were limited in their operating hours (the gaming day began at 10 a.m. and ended at 4 a.m. most nights, 6 a.m. on weekends and holidays). Commission rules mandated the percentage of floor space that could be allocated to slot machines, the operating hours of restaurants, and the entertainment options the casinos offered. This went far beyond ensuring fiscal accountability and fair dealing, and represented a never-before-seen intrusion on day-to-day management.

Perhaps the most onerous restriction placed on casinos was the Commission's table betting minimums. Under the original regulations that governed day-to-day operations, casinos had to offer $2 minimum bets at 30 percent of its tables and $5 minimum bets at another 30 percent of them. A legislative fiat designed to maximize "public participation" in gambling, the mandatory minimums prevented casino managers from maximizing the efficiency of their already limited game inventory.

The Casino Control Commission, by a 3 to 2 vote, eliminated the mandatory minimums in February 1981, after several existing and potential operators complained that overregulation was hurting the bottom line and making it more difficult to attract investment. For the next 30 years, the Casino Control Commission and Division of Gaming Enforcement only relaxed their regulatory chokehold reluctantly, after years of demonstrated decline and threats from newer jurisdictions.

For the moment, though, Atlantic City casinos seemed to prosper despite the shackles. In truth, there were plenty of signs that the money wasn't as easy as it looked—the Brighton's principal owners were forced to sell their interests in early 1981, a move that ultimately led to the property being renamed the Sands—but on balance Atlantic City was the world's most dynamic and most promising casino market in the early 1980s.

It is hard to say whose fault it is that the promise of casino gambling—a broader revitalization of Atlantic City beyond the Boardwalk and marina—always seemed just around the corner. Much of the blame should be laid at the feet of legislators and regulators; had they ruled the industry with a lighter hand and a forceful but streamlined regulatory process, it is likely that the city could have attracted significantly more investment. With gambling revenues more secure and casinos less hamstrung by arbitrary rules, operators could have focused on differentiating themselves by diversifying their non-gaming offerings, which is exactly what happened in Las Vegas in the 1990s.

With more robust non-gaming investment, Atlantic City would have been better equipped to face the competition that started with Foxwoods in Connecticut in the early 1990s and reached its logical conclusion when casinos and slot parlors opened in Pennsylvania in the late 2000s. And a more diverse industry would have required more employees, which would have boosted the city immeasurably, in addition to the boon more visitors staying longer to enjoy more varied activities would have brought.

Still, at the time the future looked bright, and it isn't hard to see why. In the 1980s, casinos brought a second chance at life to Atlantic City, and, for the time being, the people of Atlantic City made the best of that chance.

Ebb Tide

In hindsight, it was obvious: casino gambling outside of Nevada was too good a thing to be left to Atlantic City alone. There never should have been any illusions to the contrary. Indeed, there weren't; one of the reasons that the regulatory process in the first months was so rushed and haphazard was a very real fear that other jurisdictions—particularly the Catskills and Miami—would soon host their own casinos. Governor Brendan Byrne himself believed that more legalization was inevitable. A failed Florida referendum in 1978 gave the city some breathing room, but it was only a matter of time before someone else rolled the dice. The success of the Atlantic City casino industry—beating Las Vegas after less than four years of operation—guaranteed it.

For a while, it seemed like the monopoly would last, and lawmakers and industry leaders settled into complacency. That was a mistake. As it happened, Atlantic City only had about a ten-year head start on the rest of the country. In 1987, the Supreme Court ruled in its *Cabazon* decision that if a state permitted gambling, Indian reservations in that state could offer it without state oversight or intervention. The following year, Congress passed the Indian Gaming Regulatory Act, which paved the way for full-blown tribal casinos. In the early 1990s, Atlantic City got its first real competition from two Connecticut casinos, Foxwoods and Mohegan Sun.

New Jersey casino regulators responded to the challenges posed by the new competition by authorizing new games like poker and keno and permitting casinos to remain open 24 hours a day. When more competition came from Delaware in 1995, the city was hurt but survived; its gaming revenues even managed to grow. Again, this led to complacency. Competition, it seemed, was nothing to worry about.

The 2006 opening of casinos in Pennsylvania, coupled with an upswing in New York gaming, however, were not so easy to weather. The advent of Pennsylvania gaming led directly to the current decline. In 2006, Atlantic City casinos brought in a record $5.2 billion in gaming win; over the previous five years, casino win had increased by nearly one billion dollars. Despite the increased competition, this looked like a market on the upswing, and a slew of ambitious projects—Gateway Atlantic City, Pinnacle Resorts' mega casino on the former Sands and Traymore sites, and MGM Atlantic City— were announced.

None would break ground. After 2006, casino win shrank and shrank until, in 2014, it fell to $2.7 billion, with no signs of a turnaround. Many projects were canceled although one, Revel, limped towards its opening, albeit in truncated form.

Then, in 2014, the consequences of the revenue slide finally became real when four casinos closed: the Atlantic Club (which had opened as the Golden Nugget), Revel, the Showboat, and Trump Plaza. As of 2015, none has reopened as a casino or in any other form, and a sale of the Showboat to Stockton University has degenerated into litigation.

In the end, though, Atlantic City survived the Great Contraction, and it will survive any other curveballs the universe tosses its way. Sure, Atlantic City isn't the global vacation destination that Alfred Heston dreamed of, but it has survived wars, depression, and an even greater decline than the current one. If there's one thing even a quick read of Atlantic City history should demonstrate, it is that the city and its inhabitants are incredibly resilient; at times the city succeeds, it seems, in spite of itself. So, after weathering corruption, crime, and corporate misadventure, a little casino competition isn't going to destroy Atlantic City.

In the current (2015) climate, maybe a re-reading of history is the best antidote to defeatism. For years, Dr. Pitney failed to get anyone excited in the possibilities of a seaside resort on Absecon Island. But he persevered, and eventually the railroad and incorporation came. For a good 15 years, Atlantic City remained little more than potential; outside of shipwrecks and drownings, it made few headlines.

Then, with more investment and, possibly, a bit of luck, the city caught on. By the 1870s, it was a town to watch, and by the 1880s, it had arrived as the "Queen of the Coast." For the next 80 years, the city kept adapting and growing. Innovations like the Boardwalk and the Miss America Pageant reflected the inventive entrepreneurship that built Atlantic City.

Currently, it seems that no amount of creativity can stem the tide of casino competition. And it can't. But Jeremiah Leeds couldn't have imagined a newly built railroad turning his homestead into a metropolis. Jonathan Pitney certainly never imagined people flocking to his would-be health resort to play quarter slot machines. It may be difficult to imagine a future for Atlantic City that doesn't include gambling as a major attraction, but the Great Contraction should have taught us that, despite what we believed in the 1980s, the casino industry is not Atlantic City's salvation. Nor is it the beginning and end of the city's appeal as a resort destination.

Contraction and uncertainty isn't a great place to stop this brief overview of Atlantic City's history, but the city right now is in a very uncertain place. It's had a fair amount of dirt kicked on it, but, if history is a guide, it would be wrong to count Atlantic City out just yet.

The United States Hotel, opened in 1854, welcomed the first visitors to Atlantic City. Expanded several times, it had an imposing presence until its 1898 closure. *Allen "Boo" Pergament.*

Captain John Young's mansion, perched at the end of Million Dollar Pier, had the address of Number One Atlantic Ocean, USA. *Allen "Boo" Pergament.*

This stylized view from Million Dollar Pier shows the classic Shelburne, Dennis, Marlborough-Blenheim, Claridge, Brighton, and Traymore Hotels. *Jersey Supply Company.*

A later look at Million Dollar Pier and the central Boardwalk and Beach. *Jack Freeman.*

An early-1950s look, again from Million Dollar Pier, at the beach and hotels of the Boardwalk. *Kardmasters.*

The Atlantic City Free Public Library's 1905 building, constructed with funds from philanthropist Andrew Carnegie, served the public until the 1985 opening of a new library. *Metropolitan News Company.*

The devastation left behind by the 1944 hurricane, seen here on Seaside Avenue. *Allen "Boo" Pergament.*

The 1962 nor'easter turned Texas Avenue into an extension of the bay. This may have been the most devastating storm in Atlantic City's history. *Allen "Boo" Pergament.*

Chalfonte-Haddon Hall in the late 1930s, when it boasted 1,000 rooms and an assortment of ocean decks, lounges, and athletic facilities. The Haddon Hall side would inaugurate Atlantic City's casino era as Resorts International. *Leeds and Lippincott Company.*

The Marlborough-Blenheim's November 1978 implosion put an exclamation point on the changes casinos were bringing to Atlantic City. Bally's Park Place was built on the site. *Allen "Boo" Pergament.*

Two

Classic Hospitality

First in Line

For most people, Atlantic City is synonymous with its hospitality industry. Since the city's first heyday in the 1870s, through the revitalization brought by casino gaming, hotels have been a major part of Atlantic City's identity. It's no surprise, then, that the first hotel built on Absecon Island was there at the very beginning.

The United States Hotel opened in 1854, the same year that Atlantic City was incorporated as a city. On May 1 of that year, voters chose the city's first mayor, Chalkey Leeds, in a meeting at the United States.

The hotel's name was apt. Atlantic City's planners, laying out city streets named after the states of the Union in the years before the Civil War, felt that, symbolically, the resort was a place for all Americans. Its largest hotel, the United States, would reflect this patriotism; it was not named for an English resort or natural feature, as were many others, but the nation itself.

The United States, like all other major hotels of Atlantic City's first years, fronted on Atlantic Avenue, which was at the time the city's major thoroughfare. Taking up land between Maryland and Delaware Avenues (today the site of a Showboat parking lot), the United States extended all the way south to Pacific Avenue and owned land extending to the ocean.

In the era before the Boardwalk, this was considered beachfront property. Horses and carriages stood at the ready to take guests down to the shoreline for their bathing pleasure. While sea bathing was a pleasant diversion, it was also dangerous. In 1855, a party of four ocean-goers chose to bathe at a spot above the usual United States Hotel bathing grounds. Unfamiliar with the area, they were swept out to sea by an undertow, and two of them perished. Such accidents were common. As a result, swimmers were urged to remain close to the "regular bathing ground," and eventually the city instituted lifeguard service.

The hotel covered 14 acres of land and, with 600 rooms at its largest, was the biggest hotel in the entire nation for a time. It was larger, in fact, than many hotels of the early casino era. The United States featured an expansive garden with a bandstand in the center for outdoor concerts, an idea that casinos would later revive. The United States, like other hotels, encouraged its guests to frequent the beach in the morning and return to its grounds afterwards; following lunch it featured concerts and dancing in its gardens.

Originally built by the Camden and Atlantic Railroad, it was soon sold to Benjamin Brown, a flamboyant impresario and promoter. Brown advertised the hotel as the most elegant and fashionable in town (which wasn't, in its first years, saying much), with walnut furnishings and gas heat and light in each room. In the 1870s, the hotel's glory years, room rates were $3.50 per day or $20 weekly. For the time, this was a considerable sum. As a result, the hotel became the favored destination for the wealthy, who rode private rail cars to the shore.

In Atlantic City's earliest years, when every visitor was greeted like a savior, the United States was the center of the action. Most special events and concerts took place there in lieu of a civic center and, until the construction of a city hall, many City Council meetings were held at the hotel.

As the resort's premium hotel, the United States hosted its share of luminaries. In July 1874, President Ulysses S. Grant spent a night at the hotel to much fanfare. Between Camden and the shore, his train made several stops, as he gave a speech at Haddonfield and accepted gifts of local wines and cigars at Egg Harbor City; these were enjoyed as the train sped towards Atlantic City. City officials declared a municipal holiday to mark the event and most of the city turned out to greet the President. That night, a gala fireworks display and ball honored Grant. Both the hotel and the city received favorable newspaper coverage as a result of the reception.

Grant's visit was the high point for the United States Hotel. Already, the tides of history were moving the center of gravity away from Atlantic Avenue and onto the Boardwalk, which was first laid down in 1870. Although the hotel was once the king of the beach, by the 1890s it found itself competing with newer, plusher hotels with better access to the city's main attractions, the beach and Boardwalk.

In a pattern that would be repeated time and again, the United States became a decaying shadow of its former self. In 1896, John Davis bought the hotel and tried to revive it, but he had no luck. In 1898, he started to demolish the proud resort, subdividing its grounds into lots. While one section of the hotel, converted into a rooming house, stood at States and Atlantic avenues for decades longer, the United States Hotel was eventually forgotten. Still, it occupies an important place in Atlantic City's history.

Once the city's top meeting place, and for years its leading inn, the United States Hotel set the pattern for later resort palaces. It also showed that, no matter how great the reputation or historical value, visitors would not hesitate to leave for newer, better accommodations.

The Survivor

Some historic buildings in Atlantic City, like the lighthouse, are easy to spot. Others, not so much. The former Dennis Hotel, now part of Atlantic City, is a case in point. While it's clearly not recent construction, few people walking its corridors have an appreciation for just how long the Dennis has been part of the city. It is, in fact, older than even the Boardwalk.

Though the hotel has never been the city's tallest, biggest, or flashiest, it is one of the few classic structures that has survived the coming of casinos, and is a landmark in its own right.

The Dennis began rather inauspiciously in 1860 as a modest two-room cottage built by William Dennis at the corner of Pacific and Michigan Avenues. Dennis, a schoolmaster from Burlington, New Jersey, built the small house as a simple summer retreat for himself... and his family.

Professor Dennis (as he preferred to by known) happened to have a large extended family, with a plethora of cousins, nephews, and nieces who found excellent excuses to visit him "down the shore." A hospitable fellow, Dennis added rooms to his small residence until it boasted 22 of them.

Dennis had originally sought a refuge from the burdens of school life, and imagined himself spending quiet summers by the Atlantic Ocean, not worrying about classrooms or examinations. Instead, he found he was running a rooming house. In April 1867, he finally tired of playing host and sold his boarding house, which was well-situated in the growing resort, to a fellow Burlingtonian named Joseph H. Borton.

Borton had no pretenses; he operated the house as a hotel, which he named "The Dennis," and continued enlarging it. By 1892 it had 250 rooms (though only 15 private baths), and was one of the Boardwalk's largest hostelries.

In the fall of 1900, Borton sold the Dennis to Walter Buzby for $450,000, and Buzby continued the expansion of the property.

The Dennis witnessed some bizarre scenes: on July 4, 1901, for example, Mrs. C. J. Smith, wife of a Georgia Southern and Florida Railroad official, broke both of her legs when, suffering from "an aberration of the mind," she jumped from the hotel's second-story porch. Mrs. Smith made a fortunate recovery.

By that year, Buzby was promoting the Dennis as a year-round resort with hot and cold seawater piped into private baths. "Liberally appointed and conducted," it entertained its share of wealthy New Yorkers and Philadelphians, and was also the site for small conventions. Buzby also advertised his guests' access to the city's golf course.

Buzby kept building, adding a "fireproof addition" of 100 rooms in 1905, and again in 1911. Over the next several decades, Buzby continued to add to the hotel until it had 550 rooms. It remained a popular destination for visitors in all seasons, true to Buzby's original year-round vision.

One aspect of the Dennis now seems astounding. Since the days of Professor Dennis, it had been a "dry" hotel, in which alcohol was not served, nor intoxicated guests allowed. That changed in 1942, when Buzby finally succumbed to the will of his guests, applied for a liquor license, and opened a cocktail lounge. This was the last major Atlantic City hotel to "go wet," ending an era when, although alcohol was readily available, some visitors demonstrated their propriety by staying at non-drinking hotels. As time went on, these visitors were clearly a minority, as the Dennis's cocktail lounge shows.

In the next year, as part of the "Camp Boardwalk" program, the Dennis was converted to military use as a center for returning servicemen, and did not reopen to civilians until December 1945.

The Dennis remained in the Buzby family until 1969, when National Inns LTD, which also owned the Shelburne, bought it. Walter J. Buzby, grandson of the original proprietor, re-acquired it in 1974, but it was sold in the following year for demolition or use as a casino hotel.

The new owners, Bally Manufacturing, eventually razed the Marlborough-Blenheim next door but kept the Dennis; this allowed them to open a casino in 1979, relatively early in the game. Spending $7 million to renovate the Dennis for occupancy (thus fulfilling the requirement that the casino have a 500-room hotel), Bally's used this as their primary hotel wing until the opening of its gleaming pink glass tower in 1989.

Following a late-1990s renovation, the Dennis sported a brightly-colored façade that tied it, improbably enough, to the new Wild Wild West casino at Bally's. Some remnants of the past remain, however—Bally's still provides its guests with access to the Atlantic City Country Club, proving that, just as Walter Buzby hoped a century ago, golf would be a major attraction for guests.

Lord of the Boards

Out of the many hotels that once towered above the Boardwalk, few had as interesting a past—or as tantalizing an unrealized future—as the Shelburne. Standing next to the Dennis at Michigan Avenue, the Shelburne prospered in the city's golden age, declined in lean years, and nearly became part of the revived post-casino skyline.

The Shelburne (often misspelled "Shelbourne") had peaceful beginnings. In 1869, Elisha David Roberts, a Philadelphia Quaker, opened a wood boardinghouse on the site. He chose to name his resort after the Anglo-Irish Lord Shelburne, born William FitzMaurice Petty, who had argued in the 1770s and early 1780s for conciliation with the American colonists. Shelburne served as British Prime Minister from 1782 to 1783.

Roberts was a success as an owner/operator, luring many of Broadway's luminaries to his hotel. Often, performers in the nearby Warner Theater stayed for long stretches at the Shelburne, giving the hotel a decided show business flavor. Some of the more famous guests of the hotel included Al Jolson, Tom Mix, and Enrico Caruso.

The hotel has a place in music history: reportedly, George M. Cohan wrote the World War I-era standard "Over There" while staying at the Shelburne (though he later claimed to have penned it in New York), and in 1933 Irving Berlin wrote "Easter Parade" as a guest there.

Among all the celebrities to stay at the Shelburne, one shines particularly brightly—James Buchanan "Diamond Jim" Brady."Brady worked his way up from bellboy to railroad messenger to executive to financier, and with a fortune wrung from his Wall Street investments set out to live the good life. He had a legendary appetite, eating several steaks, lobsters, and ducks in the course of a single meal. And he had an equally large passion for Lillian Russell, the beautiful star of American stage and song.

To accommodate Russell, Brady rented an apartment for her for the then-outrageous sum of $1,000 a week. He also had a golden bathtub installed for Russell's pleasure. For his own apartment, he encased the balcony in glass and spent hours watching the crowds throng the boardwalk.

But for Brady, the hotel was more than a place to party—it was a place to convalesce. Suffering from acute indigestion in January 1917, he came to the Shelburne to recuperate, and had recovered by February. But in April he fell ill again, and died while sleeping peacefully only a day after pleasantly walking along the Boardwalk. Until its last days, the Shelburne kept a "Diamond Jim Brady" room that showcased his umbrella and other personal effects. Russell herself died there five years later.

Roberts turned the hotel over to his daughter, E. R. Ramsay, in 1904, and a year later Ramsay sold the hotel to Willis Hall, a wealthy lawyer. Hall kept Jacob Weikel on as manager, and Weikel began an ambitious expansion plan, transforming the structure into a brick and concrete giant, first with a mid-sized tower on the Boardwalk then, in 1926, with a 12-story mid-block addition.

But with the advent of the Great Depression, the hotel's fortunes dimmed. The hotel declared bankruptcy in 1931, and when Wiekel died in 1935, it lost its driving force. In 1942, the hotel was taken over by the army as part of "Camp Boardwalk," and under the ownership of the Malamut family regained some prestige after the war.

Despite a motel expansion in 1958, the hotel began to struggle again, similar to most other hotels at the time. But when state voters legalized casino gaming in 1976, the Shelburne suddenly became a hot item. The Malamuts had enthusiastically supported the casino referendum, hoping that gambling would revitalize their property. It suddenly looked like it would.

The family reportedly reached an agreement to sell the hotel for $12 million in 1977, but the pact collapsed after one of the principals realized that the buyers were, in fact, connected with the Gambino organized crime family.

A year later, two Japanese businessmen, Hiroaki "Rocky" Aoki and Takashi Saskawa signed a 30-year lease, planning to add a modern 31-story hotel tower behind the existing brick structure (which was by this time listed on the National Register of Historic Places) and add a casino. Billed as the Benihana Casino-Hotel (Aoki owned the restaurant chain of the same name), this casino would bring a touch of Asia to the Atlantic shore.

Construction actually started; crews stripped the interior of the Shelburne and razed the adjacent Empress motel. But disagreements between the Japanese investors, the Casino Control Commission, and the Malamut family followed. Aoki and Saskawa walked away, claiming to have lost $25 million. After blowing two chances to enter the casino age, the Shelburne seemed unlikely to get a third.

It didn't. In 1984, the gutted building was finally demolished. The empty lot lay vacant for over a decade as speculation swirled about what would be next for the historic beachfront tract, though with diminished interest in building new casinos, its prospects seemed dim.

Yet a happy ending—of sorts—came in 1997, when Bally's opened its Wild Wild West casino, a cowboy-themed annex to next-door Bally's Atlantic City, on the site. On land once dedicated to a British statesman, the casino now celebrated the American frontier—a fitting evolution, perhaps.

The Wooden Way

Today, the Boardwalk is synonymous with Atlantic City. It's nearly impossible to imagine the city without its characteristic wooden way. Some might think that, like the beach, it's a natural part of the Absecon Island ecosystem. But the Boardwalk was the work of very human business owners and civic boosters, who stuck with the idea despite many ups and downs.

Before the Boardwalk, most of the city's large hotels were found on Atlantic Avenue. This was when the city was still finding its way and the line between beach and city was not so hard. Within a few years, it became apparent that visitors enjoyed walking along the beach, breathing the salty air and watching the waves. They did not, on the other hand, take great delight in removing their shoes before doing so or even making more than a perfunctory effort at cleaning them off. This created a quandary: the guest may always be right, but cleaning and replacing ruined plush carpets and furniture is expensive. What to do?

In early 1870, two local hotel owners, Jacob Keim and the aptly-named Alexander Boardman, thought they had an answer. They called for a meeting of the minds at Keim's Chester County House on S. New York Avenue. Boardman conceded that while they couldn't prevent hotel guests from walking the beaches, they could give them a less messy option: "a walkway of boards on the sand which we believe will overcome our sand problems." Everyone wins: the customer gets a beachfront promenade and clean shoes, and the owners get cleaner premises.

No one could think of any strong arguments against Boardman's proposal. With $5000 in city-sponsored bonds, the City Council approved the construction of a wooden way from Congress Hall at Massachusetts and Pacific to the Excursion House between Mississippi and Missouri Avenues. Amid a parade and festivities, the innovative "walk of boards" was dedicated on June 26, 1870, only a few weeks after it was first proposed.

This first boardwalk was a far cry from the hardwood haven of today. It was a simple series of 10-foot long boards nailed together in 12-foot sections that rested on posts about a foot and a half over the sandy beach. There were no railings, and strollers too intent on watching the waves could easily fall off the boards. At the end of the summer season, the sections were packed up and stored for safekeeping until the following spring.

The idea of the Boardwalk was a great one; after guests got the hang of walking it, though, it was clear that it was too narrow. So, in 1880, an entirely new Boardwalk, featuring 14-foot long boards arrayed in 10-foot sections, was constructed. Like its predecessor, it was strictly a summer attraction, and was stowed away in winter months.

In that same year, the City Council loosened a ban on buildings near the boards (it originally forbade any structure within 30 feet), and allowed buildings within 10 feet. Though that seems like a mile today, when casinos empty directly onto (or right over, as at Caesars) the Boardwalk, that was fine for the merchants of the early 1880s, who built a series of connecting ramps and walkways.

After a serious storm in January 1884, hard-hit beach-area business owners (the boards were safely in storage) lobbied for a more permanent structure that would offer a buffer. In that year, a new walkway, raised five feet off the sands, and with higher clearances at street ends to allow for horses to pass under, debuted. Yet it didn't last. The third Boardwalk was largely destroyed in the hurricane of September 9, 1889, and City Council immediately began considering plans to put the enterprise on a more solid footing.

The following year, a 10-foot-high, 24-foot-wide boardwalk that extended from Caspian to Albany Avenues opened. This new wooden way had railings—a first—but was not long-lived.

An 1894 state law giving the city the right of eminent domain over the beachfront paved the way for the construction of a new, larger boardwalk that officially opened two years later. Built by the Phoenix Bridge Company (headquartered not in Arizona, but in Phoenixville, Pennsylvania), the new walk was 40 feet wide, leaving plenty of space for the burgeoning crowds to promenade. This is, more or less, the current Boardwalk.

The new Boardwalk was dedicated on July 8, 1896, when the wife of Mayor Franklin Stoy drove a ceremonial gold-colored spike into the boards. Though it was only a plain iron spike painted gold, and it was covered with a metal plate, thieves soon made off with it, and it has never been seen since.

Though the casino resorts of today dwarf the early bathhouses and shops that lined the early boardwalks, something of the old spirit remains. Boardwalks have become a common feature in seaside towns the world over, and the original remains world famous and a key attraction with limitless potential.

Home of the Punch

Some longtime residents may remember that the one-time Sands Hotel Casino was originally called the Brighton. Even for those new in town, the greenery in the neighborhood—Brighton Park—is a reminder that, once, the Brighton Hotel stood on the site.

In 1876, hotelier Frederick Helmsley built the Brighton Cottage, a modest rooming house that, contrary to common practice, stayed open throughout the year, hoping to lure visitors even in the deepest chill of winter. Helmsley was successful, as his cottage soon expanded into a full-scale hotel reputed, by 1881, to be one of the finest in the city. Many other hotels began adopting Hemlsley's all-year policy, leading to the emergence of Atlantic City as more than a summer vacation spot.

Long before Atlantic City became notorious as a place where Prohibition was not so strictly enforced, the Brighton may have been the first Atlantic City hotel to become famous for its alcohol. Its "Brighton Punch," a proprietary blend of rye, rum, brown sugar, and lemon juice, gained a national following; it helped that the Brighton's refusal to publish its exact recipe led to an era of mystique around the cocktail, which was so potent that women were held to a strict limit of two glasses per day.

Yet it wasn't all about the drink. The Brighton lived up to its reputation as an upscale hotel, frequently hosting celebrities and other notable guests. In the spring of 1890, Mrs. Grover Cleveland, the First Lady, chose to stay at the hotel when she visited Atlantic City, as high an endorsement as the hotel could want. Her stay yielded favorable publicity.

As with every other hotel in Atlantic City at the time, expansion was a constant. In 1892, the hotel was "enlarged and improved" and advertised that it would continue to remain open throughout the entire year. The punch was a potent selling point; even those who weren't guests stopped in for a glass—or two—of the famous concoction.

The Brighton remained, from the city's glory years through World War II, a highly regarded hotel. Along with many other hotels, it was used for about a year by the War Department as a contributor to Camp Boardwalk. After the war, the Brighton seemed primed for betting things, adding in 1948 the Pool and Cabana Club, a swimming and entertainment annex. In 1950, Alan Graff, who had been operating the hotel for three years, purchased it. He planned to continue the modernization begun by the addition of the Pool and Cabana Club, promising $1 million in improvements.

But Graff sold the Brighton in 1952 to Morris Corson. Corson attempted to keep standards high, despite the property's apparent decline. As late as 1954, the Brighton maintained its high-class label. In that year, it advertised room rates of $30 a night under the "modified American plan," which included daily breakfasts and dinners. By contrast, the Jefferson Hotel, at Kentucky Avenue "near the beach" offered rooms for half the cost.

But high room rates did not guarantee profits, and Corson began looking for a buyer. In 1955 Alfred Taxin purchased the Brighton from the Corson. Although Taxin planned no changes in the hotel's operation besides continuing a modernization program, it might have been better if he had. Business declined, and the building was ultimately demolished in 1958.

The Colony Motel, a 275-room building, replaced the Brighton in time for the 1959 summer season, fitting with a trend of the late 1950s and 1960s, as smaller motels were built to replace the aging hotels of Atlantic City's glory days; the years saw the openings of the Holiday Inn and Howard Johnson's as well. The loss of the Brighton was symptomatic of a decline that would only reverse with the introduction of casino gaming in 1978.

Appropriately, the Colony was one of the first victims of the casino boom; it was demolished to make way for a casino hotel, the first major new property to be built from the ground up since the Claridge. In a nod to history, its developers named it after the Brighton, returning that name to the Boardwalk.

In August 1980, the Brighton Casino Hotel opened to much fanfare, though it never lived up to its promise. The Brighton name soon came down, as the property became the Sands.

Though the Brighton name was stripped from the property, echoes of it remained in Brighton Park and in historical references to Brighton Punch. And the Brighton may prove to be more durable than the Sands; the ill-fated casino closed in 2006 to make way for a Pinnacle Entertainment-owned megaresort that never materialized. The land on which the Brighton once stood is empty, but there is still hope that someday, somehow, the Brighton name will come back yet again, and the wisdom of Fred Helmsley in gambling on Atlantic City as a year-round resort will be vindicated once more.

Boardwalk Heavyweight

One of the best-known classic Atlantic City boardwalk hotels, the Traymore, was also one of the earliest. Like most other hotels of the era, it went through several incarnations, and its history parallels that of the resort's hotel industry.

The Traymore began in 1879 as a beachfront, 10-room wooden cottage at Illinois Ave and the "sea end," as beachfront destinations were known in the days when the Boardwalk was laid down only in the summer. Originally a rooming house operated by M.E. Hoopes, the Traymore was named in honor of its steadiest customer, "Uncle Al" Harvey. Harvey incessantly waxed poetic over his Maryland estate, reportedly named after his Irish hometown of Tramore, a small seaside resort in County Waterford on the Emerald Isle's southern coast. To this day, there is a Traymore Lane in Bowie, Maryland.

The first Traymore "hotel" was more of a boarding house than a full-service hotel, but it stayed open year round. "Heated throughout; gas in all the rooms," announced an 1881 advertisement. This structure, though, did not last: on January 10, 1884, a fierce winter storm savaged the Boardwalk and reduced the Traymore to splinters, while the adjacent Park Parlors was left intact. The Traymore was quickly rebuilt and expanded. By 1886, it was a full-blown hotel large enough to host a reception of visiting Washingtonians. It was continually enlarged until, in 1898, it became the city's largest standing hotel, with 450 rooms.

As it stood then, the Traymore had a spacious lawn separating itself from the Boardwalk. This gave guests a pleasant space in which to meander but also served the very practical purpose of allowing a buffer from unfriendly waves. A September 1889 storm that breached the seawall did not appreciably damage the hotel itself, proving the wisdom of setting back the main building. Open all year round, the Traymore's modern appointments and luxurious rooms attracted visitors even during the slow winter months.

The Traymore continued to grow. In 1906 owner Daniel White hired the firm of Price and McLanahan to construct a new tower that brought the hotel up to the Boardwalk. Yet, for safety reasons and to keep up with the times, more renovations were in order. During the summer of 1914, White contracted with Price and McLanahan to replace the existing wooden-frame Traymore with a massive concrete structure that would rival the Marlborough-Blenheim, which William Price had built across Park Place for White's cousin Josiah.

Unlike later casino hotels that simply plunked down massive towers without regard to the surrounding environs, Price's Traymore, which was built directly behind the 1906 tower, was designed to take advantage of its ocean views: hotel wings jutted out further from the central tower toward Pacific Avenue, thus affording more guests ocean views. Commencing just after Labor Day, construction crews worked non-stop to erect the new Traymore in time for the 1915 season, and they were successful. Built with tan brick and capped by yellow-tiled domes, the Traymore instantly became the city's architectural showpiece when it opened in June 1915.

The hotel was filled immediately, and Daniel White sought to expand. He commissioned a 40-story tower addition which, unfortunately, was not built because of problems securing financing during World War I. If it had been built, this building would have been the tallest structure in Atlantic City until the construction of Revel.

Though the Traymore catered to an upscale clientele, it apparently also accepted less refined guests. In the summer of 1916, two well-dressed women were arrested for pilfering over $500 worth of hotel property, chiefly linens and bath towels. After hotel managers noticed that a number of items had disappeared, they alerted a detective, who arrested the pair just as they were checking out. Also during that summer, the Secret Service was put on the trail of a male guest who was passing forged checks in the name of a bank vice president.

Still, the Traymore prospered, and was described in 1924 as "the Taj Mahal of Atlantic City," decades before Donald Trump opened a casino resort with that name. In these years, the Traymore was one of the busiest hotels of the city.

But as Atlantic City declined after World War II, the Traymore did as well, though it promoted itself as "the fun-filled Traymore," offering package vacations with dancing in the Submarine room, free child care, and dinners at local restaurants. In the late 1960s, new owners the Loews Corporation built a 60,000-foot convention center at the property in an attempt to maintain its business.

That campaign was fruitless. In 1971, Loews closed the Traymore, citing monthly losses of $18,000. In December, the hotel's contents were disposed of in a liquidation sale.

In April and May of 1972, the Traymore was demolished in a massive three-phase series of blasts. Even in its destruction, the Traymore was outstanding. To this day, the once-famous Atlantic City hotel still holds the Guinness World Record for largest controlled demolition—with a capacity of nearly 6.5 million cubic feet, the Traymore is the largest (though not highest) structure yet demolished.

Destroyed before the passage of casino gaming gave many old hotels a second chance, the Traymore's site remained unbuilt throughout the casino era, despite several proposed resorts. It remains a prime site for development. But even if nothing ever rises again from the Traymore site, its place in history is secure.

A Central Attraction

Although it wasn't the first amusement pier built on the Atlantic City Boardwalk, Captain Young's Ocean Pier was a true groundbreaker. Though it was destroyed long ago, its replacement, Central Pier, still stands, a reminder of the distant heyday of the original edition.

In 1883, America was in the midst of incredible change. Railroads were making the nation smaller and facilitating the transportation of people and goods. Railroad companies in that year established the four time zones that remain today. Innovations in popular culture included the first Wild West show of Buffalo Bill Cody and the founding of magazines like *Ladies Home Journal* and *Life*.

The entrepreneurial spirit was alive and well in Atlantic City that year as John Applegate, a photographer, decided to follow the example of Colonel George Howard, who a year earlier had built the first amusement pier in the city. Applegate bought land at Tennessee Avenue and the sea end and began building his own amusement pier.

When it opened in June 1884, Applegate's pier had three main attractions: an ice water fountain that used more than 3,000 pounds of ice daily at its boardwalk entrance, a double-decked length that allowed strollers a clear view of the coast, and a ballroom at pier's end, 625 feet from the Boardwalk.

After seven seasons of modest success, Applegate sold his pier—for $56,000—to the duo of Captain John Lake Young and Stewart McShay. Young and McShay owned several amusements around the city together, and, under their leadership, the pier became a leading attraction in the city. Known as Young and McShay's Pier until McShay's retirement in 1897, and thereafter as Young's Ocean Pier, the pier was extended and completely renovated. This was when it truly came into its own.

There was a special auditorium for nightly dancing and shows, a convention facility, and a playhouse. Vaudeville acts were popular, as was the French actress Sarah Bernhardt. The city's first Gilbert and Sullivan opera was performed in Young's Playhouse, and it made the pier a popular destination for theatergoers.

Ocean Pier was the scene of an international incident in the summer of 1902, when a visiting Russian nobleman, Count Eugene Melrosm, was insulted and assaulted by a visiting Baltimore college student. The count's large velvet panama hat, with a seven-inch brim, somehow inspired the Baltimorean to kick him from behind and then profanely insult his headgear. When the student refused to apologize, he was arrested. Clearly, a variety of visitors strolled at Ocean Pier, though sometimes they had trouble getting along.

Though the pier was successful, it was not immune to one of the young city's worst scourges—fire. In April 1902, much of the pier was lost in a conflagration that devastated a large chunk of the Boardwalk. Several hotels were also destroyed, and fire companies from as far away as Philadelphia helped bring the fire under control. Captain Young rebuilt his pier and restored it to its former glory, only to be struck by disaster again.

Ten years later to the week, another fire swept over the pier, burning it down to the pilings. Young, already in the midst of selling the pier, did not rebuild it this time. He was occupied, perhaps, with his Million Dollar Pier, which had opened in 1906. The site lay dormant for a decade.

In 1922, the Central Pier Company rebuilt the pier, which they renamed Central Pier, to no one's surprise. Despite more fires in 1929 and 1944, Central Pier proved more durable than Young's Ocean Pier, as it hosted various exhibits for decades; other attractions included an amusement area with child and adult rides.

The pier became known for the Sky Needle, a 330-foot ride that promised visitors a 60-mile view on clear days; at the very least. As the city declined in the 1960s and 1970s, the view must have been less than inspiring, but with coming of casino gaming brought a wave of new construction.

In its later years, Central Pier became an amusement pier in the narrowest sense of the word, hosting rides and carnival attractions. Gone were the playhouse, the elegant ballroom, and the bustling convention exhibits, replaced first by skee-ball and pinball machines and later by video games.

Today, Central Pier is still plugging along, though it is a long way from its original fame as Captain Young's Ocean Pier. Both entertainment extravaganzas and convention rooms have been incorporated into casino resorts, leaving Atlantic City's piers with little more than rides and games. One can only hope that part of the on-going plan to revitalize the Boardwalk will include a return to the fantastic piers of yesterday.

Showplace of the Nation

Atlantic City's Steel Pier, jutting into the waves at Pennsylvania Avenue, is currently a thriving amusement pier. It has a long, crowded history. Encompassing everything from world-class entertainment to boxing cats and the famous diving horse, Steel Pier is one of Atlantic City's longest-lasting and most historic institutions.

Designed by Philadelphia architect John Windram and built by Atlantic City contractor Frank Souder, Steel Pier opened on June 18, 1898. On its first day, the pier opened for "free public inspection" at 9 a.m., after which the public was treated to alternating concerts by the First Regiment Band and the Hungarian Orchestra. An address by "prominent men" and another performance by the First Regiment Band closed the day's festivities.

For its first several years, military bands were a popular part of the piers entertainment. The nation's top bandleaders, including John Phillip Sousa, made Steel Pier a regular stop on their tours. In addition to martial and orchestral music, the pier also featured dance bands and a seal tank with twice-daily feedings. In time, animal acts would become a major attraction at the pier.

In 1924, a fire damaged the pier's entrance, and as part of the renovation its open arcade was converted into exhibition space. Atlantic City's piers would gain reputations as not only entertainment centers, but as exhibition halls where companies from around the world demonstrated their latest products to a national audience.

Local real estate man Frank Gravatt acquired the pier in 1926, marking a new era for the pier. He introduced many innovations, including the opening of the Marine Studio for then-municipal radio station WPG (World's PlayGround), and the expansion of exhibit space to 20,000 feet. General Motors moved into this new space, and maintained a showcase for its newest automobiles on the pier until 1968. Gravatt gave his visitors a little of everything, from opera to big bands, as well as celebrities of the moment like Gertrude Erdele, who in 1926 was famous for having swum the English Channel.

Under Gravatt's leadership, the pier became famous for its entertainment. Superstars like Bob Hope, Al Jolson, Benny Goodman, and the Dorsey Brothers appeared during that decade. Although Frank Sinatra was not impressive in his 1939 Steel Pier debut with the Harry James Orchestra, he would eventually become an Atlantic City favorite, performing for years at Skinny D'Amato's 500 Club.

At the time, the Pier was a juggernaut, extending more than 1,900 feet into the ocean, with a stadium, indoor ballroom, and no less than four theaters in addition to amusements and other attractions.

Steel Pier also garnered a reputation for its animal acts. The most famous, of course, was the Diving Horse. Wild West showman Dr. W. F. Carver originated the stunt, in which he and a horse jumped from a forty-foot tower, and his daughter Lorena inaugurated a tradition of young women riding the plunging equine into the ocean. The Diving Horse became an indelible icon of Atlantic City, and remains to this day a symbol of the city's past glory. Circus acts, including high-rise acrobats and daredevil motorcyclists, delighted crowds for decades.

Other animal acts are less well known today but no less popular in their day. During the 1930s, Steel Pier hosted a variety of spectacles, including a dancing tiger, who tangoed with Captain Roman Proske to the accompaniment of a dance band; a dog riding a surfboard; Professor Nelson's Boxing Cats (a pair of unfortunate felines outfitted with harnesses and boxing gloves); performing chimpanzees; a boxing kangaroo; Rex, the water-skiing Wonder Dog; and, perhaps a foreshadowing of Atlantic City's later emergence as the casino capital of the East, a group of card-playing cats.

The fascination with animals passed (leaving behind only the Diving Horse), but Steel Pier solidified its reputation as an entertainment mecca under the ownership of George Hamid. A former Gravatt employee who had been operating Million Dollar Pier, Hamid bought Steel Pier in 1945. The new owner continued to promote the property as the Showplace of the Nation, returning the pier's luster. In the mid-1950s, he boasted that, for a single low admission fee, visitors could enjoy more than 100 attractions, ranging from vaudeville acts, animals, movies, live music, and exhibits. Hamid's son, George Jr., assisted him in operating the pier.

The Hamids maintained their high standards, but by the 1960s, the pier, along with the rest of Atlantic City, was in the midst of a decline. A 1969 fire destroyed about a third of the pier's structure, and it limped along for the next decade. Two years after his father's 1971 death, George Hamid, Jr. sold the pier to a group led by Sherman Kendis.

Hurricane Belle severely damaged the pier in 1976, but it remained open, struggling to remain relevant. A 1977 purchase by Maryland developer Alvin Snyder, who planned to build "the world's largest casino" and hotel on the pier, fell through. The following summer, Resorts International bought Steel Pier. The 1978 season was its last as an amusement pier; although Resorts staged events sporadically on the pier, the company removed all of the remaining rides and amusements, using the site chiefly for storage.

A December 1982 storm that destroyed the Casino building, the last surviving relic of the 1898 pier, seemed to spell the end for the pier. Three years later, Resorts announced plans to renovate and extend the derelict pier that ultimately came to nothing. It would take the development of the adjoining Trump Taj Mahal to revive it.

Steel Pier was a part of the Taj Mahal's design early on, but when the casino finally opened in 1990, the bridge connecting the pier to the casino was (and remains) vacant. Still, in 1992, the pier resumed operation as an amusement park, and it continued to operate under Taj's auspices until 2012, when it was sold to Steel Pier Associates, a group comprised of the Catanoso brothers and architect Paul Steelman.

The new owners breathed new life into the pier. Operating in its third century, Steel Pier promises to be part of Atlantic City for a long time to come.

Pier Pressure

In the late 19th century, piers were the most exciting entertainment option in Atlantic City. Incorporating concert space, exhibition rooms and dance floors, they were always popular among visitors. Later, the piers changed from entertainment venues to amusement parks, with rides and other attractions. Steeplechase Pier, initially built as Auditorium Pier in 1899, was one of the first to make this switch, and though it is now gone, it still occupies an important place in Atlantic City history.

Even before it opened, Auditorium Pier was steeped in controversy. The owners of the city's existing piers, the Heinz (formerly Iron Pier), Steel and Ocean Piers, weren't eager to welcome new competition for the limited tourist dollar. They were less than happy when a group leased a piece of Boardwalk land near Pennsylvania Avenue and started building a fourth pier.

Much like some casino operators in later decades, the pier operators tried to prevent the new competitor from opening, rather than upgrade their own facilities in face of the challenge. They circulated a petition; since the pier would only be 500 feet long and not the usual 1,000, they demanded that the city council take action.

Several hotel owners signed the petition, and even as construction continued, the city refused to allow the pier to connect to the Boardwalk and passed an injunction preventing its opening. After its owners tacked on an additional 500 feet, the city permitted the pier to open.

Less than a block from Steel Pier, the newcomer had trouble establishing itself. In 1902, George C. Tilyou bought Auditorium Pier. Tilyou hailed from Coney Island, where he was a noted impresario, opening the resort's first theater and building one of the earliest Ferris wheels. His iconic Steeplechase Park included such rides as the Human Roulette Wheel, Human Pool Table and Barrel of Love.

Looking to turn business around, Tilyou brought in the top entertainment draw of the day—John Phillip Sousa, whose 85-piece band was known for its romping military marches. People flocked to see Sousa, but unfortunately, since the bandstand was outside, they could catch a free show from the beach.

Rather than compete head-on with the other entertainment piers, Tilyou decided to stick with what he knew best. In 1902, he renovated the pier, keeping an auditorium but adding slides, rides and similar carnival attractions. He renamed the structure Steeplechase Pier, after his famous Coney Island resort.

Known as "the funny place," the pier boasted, for a time, the world's largest electric sign—a 27,000-light-bulb behemoth that advertised Chesterfield cigarettes. Its whimsical rides appealed to vacationers' lighter sides, and the pier became remarkably successful. Even after Tilyou's death in 1914, the pier's managers continued in their winning ways.

Steeplechase suffered a devastating setback on Valentine's Day 1932, when a fire, fanned by strong ocean winds, destroyed nearly all the pier. But the pier was rebuilt, opening partially that summer and later restoring some of the pier's former splendor.

For more than 40 years, Steeplechase Pier continued to draw visitors; Marie Tilyou, George's daughter, remained president of its operating company into the 1970s. But with the city's decline, the pier, along with the rest of the Boardwalk, fell on hard times.

The advent of casino gaming didn't do much to help Steeplechase Pier. The pier passed into the hands of Joseph Bradway, who sold it to Resorts International in 1982. In 1984, structural weaknesses forced Steeplechase to close, and four years later, a fire gutted most of what remained. Any hopes of a revival were dashed in 1996 when the pier was finally demolished.

Though Steeplechase Pier is long gone, photographs and memories remain. Never as celebrated as Steel Pier or ornate as Million Dollar, it was nevertheless one of the best-known spots in a town famous for fun.

The Concrete Palace

The smashing success of Resorts International in May 1978 sparked a heady period in Atlantic City's history. Every day, it seemed, developers rushed forward with new and grandiose plans for remarkable casino hotels that would restore the luster to the oceanside resort. Often, though, these plans meant the demolition of older buildings. One of these, the Marlborough-Blenheim, was truly historic, and its loss is still felt today.

This ornate hotel began, like most classic Atlantic City hotels, far smaller than it eventually became. In 1901, hotelman Josiah White III and his son John bought a near-Boardwalk site on Ohio Avenue which then housed the Sacred Heart Academy. The next year, they opened the Marlborough House.

The Marlborough House, named for a British dukedom whose descendants include Winston Churchill, was designed by William Lightfoot Price, a ground-breaking architect who would also build the Traymore. Its subdued Queen Anne-style design made it a pleasant, though unexceptional, addition to the Boardwalk. Contrary to some reports, the Marlborough was not the first Atlantic City hostelry to offer indoor hot and cold running saltwater—that distinction belongs to the Luray Hotel, a Kentucky Avenue property also owned by the Whites that was destroyed by the great blaze of 1902.

Also in that year, the Marlborough's next-door neighbors on the Boardwalk, the Children's Seashore House, moved to Richmond Avenue and the Boardwalk. To the consternation of the Whites, an amusement company acquired the property and erected a roller coaster on it; the Whites viewed the noisy ride as unattractive and likely disturbing to their guests. The Whites solved the problem by buying the land themselves.

On the Seashore House site, the Whites built a new hotel, the Blenheim, retaining Price's firm Price and McLanahan to design it. The addition was named for the Palace of Blenheim, Marlborough's ancestral home, built starting in 1705 by a grateful Queen Anne to reward John Churchill, the first Duke of Marlborough, for his heroic leadership in the War of the Spanish Succession. When the "million-dollar annex" opened in March 1906, the hotel's name was changed to Marlborough-Blenheim.

With the Blenheim, Price made an unparalleled aesthetic and engineering statement. Famed inventor Thomas Alva Edison assisted in the innovative use of reinforced concrete in the hotel's construction, and its Spanish/Moorish theme, along with its signature dome and chimneys, represented a distinct step forward from earlier, classically-influenced, building designs. It was about as different from existing hotels as Tropicana's Quarter is from, say, the Shore Mall. It was also the Boardwalk's first "fireproof" hotel and the first to feature a private bath in each room.

Together, the Marlborough-Blenheim complex was a Boardwalk centerpiece for decades, and the White family remained influential. Charles White, one of John's brothers who helped run the hotel, served as mayor of Atlantic City and a state senator.

In August 1942, Colonel Robert P. Glassburn announced the Army's plan to commandeer the Marlborough-Blenheim, part of the military's "Camp Boardwalk" takeover of Atlantic City hotels for training and recuperation purposes. The hotel was returned to civilian use in early 1944.

In the 1960s, the Marlborough-Blenheim added motel wings, conference rooms, and a new pool as its operator, Josiah White IV, continued to run it with the same determination as his grandfather.

The advent of casino gaming in 1976 seemed to promise brighter days for the hotels. Reese Palley, an active booster of casino gaming, bought the hotels in 1977 and announced plans to preserve the Blenheim half of the hotel and to replace the Marlborough with a modern 750-room casino hotel. Palley succeeded in having the Blenheim placed on the National Register of Historic Buildings (which would translate into tax savings of over $1 million a year), but he soon stepped aside as Bally Manufacturing bought a controlling interest in the project.

Bally then switched architects and announced plans to raze the Marlborough, Blenheim, and the adjacent Dennis Hotel to build a sprawling "Park Place casino hotel" featuring an octagonal 385-foot hotel tower. Preservationists were aghast, but Bally cited the difficulties of bringing the old structures up to code.

The Marlborough-Blenheim closed in October 1977; at the time, Bally was mum about its plans, holding out the possibility that the hotels would, in some fashion, be saved. But that was not to be; it was more cost effective to keep the older Dennis hotel operational while razing the Marlborough-Blenheim.

In 1978, the Baroque domes of the Blenheim came tumbling down in an implosion; work on a "modern" casino hotel commenced. The next year, Bally's Park Place opened as a 51,000 square-foot casino complex tacked onto the renovated Dennis Hotel, becoming the city's third casino hotel. Eventually, Bally's added its hotel tower, a towering pink-glass monument to reinvention.

Today, the Marlborough and Blenheim are little more than fading memories. When the Blenheim was imploded, more than a historic structure was lost—Atlantic City lost some of its personality.

Garden Spot

G arden Pier wasn't one of the first piers in Atlantic City, nor is it one of the largest. But it has become one of the longest-lived structures on the island, and if not one of the better known attractions, certainly one of the most beloved.

Louis and Alfred Burk, who had made their money in meatpacking in Philadelphia, spent much of 1912 building the pier, which cost $1.5 million. The pier opened on January 19, 1913, at a time when the amusement business was booming. So even though the promenade had many attractions, a theater was the chief draw. Perched on the end of pier, the showroom could be seen from the foot of the structure, since stores and exhibit space lined its sides, while the center was taken up by a large series of flowerbeds.

These plantings gave the pier its name. The idea of a "garden" floating over the Atlantic Ocean was a striking one at the time, and a way of distinguishing Garden Pier from its numerous competitors.

In the pier's early days, vaudeville reigned supreme in America. A night of this variety entertainment could include everything from dancers and singers to comedians and animal acts. Garden Pier's theater became a stop on the Keith circuit, which was one of the nation's most popular vaudeville tours.

For a while, Garden Pier hosted one of the most unusual spectacles in Boardwalk history. In 1916, the Underwood Typewriter company set up a working typewriter that was a typical Underwood Number 5 model, although it was 1,728 times the usual size. It's unclear today why this was considered a good idea, although it's easy to surmise that it was a marketing gimmick, and no explanation survives of the importance of 1,728. Why not 1,700 times the size, or 1,800?

As it was built, the typewriter weighed 14 tons. It stood 15 feet high and was 21 feet wide. The giant used 9 foot by 12 ½ foot pieces of paper, on which its managers printed a variety of messages, usually welcoming congratulations to various convention groups.

The behemoth was first displayed at the Panama-Pacific Exposition in San Francisco, then dismantled and shipped to Atlantic City, where it was reassembled on Garden Pier. After several years there the giant machine moved to Convention Hall, where it remained until it was disassembled and melted down for scrap during World War II.

The pier also hosted shows and exhibitions like the meeting of the Kennel Club of Atlantic City, which tended to be dominated by New York and Philadelphia canines. As vaudeville fell out of favor, the theater presented concerts and other fare, but the odds were stacked against Garden Pier. When the city's center of gravity shifted towards what's today called the "Center Boardwalk," the pier began to decline—as shown by the giant typewriter's move to Convention Hall.

Still, the pier witnessed some crazy stunts, like Mike Gillette's summer 1932 attempt to set a flagpole-sitting record; after 54 days at the top of a 20-foot pole, he lost his grip and fell to the ground, where doctors pronounced his physical condition as "poor."

They could have classified the pier's prospects as similarly dire. In July 1934, the Garden Pier theater closed "because of lack of patronage," cutting short what promised to have been a thrilling summer series of operettas that had started with "The Chocolate Soldier." The pier continued to host conferences and other gatherings, but it was clearly having troubles; in 1937 it was auctioned off.

In 1940, the pier fell into receivership, as the city's tax collector attempted to pay $80,000 worth of claims against the pier. The property began to decay. Though the city was under the pressure of wartime mobilization, local citizens couldn't tolerate such a prominent landmark becoming dilapidated. So in 1944, the city, after it acquired the property in a tax sale, razed all of the buildings on it, leaving only the pilings and deck. It appeared that, after three decades, the pier was finished.

But historically minded members of the city administration had other ideas. A portion of city luxury taxes funded the rehabilitation of Garden Pier. Just in time for the city's 1954 centennial celebration, the pier re-opened with a concert stage, art gallery, and space for community groups. Weekend band concerts attracted crowds of nearly 5,000 people. The pier was back.

In a nod to the pier's history, members of the community were allowed to maintain garden plots in the center of the pier, making it a "garden" yet again.

Today, the pier still hosts the Art Center, as well as the Atlantic City Historical Museum. It is fitting that one of the surviving reminders of the city's heyday now memorializes the city's history.

A Good Dining Deed

The Knife and Fork Inn is one of the oldest restaurants on Absecon Island, and as befits an Atlantic City institution, it's not without its share of controversy.

The iconic building has been standing guard over the intersections of Atlantic, Pacific, and Albany Avenues for nearly a century. In many ways, it's the beginning of Atlantic City. After all, Pacific Avenue starts in front of it, and most of the city's tourist attractions lie beyond it, heading uptown. Today, since it is surrounded almost completely by parking lots and vacant land, it's even more conspicuous.

The narrow, four-story, Flemish-influenced building opened as a men's club in 1912. Its members enjoyed good food and fine liqueurs, as did members of similar clubs in most cities around the United States. In 1920, they met the onset of Prohibition with jeers. While others continued to drink on the sly, sipping from hip flasks, the club's members insisted on serving alcohol openly. A federal strike force attacked this hotbed of lawlessness by raiding the club and demolishing its bar.

The club never really recovered from the raid and, in 1927, sold the building to Milton and Evelyn Latz, who converted it into a restaurant. As a restaurant, the Knife and Fork continued the exclusive ways of the club, quickly establishing itself as a necessary stop for all gourmets visiting Atlantic City.

The menu featured primarily seafood, although jumbo lamb chops were also popular.

The building's architecture—tied to its origins as a private club—was as exemplary as its food. With its dining spaces spread out over several small rooms on multiple levels, the Knife and Fork seemed far more intimate than other restaurants its size.

After Milton's death in 1948, his two sons Mack and Jim took over the restaurant. Despite the eatery's continued popularity, the brothers could not get along, and eventually (in 1986) Mack took sole possession of the family business, with Jim remaining in control of the adjoining parking lot.

Ironically, as the rest of Atlantic City crumbled in the 1960s and 1970s, the Knife and Fork got better. A *New York Times* review printed on the very day that the disastrous 1964 Democratic National Convention began said that the Inn stood out "like a good deed in a naughty world." In a city where a top steak house featured pulsating red lamps on each table to hail waitresses, the Knife and Fork was the epitome of class.

As the city continued to deteriorate, however, the Knife and Fork only shone by comparison. In 1970, a reporter chronicling the city's centennial took a dim view of the Boardwalk's offerings: the hotels were decaying, many of them being renovated into apartments, and there was little to do besides play bingo and eat salt water taffy. Hoping to escape the hot dogs and frozen custard stands, he headed down to the Knife and Fork, where for a moment he felt transported back to Atlantic City's golden age. Then, a waitress tied a plastic bib around his neck.

Casino gaming's arrival in 1978 first helped the Knife and Fork. Since many casinos didn't have restaurants to rival the Latz's, they sent their best players there and picked up the tab. That year, the Inn was immortalized in Louis Malle's *Atlantic City*, as Burt Lancaster and Susan Sarandon ate lunch in one of the film's more atmospheric scenes.

The early 1980s were a boom time, with everyone from Bob Hope to notorious mobster Nicky Scarfo making themselves frequent guests. But then, as casinos upgraded their own offerings, the flood of customers slowed. In December 1996, Mack Latz closed the Knife and Fork, insisting that he was getting old and was tired of running it.

The building sat vacant until early 1999, when Latz's son Andrew secured a lease. In April of that year he re-launched the Inn. The reopening was one of the most highly anticipated events in Atlantic City restaurant history, and the rave reviews picked up where they'd left off.

It seemed to be a storybook ending—family business stays in the family—until September of 2003, when Mack stopped negotiating to sell the Inn to Andrew and instead offered it to the Dougherty family, who owned long-time rival Dock's Oyster House.

After a protracted legal battle, Frank Dougherty officially purchased the Knife and Fork in early 2005, and embarked on a renovation and restoration plan that many say has restored the landmark to its original luster.

Seafood and chops are still at the center of the menu, and for those looking for an authentic taste of Atlantic City before the casino era (the restaurant's website proudly advertises that Nucky Johnson ate there), dinner at the Knife and Fork may still be a winning bet.

Million Dollar Address

Once called Million Dollar Pier, the promenade that is now home to The Playground has a fascinating history. With any luck, its fourth incarnation will combine the ambition of its second with the staying power of its first.

In early 1906, Captain John L. Young announced his plans to build a new pier at Arkansas Avenue. A former lifeguard, policeman, fisherman, and carpenter, he already owned the six-story, unfortunately-named Bleak House hotel on Tennessee Avenue and the Boardwalk and Ocean Pier, the former Applegate Pier, also at Tennessee Avenue.

Though the location is considered the center of the Boardwalk today, at the time skeptics thought it was too far away from the action, which then was concentrated farther uptown. Still, Young insisted that his pier, which he estimated would cost a million dollars, would be a success; the name was as good a reminder of the pier's ambitions as any, and it stuck.

He was right. The pier opened on June 26, 1906, and was an immediate sensation. Strollers flocked to see the attractions, which included a ballroom which Young claimed was the world's largest, a course used for horse shows, a replica of a Greek temple, exhibition space, and a series of aquariums.

Young kept up with the times by installing scoreboards at his Ocean and Million Dollar Piers to display the tallies of baseball games. He also hosted horse shows, where the winner took home a blue ribbon and the enviable title of "Best in Show." They were so successful that by 1910, spectators began to complain that the hippodrome was overcrowded.

Million Dollar Pier is probably most famous for its "street" address, Number 1 Atlantic Ocean, USA. The address was actually that of Young's mansion, which he built in the center of half block-sized plot suspended over the ocean on his pier. Young had already lived on Ocean Pier, and he decided to build his dream house on his new creation.

Made entirely from reinforced concrete, Young's 12-room house reflected its designer's tastes—the *New York Times* claimed he was a lover of "anything showy and elaborate and everything that smacks of the marine." So his reception hall featured furniture made in Germany, which Young designed himself. The backs and seats of his chairs and tables were carved to resemble seashells, while their arms and legs looked like sea serpents and other aquatic creatures. He covered the walls in green burlap bordered with a priceless moth and butterfly collection.

The house, topped with a domed observatory that Young himself never used, even had a basement, which housed the laundry room, heating and cooling devices, and the lawn equipment—Young's showplace was surrounded by a lushly manicured lawn and gardens. The Wizard of Menlo Park, Thomas Edison, was a frequent guest, and himself designed the elaborate system that washed the house and grounds in pastel light.

Million Dollar Pier hosted the first Miss America Pageants, Sarah Bernhardt's first Atlantic City concert, and scores of big bands, vaudeville acts, and dance marathons. For younger guests, attractions included carnival games and thrill rides.

Despite its popularity, the pier, like much of Atlantic City, suffered through a period of decline. By the time the city's first casino opened in 1978, it was literally a shell of its former self. In 1981, shopping mall developer Kravco bought the pier, which by then had only a carousel, funhouse, and a smattering of cheap rides. They announced plans to demolish the wooden pier and replace it with a concrete and steel edifice to be called Ocean One.

The name was a leap into the future, but it also recalled the past, particularly the address of Young's seahouse. With three decks of stores, restaurants with ocean views, and a top-deck miniature golf course, Ocean One promised to bring Atlantic City retailing and non-casino leisure into the 1980s.

Unfortunately, the mall mostly stayed in that decade. Despite its early hoopla, it proved less durable than Young's original, and before it reached its 20th birthday, it was consigned to the scrap heap. In 2002, Park Place Entertainment—which had bought the mall—announced plans to redevelop it as a Monopoly-themed attraction called "Park Place on the Boardwalk." Soon after, the company would switch gears (dumping the Monopoly theme and even changing its own name to Caesars Entertainment) before being bought by Harrah's Entertainment.

With the opening of the Pier at Caesars in 2006, a new era in the pier's history began. Yet it was to be short-lived. The property was sold in a foreclosure auction 2011 and seemed, like many casinos, to be condemned to a slow drift toward a quick end.

In 2015, though, Philadelphia developer Bart Blatstein bought the mall and transformed it, with the help of architect Paul Steelman, into the Playground, which mixed shopping, dining, and live entertainment. It gave the address—one of the city's most storied— yet another lease on life. Catering to a younger demographic, it promised to help revive the city's appeal for a new generation.

Captain Young, who passed away in 1938, would no doubt approve of the new project's ambition, and the inveterate showman would have his fingers crossed for the new owner of his one-time mansion and showplace.

The World's Meeting Place

Most Atlantic City residents and visitors know that Boardwalk Hall, near the center of the Boardwalk, is among the city's most historic structures. From its inception, it served many functions, and at least twice hosted events of deep historical importance.

Conventions were important to Atlantic City from the 1880s onward. Meeting in the ballrooms of hotels and piers, business and fraternal groups helped to fill hotel rooms. Recognizing the importance of convention groups to the city's tourism, officials announced plans as early as 1905 for a major convention hall on the Boardwalk. Those plans amounted to nothing, but the idea of a large convention hall remained.

In the years that followed, the concept gained momentum. In the early 1920s, Atlantic City's reputation as a convention grew rapidly. National groups like the National Electric Light Association, National Railroad Car Builders, and National Dairy Association held regular meetings there, usually on Million Dollar Pier. As the gatherings got larger, they outgrew the pier. In order to prevent other cities from swiping this lucrative business, Mayor Edward Bader proposed building a large convention hall.

Bader purchased land on the Boardwalk between Mississippi and Florida avenues that had been the site of Rendezvous Park. This amusement park featured carnival games, a dance hall, a bathhouse, a restaurant, and a "scenic railway." The park opened in May 1921, but lasted only one summer; it was razed by a fire in September of that year.

After Bader's death, his successor, Anthony M. Ruffu, saw that the building was completed as planned. Construction began in late 1924 and cost nearly $13.5 million. The building itself was an architectural marvel. The main hall, 488 feet long and 288 feet wide, was large enough to hold a regulation football field. The curved roof peaked at 137 feet. Built with no supporting pillars, for years it was the largest unobstructed room in the world.

The building opened as Convention Hall on May 31, 1929, which was the same year as the Atlantic City Diamond Jubilee and the Golden Jubilee of Light, the national celebration of the 50th birthday of Thomas Edison's incandescent light bulb. As the National Electric Light Association was one of the city's major convention groups, they made the most out of this coincidence. On the night of its dedication, Convention Hall and the entire Boardwalk were bathed in gold lighting, and the battleship *Wyoming* trained its lights on the hall from offshore.

Convention Hall had, for decades, the world's largest pipe organ, which had over 32,000 pipes. During the 1930s, the Atlantic City Seagulls, a semipro hockey team, made their home in the hall. Beginning in 1941, the Ice Capades visited every summer, and the Miss America pageant became an annual rite of September. Thousands of conventions, exhibitions, and shows made use of the Hall from its beginning.

In 1935, Convention Hall was the scene for an epic moment in labor union history: the creation of the CIO (Congress of Industrial Organizations). The American Federation of Labor, the country's dominant union organization, placed an emphasis on craft-based unions and disdained mass organizing along industrial lines. John L. Lewis, leader of the United Mine Workers, disagreed. Tensions between AFL leaders and upstart industrial unionists came to a head during the AFL's 1935 convention. Lewis, angered at comments by carpenters' union president William Hutcheson, knocked the craft unionist to the ground with a single punch. Following his Convention Hall fisticuffs, Lewis and other industrial unionists organized the CIO, which became a rival to the AFL before the two groups merged in 1955.

Convention Hall stepped again onto the national stage from August 24 to 27, 1964, as the host of the Democratic National Convention. That year, Democrats mourned the loss of John F. Kennedy and nominated Lyndon Johnson for re-election as President. Johnson announced his running mate, Hubert H. Humphrey, at the convention.

But the 1964 convention is most significant for a watershed

moment in civil rights. The Mississippi Democratic Party, still committed to segregation, refused to back Lyndon Johnson, who had signed epochal civil rights legislation into law. Civil rights organizers, angry over their lack of a voice in the state party, sent a rival group of delegates to the convention as the Mississippi Freedom Democratic Party. The group took its case to the credentials committee, which did not seat them. National television news covered the MFDP's attempt to be seated, which focused attention on the issue of African-American voting rights in the South; the next year, President Johnson would sign important voting rights legislation.

Convention Hall adapted to the times; the West Hall added 200,000 feet of convention space in 1971, and the main hall hosted several world championship boxing matches in the 1980s, as well as two consecutive World Wrestling Entertainment "Wrestlemania" extravaganzas in 1988 and 1989.

With the opening of the new Atlantic City Convention Center in 1997, the boardwalk facility was renamed Boardwalk Hall. Calling itself "America's Seaside Entertainment Center" and still hosting Miss America each year (after the contest's Las Vegas sabbatical), Boardwalk Hall continues to do its founders—the visionaries of the 1920s—proud.

Organic History

When it opened in 1929, Atlantic City's Convention Hall was considered a symbol of excess. Six years later, the *New York Times* dubbed it "the greatest convention hall in the world," noting at the same time that the city had flung itself into bankruptcy to build it.

One of the most excessive—and impressive—features of old Convention Hall, the pipe organ, is still part of Boardwalk Hall today, though it's fallen into disrepair. In many ways, the story of the Boardwalk Hall Organ is the story of the city itself, told in a microcosm.

Though the Hall itself opened in May 1929, the organ wasn't finished until December 1932—tough years, when the city and the country struggled through the worst of the Great Depression. Like the election of Franklin Delano Roosevelt a month earlier, the organ's debut was a sign of hope.

One of the city's more important citizens designed the organ. Emerson L. Richards was a longtime state senator who, in 1918, oversaw a marathon six-week legislative session that revised enormous parts of the state's law books. He served as an assemblyman, state senator, and acting governor, and was the majority leader in both houses. A lifelong Republican, he was for a time an active major with the U.S. army while serving in the Senate.

Richards was also a musician, and, when his hometown opened the world's biggest meeting hall, he figured that it needed the world's biggest pipe organ. According to Dennis McGurk, the organ's longtime curator, Richards was interested only in building an organ bigger than the one in Wanamaker's Philadelphia store (now Lord and Taylor), neglecting the affect of weather and location on it.

Richards designed a behemoth of an instrument—it officially had 33,114 pipes, though most experts maintain that it "only" had 32,000. Still, it was massive, and with more pipes, manuals (keyboards), and stop keys than any other organ. Its tallest pipe measures a full 64 feet. It was later recognized by the Guinness Book of World Records as both the largest and the loudest instrument in the world.

Built by Midmer-Losh, a Merrick, New York organ builder, the organ was rather unpopular when it debuted. Several residents objected to footing the $350,000 bill for an instrument regarded as a rich man's toy. Mimder-Losh was forced to sue the city to collect payment, and ended up insolvent despite winning the case. Perhaps for that reason, Convention Hall's managers chose to downplay the grandiosity of their organ, hoping to avoid further controversy by keeping a low profile.

The organ was used for everything from serious classical music to accompanying ice skaters until it fell out of use in the 1970s. By the late 1990s, it was rarely used, though organ enthusiasts from around the world regularly made pilgrimages to play the mammoth instrument.

From the start, maintenance was a constant struggle. The great hurricane of 1944, which put some highways under as much as five feet of standing water, flooded the Hall and the organ's compressors; the damage was never completely repaired. Through the years, assorted floods, leaks, animal interlopers, and dust did their damage, shutting down various parts of the organ.

Renovations to Boardwalk Hall haven't been kind to the organ, either. In 1998, the organ's Right Stage chamber was operable—before work on the Hall began, organ aficionados recorded a performance of the instrument. The $90 million overhaul that ended in 2003 won awards for restoring the Hall to its former glory, but wreaked havoc on the organ. Unskilled workmen bent pipes, improperly insulated wires, and deliberately cut cables, effectively destroying what had been one of the few still-working sections of the organ.

Around the time of Boardwalk Hall's reopening, experts estimated the cost of the organ's rehabilitation at around $10 million. In 2003, the New Jersey Sports and Exposition Authority won a $100,000 "Save America's Treasures" grant to "support restoration of the organ." This led to a systematic campaign to restore the famous instrument.

The NJSEA formed the Historic Organ Restoration Committee, a non-profit group, to oversee the overhaul of the organ. It enacted a

15-year restoration plan which, by 2015, had returned enough of the organ to functionality to permit free daily concerts, which were held weekdays from May through October. The group estimated that the organ would be completely restored by 2023, 89 years after it first played.

Once left derelict, the organ's return to performances symbolizes, hopefully, the continuing rebirth of Atlantic City as both a city and a vacation destination.

Seaside Skyscraper

The Atlantic City skyline has been completely remade since the legalization of casinos in 1976. The Claridge tower, one of the old stalwarts of the Boardwalk, is now considered venerable, but it too was once the symbol of a newer, more modern Atlantic City. The Claridge's life as a hotel is as interesting as its afterlife as a casino.

The Claridge was a relatively late arrival to the Boardwalk. Before the high-rise hotel occupied the land at Pacific Avenue and Park Place (once Belmont Ave.) behind today's Brighton Park, this piece of prime real estate wasn't empty. In 1872, the wife of Philadelphia saw manufacturer Henry Disston built a lavish summer home for her husband there. Though Disston died only six years later, the land remained in his family until 1926, when the Sealands Corporation bought it for $2 million.

The Sealands Corporation began planning to build a large skyscraper on the site, and decided to name the new hotel after a famous London hostelry, Claridge's. Claridge's roots went back to 1812, but it first achieved fame in the 1860s, when it was one of the city's poshest resorts. Completely demolished and replaced by a modern hotel in 1898, Claridge's remained one of Europe's most exclusive hotels, and is still open.

The Atlantic City Claridge (at some point, the builders opted to drop the apostrophe and "s") was planned to be just as fancy as its London namesake. Philadelphian Charles H. Roberts, the building's architect, capped the 24-story structure with an iconic five-story cupola. The twenty-third floor had a large solarium, and the entire structure contained over 400 rooms, with running fresh and salt water baths.

The Hotel Claridge cost $5 million to build and was, at the time, the city's highest tower. Planning for the hotel started during the roaring Twenties, when the stock market was booming and the future seemed to be getting constantly brighter. Atlantic City was in the middle of a boom, enjoying record visitation levels, rising convention sales, and the newfound success of the Miss America Pageant.

Few would have predicted, at the time, that the Claridge marked the end of an era. Despite its high hopes, when the Claridge finally opened, on December 17, 1930, the future looked anything but bright for the United States and Atlantic City. The Great Depression was getting worse, as more Americans were losing their jobs—and their hope—with each passing week. With the Depression, the bottom dropped out of new hotel construction, and no further skyscrapers would be built until the advent of casino gaming, nearly a half-century later.

Despite the Depression, the Claridge did a steady business in the 1930s, hosting visiting dignitaries, millionaires, and convention groups. One highlight included the Boardwalk Persian Cat Club's annual competition. Throughout the decade, the hotel remained a bright spot amid the gloom.

In World War II, the Claridge was an essential part of "Camp Boardwalk," the American military's conversion of resort facilities to wartime use. On July 7, 1942, it became the fifth Atlantic City hotel "drafted" for the duration of the conflict. The hotel was most famous as the birthplace of the United Nations Relief and Rehabilitation Agency—the Claridge hosted the group's first session in November 1943.

After the war, the Claridge resumed its place as a major hotel, welcoming visitors and hosting numerous convention groups.

But as the city fell on hard times in the 1960s, so did the Claridge. While most of the classic hotels were torn down or converted to apartments, the Claridge hung on, barely. It slid into receivership in 1971. In 1973, the state ordered the hotel closed for failure to adhere to safety guidelines.

The Claridge remained closed, and when was auctioned off after bankruptcy proceedings in May 1976, just months before the legalization of casino gaming, the court found no takers. Its mortgage holder, the Guarantee bank, could not give the property away for $1.5 million.

The advent of casino gaming boosted the Claridge's value, strictly because of its potential for use as a gambling hall, not its past. It sold in March 1977 to a group led by Connecticut entrepreneur Fiore Francis D'Addario and New Jersey developer Daniel Rizk for $3.5 million. After the sale, hundreds of pieces of hotel property were auctioned off, including the desk that Lyndon Baines Johnson wrote his will on and a bed in which Frank Sinatra once slept.

In 1979, D'Addario was ready to follow through on plans to renovate the Claridge, add additional rooms, and open it as a casino. He hired the Del E. Webb Corporation, then the nation's biggest casino operator, to manage it. But Del Webb proved to be a liability, as the company had difficulty getting licensed by the stringent Casino Control Commission. The casino struggled from its opening in July 1981, and Del Webb sold its interest in 1983, though it continued to manage the casino.

Over the next 20 years, the Claridge remained competitive, taking advantage of its status as the city's smallest casinos by reminding patrons that "smaller is friendlier." But smaller wasn't more profitable, and the casino sank into bankruptcy in 1991 before being bought by Park Place Entertainment in 2001.

Sold by Park Place successor Caesars Entertainment in 2014, the Claridge still stands tall over the center Boardwalk. Without a casino, the Claridge will remain a link to Atlantic City's past and is perhaps, a sign of its future.

Kentucky and the Curb

Today most Atlantic City entertainment happens in casino lounges and showrooms, but in the 1940s and 1950s, many of the city's superstar performers could be found on Kentucky Avenue, particularly at the Club Harlem. For over 50 years, the Club Harlem stood at the top of the city's vibrant entertainment scene.

The Club Harlem opened in 1935, when Leroy "Pop" Williams converted the existing Fitzgerald's Auditorium into a new venue. Williams hired Sam Singer, a former bootlegger, to manage the club. Like many other nightclubs of the time, entertainment was not the only attraction: illegal gambling drew many customers. During the day, Singer ran a profitable horse room, where visitors could bet on horse races from around the nation thanks to a hookup to the "race wire," a clandestine telegraph signal.

Pop Williams, who was the club's principal owner, was an early black entrepreneur in Atlantic City. Though his club occasionally featured white performers, and white visitors were common, it did something that most Boardwalk hotels in the 1930s and 1940s did not—actively catered to black guests. In a 1987 interview with the *Philadelphia Inquirer*, Atlantic City music legend Chris Columbo recalled that, denied entry to "white" hotels, "all we had was… Kentucky and the Curb," as the famous stretch of North Kentucky Avenue was known. Other popular hangouts included Grace's Little Belmont, Jerry's Barbecue, Catfish's piano bar, and the Wonder Garden bar.

Though the club was popular, and Williams did not lack for financing, he took on two white partners in 1951, Ben Alten and Jack Southern. Williams wanted to expand, and at the time banks would not lend money to black businesses. So, a "partnership of convenience" was formed. But Alten, who handled the books for the club, became one of its leading advocates, and was known for decades for his good humor and excellent business sense.

Inside, the club had a main showroom seating about 900, and a bar area with two bandstands that provided continuous music. Nearly every black entertainer of renown played the Club Harlem at one point or another, from Billie Holiday and Cab Calloway to Diana Ross and James Brown. Comedian Slappy White and Larry's Steele's Smart Affair—a revue extravaganza featuring dance production numbers—warmed up the crowds for the headliners.

The club justifiably has a prominent place in Atlantic City history, but it is nationally significant as well. Billy Daniels found his career-making hit "That Old Black Magic" while working at the Club Harlem in 1942. Needing an uptempo opening, he spied a copy of the "Black Magic" sheet music on the club's piano. With a revamped arrangement, he rode the song to international stardom.

Daniels' was one of several careers made at the Club Harlem. Sammy Davis Jr. performed there as the child star of the Will Mastin Trio, and former Atlantic City mayor James Usry worked there for 15 summers.

During the hectic summer months, the Club ran at all hours. On Saturday nights, the club had four shows at 10 p.m., midnight, 2:30 a.m., and the "breakfast" show at 6:00 a.m. The breakfast show was hardly a filling brunch—customers had better luck getting scotch and soda than ham and eggs—but it was usually the best show—musically—of the night. By that hour, entertainers appearing throughout the city, came to "sit in" at Kentucky and the Curb.

With the city's decline in the 1960s and 1970s, the Club Harlem also encountered troubled times. A 1972 shootout between two rival Philadelphia gangs—on Easter Sunday morning, no less—ended with five dead and dozens injured. After that, business slowed.

The Harlem's owners had hoped that the arrival of casino gaming in 1976 would lead to a revival, but gaming regulations stipulated that any casino must have a 500-room hotel, thus barring the club from installing slot machines or table games. After struggling for over a decade, the Club Harlem closed its doors forever in 1986, and was torn down in 1992.

With a renaissance for Atlantic City overdue, perhaps the time is right for the Club Harlem's rebirth, either as part of a larger complex or as a standalone club. Returning the Club Harlem's name to the Atlantic City skyline would be a fitting tribute to the legacy of Williams, Alten, Columbo, and all of the entertainers and patrons who made the Club Harlem such an integral part of Atlantic City's nightlife for generations.

At the Five

Just as it's known for its casinos today, Atlantic City was once famous for its nightclubs. These were intimate, smoky lounges where visitors could see some of the day's biggest stars, live and in person. Atlantic City had many legendary rooms, but the most famous might have been the 500 Club.

The "Five," as it was popularly known, had humble beginnings. Phil Barr, a former trolley conductor and boxing promoter, moved to Atlantic City from Philadelphia in the mid-1930s, intent on opening a nightclub. In 1936, he bought and demolished two houses at 6 South Missouri Avenue, then built a two-story brick building. The nightclub occupied the ground floor, and above it Barr lived in a comfortable apartment.

The 500 Café (the club's original name)was a small operation. During the day, a race-betting operation (illegal, naturally) attracted a stream of horse-lovers, and at night singers and dancers graced its small stage.

At the time, horse betting was rampant throughout the city, but there were not many full-fledged casinos. In 1941, Barr approached Paul "Skinny" D'Amato, the young part-owner of Luigi's, the most popular illegal gambling den, with a proposition: bring his magic to the Five. Though D'Amato initially rebuffed Barr, they eventually agreed on terms and D'Amato opened up a major casino behind the Café.

After a gambling raid that sent Barr to prison, the Café closed for several months before D'Amato assembled a partnership to buy it. In May 1943, Skinny and his partners assumed control of the small club. The opening night was a fraught affair: D'Amato was so undercapitalized that he had to send his brother to a liquor store to buy bottles of liquor, a few at a time, barely balancing the cash register with his customer's drink orders. But the new ownership was a success, and business was good.

In June of 1946, D'Amato bought out one of the partners, and the venture was renamed the 500 Club.

This is when the Five's glory years began. Through his connections in the entertainment community, D'Amato brought the biggest stars of the day—from Liberace to Sammy Davis Jr.—to perform in his club. It's impossible to estimate how many people visited Atlantic City in these years just to see the acts at the 500 Club, but it's a large number nevertheless.

D'Amato did more than showcase existing performers: he launched new acts, most famously on July 26, 1946 when Jerry Lewis and Dean Martin first performed together on his stage. Martin and Lewis spent much of the next decade as one of the most esteemed attractions on radio, and television, and they starred together in 16 movies.

Martin and Lewis's runaway popularity helped elevate D'Amato's star as well, and even those who didn't know much about Atlantic City learned that the 500 Club was one of the country's top entertainment venues.

D'Amato's biggest star, though, was Frank Sinatra. The two became friends in the late 1930s, and though Sinatra's career dimmed in the late 1940s, the nightclub owner maintained an unshakeable conviction in the singer's talent. When Sinatra was at a professional and personal low point in the summer of 1951, D'Amato brought him in to sing at the 500 Club. The crowds flowed out of the club into the street, proving Sinatra's continuing appeal.

Later, when Sinatra's career revived, he continued to perform at the 500 Club, out of gratitude to D'Amato for his friendship. Each year, his August stints at the Five would draw tens of thousands of visitors, despite the city's waning popularity.

But Sinatra and D'Amato couldn't hold off the wolves forever. Sinatra made his final 500 Club appearance in 1964, the same year that coverage of the Democratic National Convention revealed to the public just how dilapidated Atlantic City had become. The 500 Club continued, but part of the magic was gone.

What the city's diminishing appeal couldn't squelch was claimed by disaster. On June 10, 1973, a massive fire gutted the 500 Club, ending an Atlantic City institution. In many ways, this was the day that the old Atlantic City died.

It would take another three years, and the successful casino referendum, for the resort to begin building for the future. Though Skinny D'Amato didn't reap the bonanza of legal casino gaming, he was one of its boldest proponents.

Without Skinny, it's safe to say that Atlantic City wouldn't have been half the place it was in its post-war silver age. His 500 Club kept the resort afloat in tough times and pointed the way to the future.

Eat Where They Are Caught

Today, Atlantic City's nautical tradition is all but forgotten. Bus schedules mean more in today's fast-paced tourist town than tide tables. But in its earlier days, the sea was a major attraction, and for many a way of life. One of the most famous to wring a living from the ocean was Captain Clarence Starn, whose namesake Inlet restaurant was a seaside staple for decades.

Starn, born on November 19, 1890, went to sea at the age of 14. He served his country in the Merchant Marines during the First World War, and, still in love with the ocean-going life, began running both fishing and excursion boats in Atlantic City (in the summer) and Miami (in the winter).

The captain made headlines early in his career. In April 1921, his ship docked in the Inlet with a baffling catch: a two-ton leviathan that none of the veteran sea dogs on hand could identify. Starn had caught the "sea monster" in a mackerel net 60 miles off the Jersey coast and brought it back to shore after a prolonged fight. Though impressed with his catch, no one could identify the 20-foot long fish.

Starn's heroics also saved lives. In August 1926, a yacht under his command rescued two fisherman whose boat had capsized in rough seas.

But Starn achieved some of his greatest notoriety five years later, when he was arrested, along with two other Atlantic City-based sea captains, on charges of assisting Cuban revolutionaries. In the summer of 1931, Starn and the others were implicated in a plot to ferry 75 "freedom fighters" from the U.S. to Cuba. Starn protested that he had only agreed to take a group of men on a fishing trip. With the other captains, Curtis Hilton and Harold Fiddler, Starn was ultimately exonerated.

The captain's lasting fame lies not in his aquatic exploits but in his restaurant. Opened in the summer of 1940 at the Inlet terminus of Maine Avenue, Captain Starn's Restaurant was among the island's finest seafood stops for nearly 40 years.

Starn used his restaurant to incorporate exhibits of performing sea life and a fish market into the site. A fleet of 13 vessels, including double-decker excursion boats, deep-sea fishing vessels, and an open-cockpit speedboat named Miss Atlantic City docked on the pier.

Visitors to Atlantic City made Captain Starn's one of the city's top attractions. While it offered steaks and chops, seafood was the star, with fried shrimp, battered haddock, scallops au gratin being perennial favorites. The must-have item, the baked lobster, was served with baked-clam or crabmeat stuffing. Diners rarely went home hungry from Captain Starn's. By 1955, he was even marketing pound-sized cans of lobster. "Captain Starn's Canned Lobster" sold in stores as far away as New York and Chicago.

A separate clam and oyster bar provided a less formal option, while the main dining room, done up in white-paneled wood and decorated with paintings of fishing boats, was both spacious and relaxing.

In the restaurant's later years, photographs, plaques and awards belonging to Clarence Starn bedecked the walls. Life preservers with printed slogans also provided a homey seagoing touch with phrases such as "Eat Where They Are Caught," "We Have Our Own Fishing Boats," and "Out of the Water and Into the Pan." Those who ate at Starn's knew that they were getting the freshest fish available.

With the decline of the Inlet neighborhood and Atlantic City in general, the restaurant went into a decline. After the Captain's death in 1969, his nephew Clarence Apel took the helm. By the late 1970s, the restaurant was losing $70,000 a year, though a shift to wholesale fish marketing, dock rental, and fuel sales buoyed the operation.

But in 1979, Starn's heirs (mostly his nieces and nephews) accepted an offer from a group led by Edward Wong to sell the site for $300,000. Wong planned to build a casino there, but, as was typical, his financing fell through, and the Starn family, having already closed and gutted their restaurant, never received their money.

Since then, redevelopment rumors have periodically swirled around the site, but little progress has been made. In a city currently undergoing a renaissance, hopefully someone will emerge to return Maine Avenue to its former glory.

Diamond Dining

The Atlantic City area is famous for its share of restaurants, but one of the most storied is the Ram's Head Inn, about eight miles from the shore on the White Horse Pike.

The story of the Ram's Head Inn begins with Fred and Ethel Noyes. Fred, born in Philadelphia in 1905, was an artist who, after serving in World War II, opened a small Absecon antique shop with his wife Ethel. In 1951, the Noyeses bought a rundown inn that dated from 1787 on Route 9 that, with some love and care became the Smithville Inn. By the early 1970s, they had expanded their holdings to include an entire historic village.

In 1974, Fred and Ethel sold the Towne of Smithville. But they weren't done with the hospitality business. Two years later, they bought the Dutch Barn, an established restaurant. The Barn had been a quiet, rustic eatery that was far from memorable. The Noyeses wanted to create something that was, if nothing else, memorable, so they completely overhauled the decades-old building to create, as they put it, "a lovely restaurant devoted to dining." But they offered more than just a dining room. Meals were served in six exquisitely decorated rooms, with a library converted into a bar, a formal reception hall, a gift shop, and an art gallery where a pianist played soft music.

When it opened in 1976, the Ram's Head Inn elevated dining to a new level. A dinner was a theatrical experience: waiters could take 20 minutes to prepare a special Caesar salad by the table, whipping together the dressing, shredding the greens, and finally adding oil and vinegar with ritualistic aplomb. A variety of meats, from trout to steak, were dramatically flamed at tableside cookers.

From the start, it was clear that this wasn't your typically casual

Jersey diner. The menu was filled with continental delights like whole roasted pheasant, lobster, and chateaubriand. The wine list was long, and expensive. And there was a dress code: men had to wear jackets.

Art was important to Fred Noyes—he'd trained as an artist and was a prolific painter. In 1973, he and his wife established a foundation that led to the opening of the Noyes Museum, which still embraces Noyes's vision of collecting American fine art, particularly works by New Jersey artists. Displaying art—including his own paintings—at the Ram's Head Inn was just one of the personal touches Noyes brought to the establishment.

In 1979, the Knowles family, led by husband and wife Harry and Doris and their sons Wade and Kurt, purchased the Ram's Head Inn. The family already owned one of New Jersey's most successful independent restaurants, the Manor, a West Orange tradition since Knowles opened it on New Year's Eve 1956, and they set about expanding their operations by buying a restaurant that had already made a name for itself.

The Knowles family continued Fred and Ethel Noyes's fine dining concept, even extending it. Under executive chef Luigi Baretto, hired in 1982, the Ram's Head has earned a mountain of culinary accolades, including an impressive run of AAA Four Diamond Awards and annual honors for best fine dining and most romantic restaurant, along other tributes, in a variety of local publications.

The new owners maintained Fred Noyes's commitment to art, and still feature paintings from local artists in the gallery. This is one of the things that makes the Ram's Head Inn more than just another local restaurant and gives it full-fledged "institution" status. It's certainly the kind of touch that differentiates it from slickly packaged designer restaurants.

Yet the food continues to be the focus—the Inn's legendary chicken pot pie, delivered to the table in a piping-hot copper kettle, is a perennial favorite, as are a variety of steaks, chops, and seafood dishes. The menu has changed with the times, now offering vegetarian alternatives. The desert car, however, is as decadent as ever.

Though many visitors to Atlantic City don't venture far from the casinos, they are missing out on a regional institution that locals have come to cherish. The Ram's Head Inn has been the *crème de la crème* of South Jersey's fine dining scene for decades, and it is a reminder that, even during the heyday of casinos there were always reasons to leave the Boardwalk.

In the Neighborhood

Mention the White House to longtime Atlantic City residents, and their first thought isn't the building with the Oval Office, but the local landmark at Arctic and Mississippi avenues.

Now part of the city's dining DNA, The White House Sub Shop dates back to October 1946, when Anthony Basile, a 20-year old Atlantic City native, home from serving his country in the Philippines, decided to open his own eatery.

Basile had deep roots in the city. His father, Natale, came to the United States from Italy in about 1905 and settled in Atlantic City, working as a cement finisher, helping to build some of the resort's best-known hotels, like the Ambassador and the Traymore.

Anthony, who attended St. Michael's school, started making submarine sandwiches at the age of 10 for an uptown sandwich shop. After coming home from the Pacific, he quickly found a newly remodeled location that, he thought, would make the perfect spot for his own shop. The building, at 1123 Arctic Avenue, had just been remodeled, with a fresh coat of white-painted stucco. Basile stood across the street looking at the place with a friend, trying to decide what to call it. After a few beers, he declared, "It looks like a little white house," and his sub shop had a name.

In 1946, a half-sub cost 25 cents; a whole one, 50 cents. Today, that wouldn't cover an order of mushrooms for a half-sub, but there's been a bit of inflation since then.

Basile worked the business on his own for a while, then welcomed his uncle Fritz Sacco as a partner in the spring of 1948. Over the next decade, the White House became a must-eat attraction for visitors to Atlantic City. People waited in line for more than an hour just to get a sub, and the White House earned its share of celebrity devotees. Dean Martin and Jerry Lewis, who first performed together onstage at the 500 Club only a few months before Basile opened the White House, were early admirers.

Sometimes, stars were so besieged by fans that they couldn't make it down to the counter, so the White House made a special delivery. Frank Sinatra and his entourage ordered sandwiches to the Claridge Hotel when he played at the 500 Club, and the Beatles got a taste of Atlantic City when they played Convention Hall in August 1964.

Joe DiMaggio was another frequent guest, usually coming in just after closing time to avoid the crowds. Former world heavyweight boxing champ "Jersey" Joe Walcott was another repeat customer.

For Basile, making great subs started with quality ingredients. Cold-cuts were sliced each day. The bread came from nearby bakeries—Formica's and Rando's—and had to be out-of-the-oven fresh. In the late 1970s, Basile estimated that his high standards cost him 5,000 or 6,000 loaves of bread a year, but his customers agreed that it was well worth it.

Since the early days, the partners kept a focus on making the best sandwiches they could. No pizza, french fries or hot dogs were added to the menu. They did, however, create their own twist on the steak sandwich, the steak submarine, as a way of offering customers a bit of variety. The steaks became as big a hit as their "regular" Italian subs.

Anthony Basile and Fritz Sacco each brought something different to their partnership. Basile was the more hands-on owner, presiding over the shop, while Sacco took care of most of the behind-the-scenes aspects of the business. Together, they built an Atlantic City icon. They worked together until the early 1990s, when Fritz passed away. Basile kept an active involvement in the business until his death on May 29, 2008.

Though the original owners are gone, the White House remains family-owned. Anthony's daughters, Genevieve (Jen) and Connie Basile, and Fritz's daughter and son-in-law, Mary and Brian Conley, now own the White House, and they continue to run it in the spirit of its founders.

"Our parents did a great job with building up White House Subs," says Genevieve Basile. "It's an honor to carry on the tradition."

Consistency, Basile says, is the key to the restaurant's longevity. "That's the most important thing. And there's no substitute for the quality of our ingredients. Our bread is hand-picked from Formica's and Rando's and delivered every hour. It's always fresh. We go back so far with them. Both businesses were started by the fathers of the current owners and handed down to the younger generations."

Basile isn't joking when she talks about consistency. One employee, Tom LaRocca, has been with White House for more than 50 years, and the average employee has been with the shop for more than 25 years. The formula is simple: create some of the best submarine sandwiches in the world, and you don't need to offer much more.

The White House has continued to be a culinary mecca in its second half-century. Daytime talk show hosts Oprah Winfrey and Ellen Degeneres have enjoyed the food, and a host of celebrity chefs, including Paula Deen, have given the restaurant their stamp of approval. The White House was even featured in the 2010 Jennifer Anniston film *The Bounty Hunter*.

A second branch of the White House opened in early 2011, on Trump Taj Mahal's retail and dining level Spice Road. So while things haven't changed much at Mississippi and Arctic, the White House Sub Shop has continued to move ahead.

Bathers frolicking in the ocean with Steeplechase Pier in the background, circa 1920. *M. & Company.*

The Marlborough-Blenheim as it appeared from the Boardwalk in 1908, two years after the Blenheim opened. *Rosin & Company.*

A straight-on beach-level look at the Marlborough-Blenheim's classic architecture. *Sithens Post Card Company.*

By the 1960s, the Traymore had been modernized and given a new white coat of paint. At the time, it had 600 rooms and the "newest and largest convention facilities in the East." *Traymore Hotel.*

"Imposing yet gracious" in this circa 1945 postcard, the Ambassador, opened in 1919, was later transformed into the Tropicana casino hotel. *E. C. Kropp Company.*

This early view of the Ambassador shows a popular early 20th century beach activity, horseback riding. *Allen "Boo" Pergament.*

Built in 1872, Philadelphia saw manufacturer Henry Disston's cottage first occupied the current site of the Claridge. *Allen "Boo" Pergament.*

The Dennis Hotel, whose first incarnation debuted in 1860 and which is still part of Bally's Atlantic City. *Allen "Boo" Pergament.*

The Shelburne was for years a popular Atlantic City hotel. *Allen "Boo" Pergament.*

After nearly a century in operation, the Traymore met its end in a 1972 series of implosions. *Allen "Boo" Pergament.*

The massive pipes that powered Boardwalk Hall's legendary pipe organ. *Allen "Boo" Pergament.*

The boxing cats, scrapping in the upper right, were among the most popular animal attractions on Steel Pier. *Allen "Boo" Pergament.*

Three

Personalities

First Family

Atlantic City was originally settled by a single family—the illustrious Leeds clan. Though today there are few signs of this enterprising bunch, the city might not be what it is today without several generations of Leeds promotion and perseverance.

The first residents of Absecon Island, the Lenni-Lenape Indians, only dwelled on the island seasonally, coming "down the shore" in the summer to enjoy the cool ocean breezes and gather shellfish and other seaside treats.

Absentee landlords had owned parcels on Absecon Island since 1695, but it wasn't until 1783 that anyone actually lived there full-time. In that year Jeremiah Leeds moved his family to a log cabin he had built himself.

Leeds was a descendant of Daniel Leeds, who had come to America from England in 1678 and published a notable almanac; Benjamin Franklin later recognized it as the first such publication south of New York. After his death, his sons continued publishing the work, and his family spread throughout Gloucester, Burlington, and Atlantic Counties.

Twenty-nine year old Jeremiah had fought for the Continental troops as a lieutenant in the Gloucester County Militia. His wife, Judith Steelman, was a granddaughter of one of Absecon Island's first land-owners, and undoubtedly was familiar with the area. So, when the young family decided to move away from Leeds Point on the mainland, this wasn't a completely new environment.

The cabin stood approximately at what is now the intersection of Arkansas and Arctic Avenues. After building it Leeds immediately set to work, planting grain crops in adjacent fields that he had cleared.

It wasn't city life—or even village life—but with a healthy supply of wild game found on the island, Leeds and his family didn't have to worry about going hungry.

Leeds saw something in what others wrote off as a desolate barrier island and continued buying land until he owned over 1,000 acres of prime beachfront real estate. He wasn't interested in subdividing it, though, and took pains to keep others from moving in. The Leeds patriarch did let mainland residents graze their cattle on his grasslands, and eventually rented a plot of land to be used for a salt-making operation.

Jeremiah had a large family; he had six children with Judith (the eldest, James, might be the influence behind Pomona's Jimmy Leeds Road), and after she died married Millicent Steelman Ingersoll, a 24 year-old widow who was a relative of Judith. The 62 year-old Jeremiah fathered four more children with Millicent after their 1816 marriage.

When Jeremiah died in 1838, his widow Millicent remained on the island, running a tavern and inn called Aunt Millie's Boarding House. Business was slow, but began to pick up in 1852, when Dr. Jonathan Pitney (the only island resident who was not a Leeds) and Philadelphia engineer Richard Osbourne interested the Camden and Atlantic Company in buying much of the Leeds' land and developing a seaside resort, linked to Philadelphia by a railroad (See "The Doctor's Dream" for the whole story).

But the Leeds family was not done with Absecon Island, and would play an influential role in the settlement, which Osbourne named Atlantic City.

Chalkey Leeds, the oldest surviving son of Jeremiah and Millicent, became the city's first mayor in 1854, a year after incorporation, serving until 1857. His mayoral campaign was a very personal affair: there were only 21 registered voters in the election, many of them members of the extended Leeds clan.

Chalkey owned a large farm which encompassed a large swatch of the Inlet: it stretched from what is today Massachusetts Avenue to the Inlet between Baltic and Atlantic Avenues. With a large number of cows and chickens, Leeds was a major dairy supplier to the earliest cottages and boarding houses in the developing resort. As the city expanded, the Leeds' family influence shrank; they sold most of their land to the Camden and Atlantic Railroad, and watched as it was leveled for development.

The mayor's younger brother Robert was the town's first postmaster, then the most high-profile federal position in the area. Chalkley lived long enough to march in a parade commemorating the city's Golden Jubilee in 1904, a full half-century after his swearing-in.

The Leeds family remained influential citizens; Sylvester Leeds, great-great grandson of Jeremiah, was a prominent real estate and hardware dealer. At the time of his death in 1936, his son James was living in Ventnor, ensuring that the family maintained a presence on the island it had helped settle.

Though the family's power would wane as that of the new hotels and amusement piers grew, the Leeds name is one that should not be forgotten. Without Jeremiah Leeds' pioneering spirit or Millicent's hospitality, it is possible that Atlantic City might never have been.

Making History

A tlantic City has seen generations of public officials and interested citizens, but few residents have left a legacy as monumental as Alfred Miller Heston, a newspaper publisher, historian and city official.

Heston descended from Zebulon Heston, a conscientious Quaker who fled England in 1684 to avoid persecution. Isaiah Heston, Zebulon's grandson and Alfred's great-grandfather, fought for the Continental Army during the Revolutionary War and was killed at the Battle of Monmouth in 1778. Another ancestor, Edward, survived the conflict and founded Hestonville, a small village that has since been absorbed into Philadelphia.

Alfred was born in Hestonville on April 30, 1854, the same year Atlantic City was incorporated as a city. He attended Central High in Philadelphia, then began learning the newspaper business. At age 20, he became editor of the *West Jersey Press*, a Camden-based paper.

It was a busy time for Heston. In 1875, he married Abbie Mitchell. The two ultimately had three daughters. Yet he was soon on the move, becoming the editor and manager of the *Salem Standard* in 1878, then buying the *Bridgeton Chronicle*.

But Heston's destiny wasn't in western South Jersey. He moved to Atlantic City in 1884, bought a share in the *Atlantic City Review*, and went to work as an editor. Three years later, he sold his interest in the *Review*, and while waiting to get back into the newspaper business, decided to write a guidebook for his new home town.

Heston's Handbook: Atlantic City Illustrated, a 250-page guide to Atlantic City, went through numerous editions, and was even sold in Europe. Packed with statistics both useful and trivial (the Boardwalk is 3.5 miles long; there are 600,000 bricks in the Lighthouse Tower), the book was a compendium of photographs of then-current and historic Atlantic City, with detailed information about the Native Americans who once lived on Absecon Island.

While the *Handbook* itself earns Heston a mention in the Atlantic City hall of fame, he wrote several other books, including an account of slavery in New Jersey and a biography of Joseph Bonaparte, elder brother of Napoleon, who lived in New Jersey for a time. Heston also bought an interest in the *Atlantic Journal*, another local newspaper, and edited it from 1888 to 1891.

In addition to his passion for history (Heston researched his own lineage back to 1277, and his *Handbook* is peppered with historical and literary references), Heston had a commitment to his community. In 1895, he was elected first comptroller of the city, and faithfully discharged his duties as a fiscal conservative opposed to corruption. The following year he was appointed commissioner of the Sinking Fund, and also served as clerk of the House of Representatives during the 51st Congress. Heston worked tirelessly to promote the city, both through his Handbook and by the creation of a press bureau.

Heston's insistence on running the city's business on a strictly square basis ruffled feathers; Atlantic City even then was known for its political corruption. It was estimated that he saved the city hundreds of thousands of dollars by rejecting bogus bills and claims during his tenure in office. That fortune should have ended up in the pockets of friends of the city's political bosses, and those bosses resolved to get rid of Heston.

In 1912, City Council refused to allow him to run for re-election. When asked the reason for his ouster, Heston said that over the past two months, he'd rejected $100,000 worth of bills that "the boss" wanted paid. Paying those bills would have been a condition of his re-election.

"I would rather go out of office with a clean record," Heston declared, "than have it said I was the tool of a political boss."

Later that year, Heston ran for the city commission, but alleged voting irregularities kept him from claiming office. Without the assistance of one or another of the factions that dominated local politics, he had little chance of winning public office again. His 1914 election as city treasurer was ultimately subverted by his political enemies. Yet his reputation was secure.

Heston made his greatest impact, however, by founding and supporting public organizations. In 1898, he was instrumental in raising money to open Atlantic City Hospital (which became today's AtlantiCare Regional Medical Center). And he served as secretary of the hospital's board of governors for the next 25 years.

Heston also parlayed his personal interest in history into an institution that would benefit the public. When Atlantic City received a $71,000 grant from Andrew Carnegie to build a library, Heston was one of the founding members of the board of trustees that opened the library in 1905. He donated his private collection of books and notes on Atlantic City's history to the fledgling institution. This provided a core of material on local history that has been an invaluable aid to researchers for more than a century.

Heston died on November 10, 1937, at the age of 83. He had been an Atlantic City resident for more than a half century, and left an impact on the city that few could rival.

In his honor, the Atlantic City Free Public Library has named its extensive collection of unique and rare materials documenting the cultural, economic, social and historical development of Atlantic City the Alfred M. Heston Collection—a fitting tribute to a public-minded man who never ceased to love history.

The Dandy Mayor

The position of Atlantic City mayor has, in the past generation, been more often than not a steppingstone to scandal and prison, with an unfortunate number of officeholders ending up in jail. But this isn't just a recent development—some early mayors had brushes with the law, as well. One of them, Franklin Pierce Stoy, better known as "the Dandy Mayor," was as interesting as any modern office-holder.

Stoy, a Republican, was first elected as a councilman at large in 1891, and then served as mayor from 1894-97 and 1900-1911 (Joseph Thompson held the office from 1898-99).

His tenure was marked by controversy. Some of his campaigns for "decency" may strike the modern reader as ridiculous. For example, in the summer of 1905, he issued an edict prohibiting women from appearing on the beach in cream-colored bathing suits. Since these were "practically transparent," particularly when wet, Mayor Stoy decreed that all women must wear dark colored swimming gear. He was also an emphatic opponent of "bathing bloomers," insisting instead that women wear full skirts while bathing.

A week later, Stoy was back on the beach, this time chasing after a traveling group of Filipino performers known as the Igorrotes. Tipped by the lifeguards that the underdressed (by Stoy's standards) tribesmen were cavorting in the surf, the mayor ordered the visitors to be ejected from the beach, and only allowed to return in "proper" beach attire.

In the following summer, Stoy announced a campaign against "untimely roistering," by which he meant people driving too fast after dark. After he was kept awake nearly an entire night by honking horns and speeding automobiles, he alerted the police to be on the lookout for anyone disturbing the peace after bedtime.

Stoy also championed a hard line against "spooning" (no less than three young visitors were arrested in August 1904 for flirting on the Boardwalk) and, in 1908, took a courageous stand against horse play on the beach. After a young woman was seriously injured when a rubber ball drove one of her hat pins into her head, the mayor confined all ball-playing and rough sporting to a small section of the beach.

Though his anti-horseplay and roistering policies might tag him as a humorless martinet, the mayor actually had a wry sense of humor. He took a liking to snakes, and allowed a five-foot rattlesnake he'd adopted on a hunting trip full run of his office. He supposedly trained it to respond to his commands (something hard to believe, given snakes' rudimentary hearing) and usually kept it on his desk while he attended to his official duties. Once, while touring the Boardwalk, he stopped at a snake charmer's booth to admire her reptiles.

He even played the hero on occasion—once, while dictating a letter inside his office, he noticed a five-year-old girl standing between the trolley tracks at Atlantic and Tennessee Avenues. He jumped out of his chair, bounded out of the building, and bundled the child off to safety before returning to work. He also happily performed weddings, and welcomed dozens of convention groups to Atlantic City.

The mayor's biggest controversy revolved around the issue of Sunday closing. During his first term as mayor, Stoy actively enforced an interpretation of the common law that required all bars and saloons to close on Sunday. In retaliation, the bar owners demanded—successfully—that Stoy himself be arrested because of his part-ownership of the Union Transfer Company, a transport company that operated on Sunday.

Perhaps because of this brush with the law, Stoy was decidedly more favorable to "Sunday amusements" during his second tenure as mayor. When, in 1907, the New Jersey legislature passed the "Bishops' law," which absolutely prohibited liquor sales on Sunday, Stoy joined with the police, media, and people of Atlantic City in publicly flouting the ban.

Two years later, Stoy was again arrested, this time for directly disregarding an order from then-Attorney General (and later Governor and President) Woodrow Wilson to enforce the Sunday closing law. He was released on $5,000 bail and continued to serve as mayor, welcoming visiting conventions and representing the city in official functions.

He was still mayor when, in July 1911, he suffered a stroke and, after a month's illness, died in a sanitarium at the age of 52. Despite his controversial tenure, the city mourned him profoundly—all public buildings were closed after his death was announced, and all business on the island stopped for three hours on July 26 as 35,000 people paid their respects. It was a fitting end to the life of a tireless advocate for the citizens of Atlantic City.

Field of Dreams

Atlantic City has had many mayors, but few have left a legacy as wide-ranging as Edward L. Bader. Bader served as mayor for much of the Roaring Twenties—when the city was arguably at the peak of its popularity as a wild vacation spot. Yet his true mark on Atlantic City goes beyond politics, extending to construction, athletics and aviation.

Born to Daniel and Sarah Bader in 1874, Bader grew up on an 80-acre farm in West Philadelphia. He attended Boon's Dam School until he turned 13, though he recalled playing hooky often. He never had any shortage of chores on the farm, and he credited this rural labor with helping him build his rugged physique.

After leaving school, Bader sold newspapers, then joined his father's new contracting business, where he handled a six-horse team. After his 1899 marriage to Katherine Helvick, he enrolled in college: first the dental school, then the veterinary school, and finally the Wharton School of Business at the University of Pennsylvania.

Bader had originally intended to earn money by playing football and attending college at the same time, but upon learning that he would have to be a student for a year before being allowed to play, he left and joined the Latrobe Athletic Association, the first professional football team in the United States. Standing 5-foot-10 and a half and weighing a beefy 195 pounds, Bader helped Latrobe win an unofficial United States Championship.

After one year with Latrobe, Bader chose to return to work full-time. Though he also played a year for a professional football team that Philadelphia Athletics owner Connie Mack fielded, his destiny was not in professional sports. Bader became a superintendent in his father's contracting company. In 1902, he came to Atlantic City to set up a garbage-collecting outfit for his father. He liked the area so much that he stayed, and two years later started his own contracting company.

After a storm washed away much of Steel Pier in 1904, many engineers insisted it could not be rebuilt. Bader sized up the challenge like he would an opposing defensive line, and decided it could. His success in rebuilding Steel Pier led to many other jobs.

His next major project put Bader on the map, literally. He paved the five miles of road from Albany Avenue in Atlantic City to Pleasantville—today part of the Black Horse Pike that passes by the field that now bears his name.

Bader's contracting business prospered for the next several years, and he built several projects in Atlantic City and up and down the East Coast. He became a stalwart Republican, was active in local charities, and was a member of the Elks, Moose, Eagles, and Knights of Columbus. Along the way he had four children, including a son, Daniel, who later became a city commissioner.

Bader also promoted his greatest passion, sports. He fielded basketball teams, organized the Blue Tornadoes—Atlantic City's first professional football team—and owned a boxing gym on North New Hampshire Avenue. He regularly brought world-class boxers in to fight at the resort, stoking interest in the sweet science long before world-title bouts sponsored by casinos. He also encouraged high school athletics, and was instrumental in the formation of Atlantic City High School's band.

In 1920, Bader's Republican friends convinced him to run for city commission. He won, and was chosen by his fellow commissioners to serve as mayor. He was re-elected in 1924.

Bader accomplished a great deal as mayor. Over the opposition of many others, he purchased land that became the city's municipal airport and high school football stadium; both were later named Bader Field in his honor. He championed the construction of the high school at Albany and Atlantic Avenues, which opened in 1923. He also acquired the land on which Convention Hall (now Boardwalk Hall) was rising at the time of his death.

In mid-January 1927, Bader was felled by a mysterious stomach ailment. Initially doctors had trouble diagnosing his illness, which they ultimately determined was appendicitis; his appendix was on the left, rather than the right side of his abdomen. At first advised to rest at home, he was moved to the City Hospital (today AtlantiCare Regional Medical Center) and underwent surgery. To speed his recovery, city policemen fanned out along the street in front of the hospital to prevent any unnecessary noises.

Originally given a good chance for recovery due to his iron physique, Bader's condition grew worse, and on the evening of January 29 he was given last rites. In addition to his family, a select few local dignitaries, including Commissioner Anthony Ruffu (who would succeed Bader as mayor), Assemblyman Anthony Siracusa, and political power-broker Nucky Johnson, held vigil at his bedside. Bader died a few minutes before midnight.

He was given a funeral fit for a man of his stature. After lying in state at St. Nicholas church, of which he was a member, his body was carried, in a 5-mile-long procession, down the White Horse Pike to Holy Cross Cemetery. Mourners of every race, color and creed bemoaned his passing, and all businesses in the city closed for two hours during the funeral as a mark of respect.

From Steel Pier to the Black Horse Pike, there are few sites in Atlantic City that haven't been impacted by Bader's vigor and determination, and he left the city far richer than he found it.

Time Keeper

Atlantic City has always been known for its entertainment. Whether bands were playing in Boardwalk theaters, ballrooms on piers, or in casino lounges, they have been a constant fixture in the resort. For more than seven decades, one man was just as regular a presence in the city's—and the nation's—music scene. From the Jazz Age to the 1990s, Joseph Chris Columbus Morris was one of the top drummers in town.

Morris, born in 1902, usually performed under the name "Chris Columbo." He moved to Atlantic City at the age of nine. It was a city filled with opportunity but also hardship. Rampant racial segregation and low wages made the town a "slave market," as Columbo recalled in a 1978 interview conducted as part of the Atlantic City Free Public Library's Living History Project.

Columbo attended local schools, starting with the Indiana Avenue School, and worked several odd jobs before finding full-time work as a drummer. He played his first gig with swing bandleader Fletcher Henderson on Steel Pier in 1921, and never looked back.

These were heady years in Atlantic City—Prohibition was in force but rum-runners flouted the law. Music was everywhere—in theaters and in speakeasies. Columbo found no shortage of work.

When he started fronting a band, he made a decision to use the name "Chris Columbo." Initially, he used the name "Joseph Morris," but promoters thought the name lacked pizzazz. So he started billing himself as "Chris Columbo," and his band became the "Crazy Chris Columbo Combo."

It was catchy, and his fellow musicians learned to respect his chops. He worked regularly at Truckson's Hollywood Grill at Tennessee and Arctic Avenues, then the Torch Club on Central Avenue between

New York and Tennessee Avenues, before leaving for the nation's music mecca, New York City.

In the mid-1930s, Columbo helmed a house band at the Savoy Ballroom. Known as "The Home of Happy Feet," the Savoy was an integrated Harlem dance hall that was memorialized in the hit song "Stompin' at the Savoy."

At the Savoy, Columbo crossed paths with some of the best-known bandleaders, musicians, and singers of the day: Benny Goodman, Duke Ellington, Count Basie, the Dorsey Brothers, and Billie Holiday. Columbo worked with some of the top names in the business, and built a reputation as a spectacular drummer and bandleader.

Despite his fame in New York, Columbo continued to return to Atlantic City every summer to play at the Club Harlem. For about thirty years, Columbo made Atlantic City his home from April to September, then toured and recorded nationally for the rest of the year. Finally, in 1968, he returned to Atlantic City with the Duke Ellington Orchestra and, tired of traveling, decided to stay for good.

Columbo had a wide-ranging career as a recording artist, waxing records as a leader and a sideman. In the 1940s, Columbo, usually credited as "Chris Columbus," was an integral part of Louis Jordan's band. Jordan combined swing, blues, and rhythm and blues in a style that presaged rock n' roll. His producer, Milt Gabler, later recorded Bill Haley and several other early rockers.

Columbo also toured and recorded with Wild Bill Davis, a former Jordan pianist who introduced a widely-copied style of organ playing during his four years with the band. Davis offered a more straight-ahead jazz sound than Jordan, and his tenure with both groups speaks to Columbo's versatility.

His music took him around the world, playing a U.S.O. tour with Eubie Blake. He performed behind jazz superstars like Louis Armstrong and Ella Fitzgerald, saxophone legend Lester Young, and bop pioneers Charlie Parker and Dizzy Gillespie. His son, drummer Sonny Payne, was a mainstay of the Count Basie and Harry James bands for years as well.

Columbo continued to lead the Club Harlem house band until the venue closed. For a time, he also hosted a radio show on WFBG. "Good evening, ladies and gentleman," he began his patter each day, "This is the Captain of the Swing Ship, Chris Columbo. We're here every afternoon at 5 o'clock with a cargo of my listeners' requests." On the popular program, Columbo highlighted brilliant but underplayed artists like Woody Herman and Sarah Vaughan, brining his one-of-a-kind personality to radios throughout the area.

When the Showboat casino began offering live jazz in its New Orleans Square in the late 1980s, Columbo signed on as drummer for the Dixieland Band. Well in his eighties, Columbo played six days a week. Until a stroke that left him partially paralyzed forced his retirement in 1993, Columbo billed himself as the oldest working musician in town.

Columbo passed away in 2002 at the age of 100, having outlived all of his contemporaries. In recognition of his historic presence in the city, a section of Kentucky Avenue, home of the Club Harlem, was in 2005 renamed Chris Columbo Lane. His true memorial, though, might be in the dozens of recordings on which we can still hear his inspired drumming and the countless Atlantic City residents, musicians and music-lovers alike, whose lives he enriched.

"Pop" Quiz

B orn on April 25, 1884, John Henry Lloyd grew up in Jacksonville, Florida, seemingly destined for baseball greatness. As a teenager playing for a local semi-pro ball club, he impressed visiting Negro League players. His work as a Pullman railroad "red cap" helped him meet traveling ballplayers and talent scouts.

In 1906, team owner Ed LaMar recruited Lloyd for the Philadelphia-based Cuban X Giants (which was made up of American-born blacks, not Cubans). Starting as a second baseman, Lloyd made an immediate impact: his 10th-inning double drove in the winning run in his first game. It was a fitting start for his outstanding career, which saw him play for several teams, including the Philadelphia, Leland and Lincoln Giants; the Chicago American Giants; the Lincoln Stars; the Brooklyn Royal Giants; the Columbus Buckeyes; the Hilldale Club; and Atlantic City's Bacharach Giants.

The Bacharach Giants started as the Duval Giants in Lloyd's home town of Jacksonville, and when the team moved to Atlantic City in 1916, its owners thought it politic to rename the Giants after the city's current mayor, Harry Bacharach. And though Lloyd had many more stops after the Bacharach Giants, he chose to make Atlantic City his off-season home in 1919.

Lloyd never played for the Phillies, Athletics or any other major league baseball team. When he was at his prime, black ballplayers were not welcome in "organized baseball" (the professional major and minor leagues) in any capacity. In 1912, manager John McGraw of the New York Giants sought to bring him to the major leagues, but was unable to break the color line. It would take another generation for Branch Rickey of the Brooklyn Dodgers to make history by fielding Jackie Robinson.

Lloyd gained renown for both his hitting and his fielding, chiefly at shortstop, and early on was regarded as a "smart" player—even before he retired, younger players called him "Pop" because of his wisdom. He had a lifetime batting average (.368) higher than Ty Cobb's, and was known for both power and speed. Despite his fierce competition on the field, he was a complete gentleman off it. Lloyd neither smoked, drank, nor cursed, which enhanced his reputation as an elder statesman of the game.

Honus Wagner, on hearing that Lloyd was called the "black Honus Wagner," said it was an honor to be compared to the Negro Leagues star. Babe Ruth said Lloyd was the greatest player of all time, bar none.

After a 27-year career, Lloyd retired from professional baseball in 1931. But he continued to play with and manage the Johnson Stars, a local semi-professional team named for Atlantic City power broker Enoch "Nucky" Johnson. He also continued to play first base (a position that didn't require the physical pyrotechnics of shortstop) until 1942, when he turned 58. After he retired from playing, Lloyd continued to manage the Johnson Stars and, later, the Farley Stars.

In an era before lucrative endorsement contracts or pensions for players, Lloyd took a job with the Atlantic City school system. For many years, he served as a custodian at the Indiana Avenue School, and later took the same job at Atlantic City High. For decades, students gathered to hear "Pop" tell stories of his time in the baseball spotlight. Lloyd also served as the city's Little League commissioner.

In 1949, the city honored him by naming its new ball field Pop Lloyd Stadium, dedicating the diamond as "an everlasting monument to a humble, beloved American whose life has been devoted to baseball, his job, and the development of American youth."

On March 19, 1964, Lloyd died at the age of 79. He was not forgotten by the custodians of sports history. In December 1974, he was inducted into the Black Athletes Hall of Fame alongside heavyweight boxer Jack Johnson, Chicago Bears running back Gale Sayers, Los Angeles Lakers great Elgin Baylor, and baseball players Roy Campanella and Roberto Clemente. On August 8, 1977, Lloyd was finally inducted into the Baseball Hall of Fame in Cooperstown, New York, taking his rightful place among the legends of the game.

Yet in Atlantic City, Lloyd's adopted home, the stadium that bore his name languished in a pitiable state of decay. By the early 1990s, the ballpark was a crumbling, trash-strewn wreck of a field. The Committee to Restore Pop Lloyd Stadium, a group of local volunteers, led efforts to raise money to finance a much-needed renovation.

The result was a restored stadium that opened on April 29, 1995, with a refurbished grandstand, new lights and fences. A commemorative statue of Lloyd now welcomes visitors to the park. It's a fitting tribute to an Atlantic City legend.

The Star Maker

Today, most of the entertainment presented in Atlantic City comes courtesy of seasoned veterans and nationally-known recording artists. Once, however, the city was a mecca for amateur performers seeking applause—all courtesy of one man, whose name became synonymous with young talent. Tony Grant's Stars of Tomorrow show, for decades, gave thousands of children their first taste of the performing arts.

Grant's show, a staple on Steel Pier for 32 years, featured several talents before they were famous. Singers Connie Francis and Frankie Avalon and Broadway star Andrea McArdle are some of the best-known graduates of Grant's revue.

Born Antonio Grande in Wilkes-Barre, Pennsylvania in 1907, Grant evinced a love of show business early on. In his sophomore year of high school, he represented his hometown in a statewide dancing contest. He took first place, and never looked back.

Grant subsequently dropped out of school to take a job as a dancer with the Guy Hall band, as part of a traveling vaudeville show. Paying $150 a week—about $1,900 in value today—this was a good job doing what he loved. He then went out on his own as half of the Two Barons dancing team on the vaudeville circuit.

When the market for touring dancers dried up, Grant returned to Wilkes Barre, where he ran a dance studio with his wife, Topsy.

Grant moved his school to Ventnor in 1945. He'd been traveling to the area for a while, bringing students from his dancing school to perform in Daddy Dave's Juvenile Revue, a featured attraction at Steel Pier's Little Theater. "Daddy Dave" Tyson, who billed himself as "the Radio Friend of the Kiddies," ran shows with child talent from the early 1930s until his death in 1947.

After Tyson's death, Grant took over the show. It was a chance he was ready to take. In a 1973 interview with the *New York Times*, he spoke about his commitment to his child stars.

"This is not a job," he said. "It's something I believe in. When I see the children progressing from the first day they arrive until the last day of the engagement, it makes me so proud."

When Grant took over the children's revue, it had about 16 young performers in each show. Over the years, he enlarged that number to 250. Children came to Atlantic City from across the country to audition for Grant in hopes of landing a spot on his show. At its busiest, Grant auditioned 5,000 different acts each summer.

Grant soon found a steady format for his shows. A child act, be it singers or dancers, performed once in each show for seven days straight. After that, another act had its chance. With 12 acts in each show, Grant had his hands full. At one point, he presented eight shows per day but soon reduced that number to allow his young charges to enjoy their week in Atlantic City.

By the 1970s, he had settled on using three separate casts to stage three shows per day—at 11:30 a.m., 1:30 p.m., and 6 p.m., thus giving audiences in the 1,700-seat theater ample opportunity to see a show, but allowing plenty of time for the youngsters to visit the beach.

Early on, he had a keen eye for talent. In 1948, 10 year-old Concetta Franconero was a featured performer, playing the accordion and singing. Grant handed her two records, one in Spanish and one in French, and told her she'd be singing them the next day. Though she had no familiarity with either language, she mastered each song under his guidance and performed them to rave reviews. As an adult, recording as Connie Francis, the popular star recorded songs in 13 different languages.

Featuring stars from four to 19 years of age, the shows became an institution at the Steel Pier, known as "the Showplace of the Nation." The Midway theater, which hosted the shows, was the only venue in the United States solely dedicated to juvenile performers. The Stars of Tomorrow remained a fixture on the pier through good times and bad.

Grant's son, Tony Grant, Junior, followed him into the theater, becoming assistant producer and director of the show. His grand-daughter Roxanne got started early, working as a stagehand, and eventually emceed the shows.

"It was an unbelievable experience," she remembers today of her time with her grandfather's productions. "It was like a family there on the Pier—everyone was so close. And we'd have celebrities coming over all the time to the house in Ventnor."

Following Topsy's death in the early 1970s, Grant gave the Tony Grant Dance Studio to longtime dance teacher Lucille Parker, who continued his legacy by giving instruction to the next generation of dance students. And by this time, Grant's legacy was considerable. An entire generation of children had grown up performing under the watch of "Mr. Wonderful," as he was known to them.

In a 1976 remodeling, the children's theater was officially renamed the Tony Grant Theater, a mark of the respect and admiration that Grant had earned over the previous three decades. The following year, he was honored by the Dance Masters of America, an international association of dance educators, for his long work with aspiring dancers with his Stars of Tomorrow show. At the time, he estimated that he had given more than 50,000 young entertainers a chance to perform before live audiences.

But the show, unfortunately, couldn't go on forever. Steel Pier closed in 1978, and without a home the Stars of Tomorrow revue was shelved. When Grant passed away in October 1979, it marked the true ending of an era.

Today, Tony Grant alumni stay in touch through a page on Facebook (search "Tony Grant Stars of Tomorrow"). Swapping pictures and reminiscing about the old days, they are keeping the spirit of what Tony Grant started so long ago alive. And an annual reunion, which raises money for the Marine Mammal Stranding Center, makes sure that Tony Grant's legacy continues to shine.

City Painter

A tlantic City has been a stage on which dozens of notable public figures—from Thomas Edison and Diamond Jim Brady to Jay-Z and Donald Trump—have walked. Yet few people know that one of the most well-respected American artists of the 20th century was born in Atlantic City.

Jacob Armistead Lawrence's family was part of what historians call the "Great Migration," in which thousands of black southerners moved to the large cities of the north, fleeing Jim Crow and in search of better lives during and after World War I. Seeking opportunity, the Lawrence family arrived in Atlantic City where, on September 7, 1917, Jacob was born.

The family didn't stay long in Atlantic City, soon moving to Philadelphia. After his parents divorced in 1924, Jacob's life was even more chaotic, though by the age of 13 he had settled in Harlem with his mother and his siblings.

It isn't known whether he was exposed to any artistic influences during his early years in Atlantic City, but Jacob arrived in a Harlem that was bursting with literary and artistic energy. In these years, the black community in Harlem was growing rapidly, and the subsequent outburst of creativity in theater, art, and literature known as the New Negro Movement or Harlem Renaissance provided fertile ground for a young man with artistic ambitions.

Lawrence gained his first exposure to art when his mother sent him to a settlement house where painter and muralist Charles Alston taught an arts and crafts class. Experimenting with color and texture, Lawrence knew that he wanted to become an artist. In his late teens, when Alston created a community workshop in his studio on West

141 Street, Lawrence rented a corner in which he painted while listening to poets and authors like Countee Cullen, Claude McKay, and Ralph Ellison discuss art and the day's events.

By the age of 19, Lawrence had begun painting scenes of everyday Harlem life. Between Alston's workshop and hours spent absorbing the works hanging in the Metropolitan Museum of Art, Lawrence had begun to create an artistic style of his own.

Lawrence called that style "dynamic cubism," and it was informed by both European masters like Picasso and Matisse and the vibrant colors of Harlem. His paintings were, at the same time, both realistic and abstracted.

Lawrence's first major series of paintings depicted Toussaint L'Ouverture, the freed slave and Haitian general who helped to lead the first successful slave revolution in the Americas. When he was 21, these paintings were exhibited in a museum show—a tremendous honor for such a young talent. It was a portent of things to come.

Series of paintings about noteworthy African Americans like Harriet Tubman, who helped establish the Underground Railroad that spirited fugitive slaves to freedom, and Frederick Douglass, the famed abolitionist, followed.

In 1938, Lawrence secured a position on the Works Progress Administration's Federal Art Project. This was a New Deal program that put artists to work creating pieces for libraries, schools, and hospitals. For the next year and a half, Lawrence had a steady income and the chance to work on his craft.

With his status as an artist secure, Lawrence returned to his roots, creating a series of paintings that he called *The Migration of the Negro*. This collection reflected the Great Migration that had brought his own family, ultimately, to Harlem, with a stop in Atlantic City. He drew on both his own memories and historical research to create source material for the 60 paintings that made up the cycle of paintings.

The paintings, which chronicled the Great Migration from the first inklings of movement in the South to the adjustment to the massive cities of the North, earned Lawrence a good deal of fame. In November 1941, about half of the series was reproduced in *Fortune* magazine, the first time that the publication had given such attention to an African American artist.

Also in this year Lawrence married artist Gwendolyn Knight. Another personal milestone came when he was invited to exhibit in

New York's prestigious Downtown Gallery. Once again, as the first black artist to be represented by a major New York Gallery, he was making history.

The Second World War, however, forced Lawrence to interrupt his artistic career, though he couldn't avoid another rendezvous with history. He joined the Coast Guard, where he served aboard the first racially-integrated ship in Coast Guard history. He was ultimately appointed to a post as a combat artist, though none of his paintings from the time survive.

After the war, Lawrence continued his career, painting and teaching at the Pratt Institute in New York City, Brandeis University, and the University of Washington. One-man exhibitions in New York, Baltimore, Portland, Boston, and Washington featured his work.

In 1965, when paintings from his *Migration* series were shown in Nigeria, Lawrence crossed the Atlantic and spent eight months living and painting in the African country.

During the late 1960s, Lawrence's works were exhibited in a Manhattan gallery owned by Terry Dintenfass, who coincidentally also hailed from Atlantic City, and had operated his first galleries in Boardwalk hotels.

Living in Seattle, Washington, from 1971 onwards, Lawrence continued to paint. In 1983, he was elected to the American Academy of Arts and Letters, a select honor society of 250 architects, composers, artists, and writers. Seven years later, President George H.W. Bush presented him with the National Medal of the Arts, the highest award given to artists by the United States government.

When Lawrence died on June 9, 2000, he was hailed as one of the foremost modern American painters and chroniclers of black American life. Honored throughout his career, Lawrence's artistic legacy is secure.

Though he didn't spend much time in Atlantic City, the seaside town should be proud to claim him as its son.

The Boardwalk Emperor

Atlantic City did not become America's Playground overnight. Rather, it was built up, over many decades, by the hard work of many men and women. Some were unknown, some were famous, and some were infamous. One of the best-known and most influential was Enoch "Nucky" Johnson, who put his own stamp on the city during what was arguably its most successful era.

Johnson has attained a measure of recent celebrity thanks to the HBO series *Boardwalk Empire,* which chronicles goings-on in Atlantic City during the reign of Nucky Thompson, a thinly fictionalized version of Johnson. The Atlantic County kingmaker's real life, however, is more dramatic than anything dreamed up for the screen.

Nucky Johnson was born in Smithville in 1883, son of a farmer who became Atlantic County sheriff and a political power in the then-dominant local Republican party. After serving as undersheriff, Nucky, an Atlantic City High School graduate (class of '00), was elected to the office of sheriff himself in 1908.

The position, as Johnson re-interpreted it, involved more than simple law enforcement. In fact, much of his success—and his wealth—came because he learned when *not* to enforce the law. Under his watch, gamblers and prostitutes openly plied their wares—provided, of course, that they returned a fair share of their earnings to Johnson and his associates.

His financial base established, Johnson worked his way to the top of the Atlantic County political pecking order, securing himself a place on the Republican County Committee, where he could maintain firm discipline within his party. Not even the election of

Woodrow Wilson, a reform-minded Democratic governor, could derail Johnson's rise to the top. In 1914, after Wilson had left the New Jersey governor's mansion for the White House, Johnson was appointed to the post of county treasurer. Officially, he was in charge of the county's finances, but in fact he entrusted the actual business to underlings.

Johnson's regime, which had weathered the reformer Wilson, enjoyed the boon of a quixotic national drive for progress, Prohibition. In 1923, Johnson reportedly struck a deal with New York underworld boss Lucky Luciano—he would guarantee protection for bootlegged liquor landed in Atlantic City for Luciano and his associates in exchange for a 10 percent cut of the syndicate's entire operation.

That was a huge sum, but it was a good deal for Luciano, particularly since Johnson agreed to allow him exclusivity. So while he could land cargo at will and be assured that it would arrive it its destination, his competitors were sure of only one thing: that if they tried to work in Nucky Johnson's fiefdom, they'd be mercilessly targeted by the local police.

The cash coming in from Luciano's enterprises only bolstered Johnson's political power. At the height of Prohibition, he was making more than a half-million dollars a year from vice alone. As Prohibition continued, he became the undisputed king of Atlantic City, a man whose influence stretched to the statehouse and beyond.

In these years, Johnson leased an entire floor of the Ritz Carlton hotel and held court on the Boardwalk, where he dispensed charity (he was notoriously generous), business advice, and political favors. At night, dressed in one of his hundred tailored suits, he'd make the rounds of the city's nightclubs and gambling spots.

Johnson even became a fixture in Manhattan's star-struck night-life, where he gained a reputation as one of the hardest-partying—and most generous—men who'd ever done the town. He dated showgirls, befriended celebrities, and had front-row seats for the biggest sporting events of the era.

The political boss was able to enjoy himself so thoroughly after dark because he took care of business during the day. He developed a finely-honed political organization that had a single aim: the promotion of Atlantic City as a tourist destination. In order to do this, of course, Johnson had to remain in power, which required both money and votes. He ensured that there was never a shortage of either for him or his associates, and he personally hired public workers in the county, only choosing those whose loyalty was guaranteed.

But the good times couldn't last forever. In 1933, Prohibition ended, and in 1936 the federal government began investigating Johnson's empire. With Johnson's army of followers obstructing agents at every turn, the investigation did not run smoothly, but in 1939 a federal grand jury indicted Johnson. The case finally went to trial in 1941. All of his power was for naught, as he was convicted of tax evasion and sentenced to 10 years in prison.

Released after four years, Johnson refused to return to power, content to merely advise the city's new power brokers. In 1968, in a Northfield nursing home, Johnson passed away at the age of 85. His death, coming at the nadir of Atlantic City's reputation as a tourist town, emphasized the ending of an era.

Political Juggernaut

Most local residents and auto visitors to Atlantic City who've taken the Atlantic City Expressway or been in the city's marina district know at least the name Frank S. Farley. He's been honored by having both an Expressway service plaza and Atlantic City's marina named for him. These are appropriate honors, since without Farley, Atlantic City might not have enjoyed much development in the mid-20th century.

Farley was born in 1901, the last of 10 children in a poor family on the North Side of Atlantic City. Despite his family's poor social standing, he was a popular and athletic young man who was nicknamed "Happy" for his cheerful disposition. Later, this was shortened to "Hap."

The quintessential team player, Hap learned about politics from his father Jim, secretary of the Atlantic City Fire Department and a mid-level worker in the county Republican machine. After attending the University of Pennsylvania and Georgetown law school, Farley returned to Atlantic City and began practicing law.

His legal career didn't quite take off, so Farley decided that politics would be a better place to make his mark. At the time, Nucky Johnson's organization had a secure hold on the Atlantic County Republican Party and both county and municipal government.

With the approval of Johnson, Farley ran for the state assembly in 1937. He was successful, after being re-elected twice, he won a seat in the state Senate in 1940.

This was a tumultuous time in Atlantic County politics. With the threat of prison hanging over Nucky Johnson, the leadership of the political machine was in doubt. The ultimate prize—control of

Johnson's organization—might be up for grabs to the man who knew how to play his cards right.

Farley, by cultivating the right friends and carefully neutralizing his rivals, quickly assumed Johnson's role, following Johnson's 1941 conviction and prison sentence, and a brief power struggle with Atlantic City mayor Thomas Taggart. Taggart had been popular, but made the mistake of alienating the local vice magnates with his reform talk and hardline anti-crime initiatives. When the smoke cleared, Taggart had been stripped of power and Farley was in command.

Getting power was one thing; keeping it was another. Farley intended to maintain his position by convivially trading favors with his fellow senators and always keeping an open door to his constituents. He quickly earned a reputation among his peers and everyday citizens as a man who always tried to help and never failed to keep his word.

A hard-working senator who missed only three legislative sessions, Farley, with his re-election perpetually secure, became a dominant figure in the statehouse. The fact that he wasn't ambitious for higher office greatly increased his effectiveness; while other state senators jockeyed for the chance to run for Congress or the governor's mansion, Farley was content to rule Atlantic County from his state senate office. Since he wasn't a threat to anyone's statewide aspirations, he had no real rivals in the senate.

Within time, Farley was arguably the most important politician in the state. He carried with him the votes of seven South Jersey senators and, through his chairmanship of the Judiciary Committee, had the final say on the elevation of judges to the bench. No one could get anything accomplished in New Jersey without Farley's approval.

In 1950, a trio of police officers became disgruntled by Farley's refusal to guarantee a pay raise. They began raiding bookmakers and numbers banks under Farley's protection. Hap Farley was facing his biggest challenge yet. The Kefauver Committee, a congressional body charged with investigating crime, gathered evidence of corruption in the city. Farley's chosen ticket squeaked out a win in the 1952 election, ending the threat. His power secure, Farley returned his focus to the statehouse.

There, Farley used his leverage to greatly benefit Atlantic County. He pushed to build the Atlantic City Race Course in the mid-1940s, though it was later learned that he was a stockholder in the company that built and operated the race track. He also brought pari-mutuel horse betting to New Jersey, which greatly helped the racing industry.

Farley was critical in passing the bond issues that allowed the construction of the Garden State Parkway and the Atlantic City Expressway. Today these roads benefit the entire state, but at the time northerners derisively referred to the Parkway as "Farley's Folly."

He was also instrumental in the creation of Stockton State College and Atlantic Community College.

After 34 years in the legislature—the longest tenure in New Jersey history—Farley lost re-election in 1971 to Democrat Joseph McGahn. Now in his late 60s, he never ran for office again, though his embrace of casino gaming in 1976 helped to win support for the referendum that legalized casinos for Atlantic City.

The next year, he died at home in Ventnor. Though he didn't live to see the revitalization of Atlantic City, this political juggernaut left a legacy that will never be forgotten.

A jitney letting off passengers near the War Memorial at Albany and Atlantic Avenues in the 1950s. *Allen "Boo" Pergament.*

A more recent photo of a jitney near North Carolina and Pacific Avenues. *Robert Rossiello.*

The Warner Theater, opened in 1929, was as opulent a movie palace as was ever built in Atlantic City. *Allen "Boo" Pergament.*

The front of the Warner Theater, incorporated into Bally's Wild Wild West's Boardwalk frontage, slyly combines old and new Atlantic City. *Robert Rossiello.*

An Atlantic City staple from 1940 to 1979, Captain Starn's offered seafood caught by the Captain's own fleet of fishing boats. *Tichnor Bros.*

This photo of Starn's pier shows just how popular the Inlet eatery was. *Allen "Boo" Pergament.*

Enoch "Nucky" Johnson, who held court at the Ritz Carlton, ruled Atlantic City during its wild Prohibition years. *Allen "Boo" Pergament.*

Johnson's successor, Frank S. "Hap" Farley, shaped Atlantic City as profoundly as anyone in the 20th century. Among other accomplishments, he made the Atlantic City Expressway a reality. *Allen "Boo" Pergament.*

Four

The Community

Lighting the Way

Today, Atlantic City's skyline is distinguished by its towering casinos. Before the city had any legal casinos or even high-rise hotels, its dominant architectural statement was as functional as it was noticeable: the Absecon Lighthouse.

In the 1850s, as Atlantic City was establishing itself on the coast of the ocean of the same name, local leaders became increasingly concerned about the navigational hazards the sandy beaches of Absecon Island presented to mariners. Sailors had taken to calling Absecon Island (or at least the northeast end of it) the "Graveyard Inlet," something that, local promoters realized, was hardly a boon to development. For years, they had complained to state and federal authorities that, without a lighthouse to warn ships of the danger, vessels would continue to run aground, causing a loss of life and property. But it was not until the 1854 wreck of the *Powhattan* that Congress finally took action, buying land at Rhode Island and Pacific Avenues and entrusting construction of a new lighthouse to the Army Corps of Engineers.

One of the army officers involved with the lighthouse's construction is immediately familiar to Civil War enthusiasts: Lieutenant George Meade, who would ultimately rise to the rank of general and command the victorious Army of the Potomac at the Battle of Gettysburg. The lighthouse was finished in late 1856 under the guidance of Lieutenant Colonel William Reynolds, and was first lighted on January 15, 1857.

The light could be seen from 19.5 nautical miles out—about 22 ½ standard miles—and successfully kept ships from foundering on the Absecon Island coast, although shipwrecks remained a hazard into the 20th century. The red brick tower stood 171 feet tall—making it the tallest lighthouse in the state and third-highest in the nation.

When first built, the lighthouse was near the lapping ocean waves, and for decades it was threatened by beach erosion. Engineers built jetties in an effort to save the lighthouse, though it appeared to be a losing battle. But luck was with the lighthouse: by the 1880s shifting currents had let the beach in front of the lighthouse stretch for blocks. This is why the lighthouse is, today, nowhere near the breakers.

In addition to its tower, the lighthouse had a keeper's house in which the lighthouse keeper resided. When first built, it was not painted, but over the years was given several paint schemes. Originally fueled by kerosene, the lamp was in 1910 converted to incandescent oil vapor and in 1925 to electric light.

As the city grew, new high-rise hotels dwarfed the lighthouse. Though it was reckoned as perhaps the best known beacon between New York and Virginia, the lighthouse was, by the 1930s, considered obsolete. Still, it remained a popular tourist attraction. But in 1933, the government decommissioned the lighthouse, citing "inefficiency and reasons of economy." On July 11, 1933, the light was dimmed. The mariner's guide shined no more.

The federal government leased the lighthouse to the city for use as a park, and in 1946 Atlantic City officially acquired the site. Yet the city failed to maintain the lighthouse and demolished two keepers' houses. Though the lamp was briefly lit in 1954 to celebrate the city's centennial and in 1963 to mark the state's tricentennial, little else was done, and the tower fell into disrepair. In 1966 the state acquired the lighthouse, which was placed on the State (1970) and National (1971) Registers of Historic Places.

The state, however, wanted to put the historic structure into local hands, although, understandably, not directly under the municipal control that had seen it deteriorate. In 1994, the Inlet Private/Public Association adopted the lighthouse and began planning its renovation. With grant money from the Casino Reinvestment Development Authority, the IPPA nearly completed restoration of the tower and a rebuilt keeper's house in 1998 before the house was lost in a tragic fire. The tower itself was spared serious damage, and work continued.

In 1999, 142 years after its lamp first shone and 66 years after its dimming, the Absecon Lighthouse reopened to visitors. Today, the Lighthouse is open to visitors and hosts many special events throughout the year. In a city where change is becoming the only constant, it remains a link to the past.

The Sweetest Storm

O cean City's caramel corn may come with or without a cover, but the Jersey Shore guilty boardwalk snack that's gone the furthest is Atlantic City's world-famous salt water taffy. Beginning as a marketing ploy in the late 19th century, salt water taffy has transcended its boardwalk roots.

Richie Brothers and Windle Hollis sold the first taffy on the Boardwalk in 1880, but errant waves created the "real" shore treat. Legend holds that on a windy 1883 night, Boardwalk merchant David Bradley's candy store at St. James Place was savaged by a storm tide. The next day, his stock soaked, when asked if he had any taffy to sell, he ruefully replied that he had plenty of "saltwater taffy."

Apparently the idea of eating candy doused by seawater—watch out for pieces of jellyfish—caught on like hotcakes, as customers lined up for it.

Though the first mention of salt water in national newspapers dates from 1893, the history of salt water taffy sellers on the Boardwalk in the 1880s is well documented. That the confection could have become nationally known a mere decade after its "invention" says a great deal about the popularity of Atlantic City.

Bradley unveiled a huge sign reading "Salt Water Taffy" over his store for the 1884 season, though he neglected to copyright the name. Bradley's rivals began advertising their own salt water taffy, and soon visitors to the shore could pick from several brands. Bradley soldiered on in the taffy business until 1939, fighting off a 1923 lawsuit from Miamian John Edmiston, who claimed that he, not Bradley, had coined the term "salt water taffy." Edmiston lost the case and soon disappeared from the city.

Whatever the real story behind salt water taffy's invention, it was by the late 1880s one of Atlantic City's hottest products. Joseph A. Fralinger (also spelled Fraelinger and Froehlinger) helped popularize the treat. Fralinger, born in Sweetwater, Atlantic County in 1848, started off as a glass blower but later moved to Philadelphia, where he ran a fish market before managing several baseball clubs.

He then moved to Atlantic City where he sold cider, lemonade, cigars and, after 1889, salt water taffy on the Boardwalk. Though he didn't invent the candy, Fralinger was the first to sell it in a durable box rather than a paper bag. Fralinger's box proved a better fit for train-riding vacationers, and taffy became a popular gift item.

Fralinger's taffy proved so successful that he was dubbed "The Taffy King." He went on to build first the Academy of Music and then the Apollo Theater. Though he sold his salt water taffy store in 1902, stores with his name still sell candy in Atlantic City, Cape May, and Ocean City.

The other legendary name in sweets came to the Boardwalk in 1905 when Enoch James, who had been making taffy for years, brought his family to town. His improved brand of taffy, less sticky and easy to chew than earlier varieties, proved popular. After James' 1906 death, his three sons Lee, Harry, and Enoch Jr. continued to sell candy and broadened their product mix to include chocolate-dipped and chocolate-center taffy.

To drum up business, the senior James gave away free samples at Arkansas Avenue and the Boardwalk to passers-by. One youngster, delighted by the bite-sized portions, exclaimed that the candy was "cut to fit the mouth." James turned this impromptu testimonial into a marketing catchphrase that the taffy seller still uses today.

Salt water taffy is a triumph of marketing. There was nothing special about the Jersey Shore that made it a better place to make or sell candy, but enterprising confectioners convinced the public that Atlantic City was the only place to get this "unique" treat. Even its apocryphal origin story is a classic case of making lemonade (or lemon candy) from lemons.

It is a lesson that today's marketing gurus would do well to emulate as they try to sell Atlantic City to 21st century audiences.

Dream of a Million Girls

Miss America is one of Atlantic City's most treasured icons. Although many local innovations, like boardwalks and salt water taffy, have transcended their Atlantic City origins, only Miss America draws international media attention every year. The contest has a long and interesting history stretching back to 1921, when Warren Harding was president, Model Ts the cutting edge in automotive fashion, and, with Prohibition just enacted, speakeasies popping up throughout the land.

Miss America began something called the Atlantic City Fall Pageant, an unapologetic attempt to extend the summer season by one week past its traditional Labor Day conclusion. The Pageant was a week of revels including a Bathers Revue (forerunner of the Swimsuit Competition), Rolling Chair Parade, Night Spectacle, and the Inter-City Beauty Contest.

This last event saw young women from Washington, Pittsburgh, Harrisburg, Ocean City, New York, Philadelphia, and Atlantic City compete in afternoon attire. The winner, Margaret Gorman of Washington, DC, was chosen by the panel of judges and the public. It was not until she returned to Atlantic City to defend her crown in 1922 that Gorman was officially named "Miss America." In that year, nearly 60 contestants, each representing a city, competed for the tiara. Fifteen-year-old Miss Columbus (Ohio) Mary Katherine Campbell, in a blaze of media coverage, became the next Miss America. The Inter-City Beauty Contest had become a truly national event.

The pageant was popular throughout the 1920s, bringing plenty of publicity to Atlantic City, but was dogged by pressure from women's groups and moral reformers (who felt that the attention lavished on impressionable young women was unbecoming). Though the context brought visitors to town and had a large economic impact, it lost money—about $50,000 a year at one point—which may have been the reason that it was discontinued in 1928. Although other cities held similar pageants, Atlantic City refused to resume the contest; a rival "Miss America" was chosen in Wildwood in 1932. A 1933 attempt to revive the pageant, with most contestants representing states, was dogged by scandal (one contestant was, in fact, married, and others were not from the states they represented).

Following a 1934 attempt to stage a beauty pageant in New York City's Madison Square Garden, Steel Pier owner Frank Gravatt championed an Atlantic City revival of the national pageant. In 1935, it was brought back as the "Showman's Variety Jubilee," and it included 52 contestants who, for the first time, could compete in a talent contest. The innovation of contests representing states rather than cities was retained, as it is to this day. Lenora Slaughter began serving as executive secretary, and helping to make the pageant both profitable and respectable.

In 1941, the name was officially changed to "Miss America Pageant" and Lenora Slaughter became the Executive Director; she would guide the pageant until her retirement in 1967; the year before, Convention Hall (today Boardwalk Hall) had become the contest's new home. During World War II, the pageant transformed itself into a patriotic spectacle as Miss America toured the country with the U.S.O. and sold war bonds. Another major change came in 1945, when the pageant began awarding scholarships, thus beginning a change from a mere beauty pageant to an organization dedicated to furthering women's education.

The pageant was first televised in 1954, and the next year Bert Parks assumed the emcee duties he would hold until 1979. Parks's singing of "There She Is, Miss America" became an essential part of the pageant's mystique, reminding viewers that, "The dream of a million girls who are more than pretty can come true in Atlantic City."

Those were Miss America's boom years; the pageant expanded in size and public recognition. By 1959, all states sent representatives to the Atlantic City pageant; in 1964, city contestants were no longer allowed. By the end of the 1950s, the pageant was a television mainstay, drawing an audience of 75 million.

Yet, as the times changed, the pageant faced headwinds. One of the most controversial pageants came in 1968, when about 100 women protested the "enslavement" of beauty standards outside of Convention Hall. These women brought along a "Freedom Trash Can," into which they threw girdles, bras, false eyelashes, and hair curlers. One participant ripped up a Playboy magazine, and another, shouting, "down with these shoes!" tossed a high heeled-shoe into the can. As the protestors denounced the Pageants for racism (there had never been a black finalist), the first Miss Black America Pageant was held in the Ritz Carlton.

The Miss America Pageant itself saw its first African-American winner, Vanessa Williams, crowned in 1983, though she later resigned the title and was replaced by Suzette Charles. The year before, Gary Collins had taken on hosting responsibilities; he would remain until 1991, when Regis Philbin and Kathy Lee Gifford became co-hosts.

In the 1990s, the Pageant became even more serious about becoming serious; winners no longer had "reigns;" they had a "Year of Service." Contestants also had official platform issues, and were seen more as advocates of social change than as attractive young women.

Some thought that Miss America would always be held in Atlantic City in September, but in 2005, pageant organizers announced plans to move the contest to Las Vegas. There, it filled the early January lull, though it was lost in the shuffle. As just another event in a city filled with events, Miss America never became a local institution in Las Vegas as it had in Atlantic City.

Perhaps that failure to connect is why, in 2013, Miss America came back to the Boardwalk, and the pageant returned to September. It was a fitting return as both the pageant and the city adjusted to hard times.

The Miss America Pageant has survived scandal, wartime shortages, and political and social upheavals. As Atlantic City looks into the future, it should keep hold of this valuable piece of its past.

Rolling Merrily Along

Rolling chairs have been, for more than 120 years, one of the most visible icons of Atlantic City. Somewhere between a rickshaw and a wheelchair, the rolling chair was easier than walking, quieter than an automobile, and less smelly than a horse. And, more importantly, it was cheaper than the last three.

Atlantic City's not the only place where guests can get pushed around, but its rolling chairs have a unique story. They first became prominent in the area with the Philadelphia Exposition of 1876. This celebration of the American centennial introduced several products to the nation, including Hires Root Beer, Heinz Ketchup, and Alexander Graham Bell's newfangled telephone. Some of the 10 million visitors to the Exposition enjoyed being pushed across the grounds in single-occupant chairs.

The chairs migrated down the shore, but their appeal was at first limited. By 1884, a Philadelphia businessman named, incredibly enough, Harry D. Shill, was renting chairs to visitors. There was a drawback, though: Shill and his competitors only rented the chairs themselves—it was up to the rider to find a pusher.

So it was mostly invalids who used the first rolling chairs, since few able-bodied strollers would ask their companions to push them around the Boardwalk.

That all changed in 1887, when William Hayday started the first true commercial rolling chair service. He provided an attendant to push the chairs and enlarged them to hold two adults comfortably.

Now riding a rolling chair was a bona fide leisure activity for couples. The intimacy of the chair had no small attraction in Victorian America, where middle-class youngsters (and oldsters, too) were expected to follow strict rules of courtship etiquette, all of which precluded casual physical contact.

The chairs were a hit. The city issued its first licenses for chairs in 1891, and they became an integral part of the contentious local transportation scene. By 1902, an anonymous visitor gave a *New York Times* reporter a stirring testimonial: "The entire population seems to be on wheels," he said as he observed the endless line of chairs snaking down the boards. "I believe it is one of the most enjoyable diversions I know."

Three years later, rolling chairs were a key attraction. "The Spring Season has opened at Atlantic City," read a March 8, 1905 advertisement for the Chalfonte. "Five miles of Boardwalk are free of ice and slush. The walking is good. The rolling chair is ditto, and golf is very popular. Now is the time for a visit."

As with any successful product, competition was fierce. In 1916 a "rate war" between upstart William Garret and the dominant Shill Company resulted in the cost dropping to a mere 30 cents an hour. Legal maneuvering, interspersed with occasional strong-arm tactics, marked the skirmishes between rival operators for the next several years.

Rolling chairs hit their peak popularity in the 1920s. During this booming decade, the Boardwalk was swamped with 3,000 of the wicker conveyances at a time. Riding in a chair was a necessary part of a shore vacation. At the time, operators charged by the hour, not by distance, showing that the experience was more about leisure than transportation.

With the Great Depression, hiring a man to push you around the Boardwalk seemed a superfluous luxury. Naturally, the economies forced by the Second World War—and the shortage of labor that followed mass conscription—hampered the growth of the industry.

After the war, Atlantic City was different. In September 1948, the first mechanized rolling chairs hit the Boardwalk: ten chairs with electric motors and chauffeurs seated behind the riders. They typically ground their way down the Boardwalk at 2.5 miles—slower than a brisk walk—and lacked the romance of the man-powered originals. Originally sheathed in sheet metal, the motorized chairs later reverted to the original wicker body.

As motels sprouted amid the aging bulks of the once-proud hotels, the rolling chair trade diminished. The advent of casino gaming in 1978 didn't appreciably help revive the rollers—most visitors were intent on gambling, and too eager to spend an hour calmly gliding along the boards.

In the 1980s, electric trams pushed out most of the remaining chairs, but in the middle of that decade Larry Belfer purchased 83 decaying chairs and re-launched the tradition.

By the middle of the next decade, nearly 200 chairs were plying the wooden way, mostly ferrying gamblers from one casino to another, though a few visitors took a page from Atlantic City history and rode for the sheer pleasure of the wind, waves, and relaxation.

Trolleying Around

Longtime residents might remember when trolley tracks ran the length of Atlantic Avenue, but, unless they are very old, they probably don't recall the oldest form of public transportation in Atlantic City—horse-drawn cars. From the city's earliest years through the 1950s, mule cars, trains, and buses gave train-riding daytrippers and residents without a car several ways to get around Absecon Island.

Public transportation started on the island in 1865, 11 years after the first train arrived in Atlantic City from Camden. Samuel and John Cordery, two Absecon brothers, rented a right of way running from South Carolina Avenue to the Inlet from the Camden and Atlantic Railroad, hitched hour horses to a pair of streetcars, and took their place in history. Four years later, an entrepreneur named William G. Bartlett bought out the brothers Cordery and replaced the horses with mules. The Camden and Atlantic Railroad, perhaps sensing a unique business opportunity, declined to extend Barlett's lease and took over the operations themselves. The service proved so popular that the Camden and Atlantic extended the line to Missouri and Pacific Avenues, where it ended at the appropriately-named Sea View Excursion House.

The mule-drawn version of the line inspired several imitators: in the days before the Boardwalk assumed its final shape, many leading hotels were far from the beach. With guests getting ever more anxious to go to the water's edge and bask in the healthy salt air, the hotels offered them a new convenience: door to dune mule-drawn carriages.

On April 23, 1889, Atlantic City moved into the electric age when it retired its mule teams and debuted the state's first electric trolley system. Initially, the mule-less cars ran from the Inlet to Kentucky Avenue, but within two months the line had been extended all the way to Albany Avenue, where a new Sea View Excursion house now stood. Four years later, the trolley line was extended all the way to Longport, replacing earlier steam-powered cars. These tracks would remain operational until the 1950s, though there was originally some controversy about them.

In the fall of 1895, Atlantic City's Mayor Stoy threatened to unleash a gang of men who would tear up new trolley tracks unless the Camden and Atlantic agreed to pay one-half, rather than the offered one-third, of repaving expenses. The railroad company, for their part, "had a big gang of Italians in its employ," and threatened trouble should the city actually begin to tear out its carefully-laid tracks. Luckily the two sides came to an agreement, and the trolley remained.

As Pacific Avenue became a major thoroughfare, attempts were made to provide convenient public transport along its length. The first came in 1895, when operators began using carettes, 40-passenger vehicles drawn by three horses. Though the carettes soon disappeared, the idea of an alternative to the trolley remained, and it proved far more successful in its next iteration.

In 1915, jitneys, or privately-owned buses, began operation. They were so successful that they pushed the trolley line to the brink of bankruptcy. The next year, at the urging of the Camden and Atlantic and local business groups, the city began regulating the jitneys, mandating fairs, routes, and operating procedures.

The city was serious about the new regulations: on a single day in September 1916, 60 jitney drivers were arrested for a variety of offenses, including overloading, crossing avenues in midstreet, reckless driving, and attempting to shorten their Albany to Maine route. The new rules put more than 300 "Jitneurs" out of business; before the crackdown, over 500 buses ran, but afterwards, only 200 remained.

The trolley line and jitneys coexisted for years, but as the city's visitation began to decline and trolley systems throughout the nation were driven out of business, the jitneys began to emerge as the winners. On December 28, 1955, bus service replaced the remaining trolleys and the tracks were soon paved over, leaving little to commemorate the earliest form of public transportation in Atlantic City.

An Atlantic City Original

The jitney is an almost-uniquely Atlantic City mode of transportation. Though the distinctive short buses seem timeless, they have been around only about 100 years. Their history, however, encompasses some of the resort's best and worst times.

In its generic sense, a jitney is any bus or vehicle that travels a fixed route, accepting and dropping off passengers along the way. Jitney buses arrived on Absecon Island in 1915, when automobiles were relatively new. Though several of the larger hotels had private motorcars to pick up valued guests from the train station, most people used trolleys to get around.

Jitney drivers charged 5 cents a head, which gave the buses their name: "jitney" was once slang for a nickel. It was a lucrative profession: At a time when $5 a day was considered decent workman's wages, on good summer days drivers made between $15 and $20 a day, and even in the offseason they could expect to make $10 a shift.

At first, jitneys were almost entirely unregulated, and they ran roughshod over the city during the 1915 tourist season. About 500 of them crowded the streets, picking up and discharging passengers willy-nilly.

There may have been some legitimate public safety concerns, but the existing trolley owners were most concerned—their income dropped by almost 75 percent. By November of 1915, the Atlantic City Traction Company was reporting an annual loss of over $100,000. Unable to pay its debts, it fell into receivership, and looked to the authorities for help.

City officials proposed more stringent regulations, but jitney drivers bitterly contested any change—in March 1916, they staged a twelve-hour strike to show the public just how indispensable they were. But the demand for regulation was indomitable, and by August the City Council had passed a comprehensive jitney regulation bill.

Jitneys were now forced to run regular routes, and the 5-cent fare was written into law. Drivers could be fined up to $100 (a good week's pay) for a variety of offenses, including overloading passengers, not following prescribed routes, and crossing avenues in mid-street.

As a result of the stricter oversights, the number of jitneys was reduced to 200. In 1917, further legislation reduced the number of jitneys to 190, where it remains today.

In the ensuing years the trolley line struggled and eventually died, while jitneys became an accepted part of the city. Once considered dangerous rebels, jitneys were now a welcome part of the city's fabric.

Even though fares rose (to a dime by the 1940s, and higher still in the future), the routes remained dependable, and riding the jitney became a necessary part of an Atlantic City vacation and an easy way for carless residents to navigate their hometown. The jitney outlasted the trolleys, which rolled for the last time in 1955 and, alongside NJ Transit buses, became an integral part of the city's public transportation, though they were privately owned.

The Atlantic City Jitney Association, founded in 1915, championed the cause of the privately-run buses from its inception. It faced its darkest days in the early 1970s, when gas rationing and the city's general decline raised the possibility that the service might disappear.

But the advent of casino gaming in 1978 brought the jitney drivers millions of new passengers, and with routes customized to serve casinos in the Boardwalk and Marina areas, jitneys adjusted to the new casino-driven resort. By the early 1980s, rides cost 75 cents, and routes were running profitably 24 hours a day.

To provide service to the city's growing casino population, jitney routes increased to four. In addition, in the 1990s the Jitney Association partnered with the South Jersey Transportation Authority to run free round-trip shuttles between the train station and the casinos.

The jitney is more than a part of Atlantic City's past; it is an indelible part of American culture. In 1982, the Smithsonian Institute received a full-size retired jitney for its collections, a fitting reminder of this humble bus's contribution to the city and the nation.

Curtain Up!

Atlantic City has long been a center for entertainment, be it in the resort's hotels, on its piers, or, today, inside its casinos. But long into the 20th century, most entertainment could be found in theaters located along the Boardwalk.

The first true theater in Atlantic City, the Academy of Music, opened in the 1880s. Salt water taffy king Charles Fraelinger built the music hall, as well as the Academy Hotel, at New York Avenue and the Boardwalk. The theater hosted a range of acts, from singers and dancers to an exposition of trained horses. Like many early Atlantic City attractions built before fire codes and modern emergency response, it was susceptible to flames, burning to the ground no less than three times in less than 20 years.

Each time, the Academy rose from the ashes. After the first blaze, the theater reopened in a scant six weeks, but after the third, the cataclysmic Boardwalk fire of April 1903, it took a full six years for the curtain to rise once more. By this time, it had been renamed the Apollo Theater.

Upon its re-opening, the Apollo became a proving ground for prospective Broadway shows. This was consistent with the usual practice: more than 1,000 plays debuted in Atlantic City between 1900 and 1935. Those that prospered by the shore went on to enjoy runs in Gotham; those that didn't quietly faded away.

In its first year of business after reopening, the Apollo presented the Ziegfield revue "The Follies of 1908," the "Honeyboy" minstrel show, and a series of plays. By the 1920s, the Apollo had been joined by the Woods and the Globe. These three stages provided the most serious drama in the city, though there were scores of others.

Over the next decade, these theaters witnessed the glory years of legitimate drama and popular stagecraft in Atlantic City. Heel-kicking revues like the Ziegfeld Follies or George White's Scandals alternated with plays like "Uncle Tom's Cabin" and "Blossom Time." Business was so good that Atlantic City was christened a "Second Broadway," and most of the popular stars of the period played in the seaside resort. Before running on Broadway, most shows enjoyed a tryout in Atlantic City's theaters.

But the golden age of Atlantic City theaters did not last forever. The Great Depression ended the run of Broadway productions, and with live entertainment diminishing nationwide, many dramatic theaters did not survive the dislocations of World War II.

Motion picture theaters to carried on the tradition. The first movie house in the city dates from 1907, when Henry Savage opened the Royal at Missouri and Atlantic Avenue. Before too long, Boardwalk playhouses were supplementing their live bills with the new-fangled flicks, and eventually several movie-only theaters opened.

George Wielland opened a string of cinema houses in and around Atlantic City, starting with the Bijou in 1911. He added the Capitol in 1919, the Ventnor two years later, the Strand in 1925, and several others into the 1940s, including the old Apollo, which became a movie theater in 1941. The Ventnor was gutted by a fire but rebuilt in 1936.

The most outstanding Atlantic City movie house, the Warner Theater, opened in 1929. This movie palace cost Harry M. Warner, the president of Warner Brothers Pictures, a fortune to build at Arkansas Avenue and the Boardwalk. Though Warner originally leased the building, two years later his company bought it, along with the rest of the shops on the block, outright. It was a jewel of a theater, with terrazzo floors and a ceiling painted blue to resemble the sky, with small lights glimmering like stars.

But even motion pictures could not save Atlantic City theaters. The Warner became the "Boardwalk Bowl" bowling alley before closing. Caesars acquired the property when it bought Howard Johnson's Boardwalk Regency in 1977 and eventually tore down the auditorium, which became a parking lot, though it preserved the façade.

Today, the Warner façade almost blends in with the Wild Wild West, which was built to incorporate the preserved frontage. For those who know to look for it, the face of the old Warner Theater is a fitting reminder of the glory days of Atlantic City theaters.

Honor Guard

Morris Avenue is not named for a city like its neighbors Brighton and Chelsea, and it's not named after a state, like most streets uptown. Instead, Morris Avenue is named for Colonel Daniel E. Morris, the city's first civil engineer and railroad surveyor. He was also the namesake of the Morris Guards, for nearly a century one of Atlantic City's stalwart civic organizations.

Edwin Smith, a member of a volunteer militia in Philadelphia called the State Fencibles Infantry, wanted to establish a similar group in Atlantic City. Working with fellow resident Joseph Shaner, they talked to several prominent local figures and received a particularly warm reception from Morris, who not only promised to support the group financially, but deeded a lot at 12 South New York Avenue to be used as an armory.

The group officially came together on March 12, 1887 in the parlor of the Malatesta Hotel, and was formally chartered on May 11. With 72 volunteers, the Morris Guards relied for their survival on rank-and-file members (who paid dues of 25 cents per week) as well as wealthy benefactors.

First and foremost, the Guards were a military organization. The group held weekly infantry drills at the New York Avenue armory, which was completed in early 1888, and kept in a constant state of preparedness. On the rooftop rifle range, generations of Guardsmen honed their shooting skills.

Soon, more than 100 Atlantic City men were enrolled in the organization, ready to serve their country should the need arise. They didn't have long to wait. In February 1898, the U.S. battleship Maine was rocked by an explosion and sank outside Havana, Cuba. Much of the public assumed that Spain, with whom the U.S. had sparred over Cuban independence, was to blame. On April 23, Congress officially declared war on Spain, and the Morris Guards immediately volunteered their services.

Acting Governor Foster Voorhees (for whom the city and township are named) accepted the offer. The volunteers mustered into the war effort as Company F of the 4th Regiment of New Jersey, U.S. Volunteers.

Lewis T. Bryant served as captain, with C. Stanley Grove and Walter E. Edge his lieutenants. Edge went on to bigger things; the newsman who founded the *Atlantic City Daily Press* (today the *Press of Atlantic City*) was elected governor of New Jersey in 1917 and served until 1919, when he became a U.S. senator. He remained on Capitol Hill until 1929, when Herbert Hoover appointed him ambassador to France (1929-1933); from 1944 to 1947, Edge served as governor again.

But neither Edge nor his compatriots found military glory in the Spanish-American War. They were sent to Greenville, South Carolina, in November 1898 (months after most of the U.S. military had already left Cuba), and awaited deployment to the Caribbean. Before they could be transferred, the war ended. The company never fired a shot in combat.

The Guards did more than train to fight, however. According to the group's original charter, they were also to "provide for the social enjoyment and mental and physical improvement of their members generally." For many years, the armory was the entertainment capital of the city, with plays, musicals and minstrel shows put on by members. The Guards also fielded several athletic teams, including basketball and baseball squads, and sponsored sports carnivals featuring everything from judo to gymnastics.

Originally constructed as a wooden building, the armory was rebuilt in 1901 in brick and stone. It had its own bowling alley and a ballroom big enough to host fancy-dress balls.

The Morris Guards also participated in many parades and events; for a while, they served as official escorts for Miss America contestants. At its peak, the organization boasted nearly 1,000 members. It was as much a part of Atlantic City as the Boardwalk and salt water taffy.

Though the Morris Guards did not serve as a unit, hundreds of its members enlisted in World Wars I and II and the Korean War. All told, eight Guardsmen perished in service to their nation in these conflicts. During the Second World War, the Guards conducted a military training program that readied civilians for service in the armed forces.

In the postwar years, the Guards began to decline. By the early 1980s, there weren't enough members to fund the upkeep of the armory, which was sold in 1982 and converted into offices.

Though the group's numbers dwindled, it retained a slate of officers who met regularly to award scholarships and keep the name of Daniel Morris—and the previous century's good work of the Guards—alive.

So Morris is a name that definitely belongs on an Atlantic City street. It commemorates not only the city's first civil engineer and a prominent early philanthropist, but one of the organizations that gave the city character for more than a century.

The Easter Parade

Atlantic City residents are familiar with the tidal flow of the tourist season. For decades, business picked up Memorial Day Weekend and flattened out after Labor Day, though the Miss American Pageant was a successful attempt to extend the tourist season by another weekend. But surprisingly enough, one of Atlantic City's biggest tourist draws for decades happened in April. Long before casinos, Miss America, or even salt water taffy, the Easter Parade drew hundreds of thousands of people bedecked in their holiday finery to Atlantic City.

The first Easter Parade was held in 1876, an early example of the lengths to which Atlantic City's boosters would go to get business. In that year, Philadelphia hosted the Centennial Exposition, a display of "high technology" and American accomplishment that featured the first telephone and typewriter; many of the gizmos exhibited can still be seen today in the Smithsonian Institution's Arts and Industries Building. But promoters figured that visitors to the exposition would like a dose of style. So they copied an informal Manhattan tradition, in which well-dressed promenaders ambled down Fifth Avenue after morning services, and held the first Atlantic City Easter Parade, giving awards to the best-dressed ladies and gentlemen.

The parade was a success, and was made an annual event. It grew in size and splendor with each passing year. By the turn of the century, it was a positive phenomenon, drawing both masses of tourists and the swanky elites of New York City, as the Absecon Island parade displaced its Manhattan predecessor as the area's top parade. The *New York Times* reported in 1902 that Atlantic City's parade was "even more charming and grand" than the New York one, as promenaders did not have to dodge carriages and could instead stroll beside "old ocean, sniffing the life-giving ozone," a reminder that Atlantic City was once promoted as a health resort.

The Easter Parade became the culmination of a week of festivities that started on Palm Sunday and lasted until Easter. Amusement piers offered symphony and band concerts and even cakewalks. A dog show on Ocean Pier in 1902 provided another high point for the week's celebrations. Though sponsored by the Atlantic City Kennel Club, the show was dominated by wealthy New Yorkers, whose canines swept the awards. The elites entertained each other throughout the week, throwing dinner parties, ping pong parties, serving each other tea, and jealously looking at each other's dogs.

In the early years of the 20th century, the parade attracted as many as 200,000 people. Easter week marked the official opening of the town's hotels for the season, and they used it to promote themselves. Atlantic City became the place to be seen. Though New Yorkers increasingly outnumbered Philadelphians, "Quakers" maintained a presence in the city. The University of Pennsylvania's Mask and Wig Club, a musical comedy troupe that still performs, put on an annual show for many years as part of Easter week.

The Easter Parade gave Atlantic City a chance to show itself off, but it also provided a showcase for fashion trends. Both men and women competed for the prizes, which included certificates and celebratory lunches, and the apparel was described as a brilliant display of color. For years, the Easter parade announced the new fashion trends. "Men's suits were loudly light and announced their coming from around the corner" in 1908. In 1952 a third of the women wore mink jackets, capes, and coats over their spring suits and dresses; pink and white Easter bonnets trimmed with tiny flowers were all the rage.

Although the Boardwalk was never formally segregated, black businesswoman Sarah Spencer Washington organized a Northside Easter Parade on Arctic Avenue in the late 1940s, providing an alternative celebration that was no less elegant. In the early 1950s, as the Boardwalk parade began to select blacks as well as whites for recognition, the Arctic Avenue parade disappeared.

Though the Easter Parade, like many other Atlantic City traditions, has dwindled in recent decades, for most of Atlantic City's history it was the defining event of the year, as throngs packed the trains, jammed the roads, and (most importantly) filled the hotels and restaurants for a week-long carnival of fashion. In 1939, it drew half-a-million well-dressed revelers, and into the 1950s it continued to draw as many as 300,000 to put on their "Sunday finest" and stroll along the Boardwalk. The parade was one of the many better aspects of Atlantic City that were lost during the decay of the postwar/pre-casino years.

Though tastes have changed, and Americans are more likely to tune into reality television than dress up in spring suits, the Easter Parade is still an important part of Atlantic City's history and can teach us a great deal about the dynamic advertising of the city in the past.

I'll Remember April

[Author's note: I originally wrote this chapter for the April 2005 issue of Casino Connection magazine. I don't see much point in rewriting the first paragraph, since it doesn't make a ton of sense to reflect on events 110 years in the past—people tend to like a nice, round number like 100.]

With last year's sesquicentennial of Atlantic City, we have the opportunity to see just how far the city has come. Once home to little more than dunes and seagulls, Absecon Island now hosts the country's second-largest gaming destination. Even over the past hundred years, Atlantic City has grown tremendously. By taking a look back at just what was on the minds of residents and visitors to the city exactly one century ago, we can greater appreciate the possibilities for the future.

Residents of Atlantic City felt a new optimism in the spring of 1905. A new, modern library had opened that winter (the building is, for the moment, still standing). The year before, the city had celebrated its 50th anniversary (called the semi-centennial), and some of the excitement of that summer's festivities still lingered.

April may be, as T.S. Eliot wrote, the cruelest month, but for guests of the Grand Atlantic hotel it began with a pleasant surprise. On April Fools Day, the hotel held a euchre party. Euchre was a trick-taking card game (related to bridge) whose popularity was matched only by whist and poker at the time. All participants received wrapped surprise presents. After cards, those in attendance danced the night away.

In a garden, spring is a time to plant, and a major project began in the middle of the month when the Chelsea Pier and Amusement started building a new 1,500-foot long steel pier and theater at Texas

Avenue. Throughout the city, hotels began opening their doors for the season, sometimes under new management. The city's newest hotel, the 10-story fireproof Chalfonte, opened for business. The Hotel Raymond, which once stood at Virginia Avenue and the Beach (now the site of the Trump Taj Mahal), had new managers in F.L. and F.J. Miller, who had previously run the Hotel Mount Vernon. The Kenilworth Inn, near the beach at Kentucky, got a new owner, Carlton Godfrey, who paid $44,000 for the hotel. Several other hotels along Pacific Avenue also boasted new proprietors, each of which had the best of hopes for the new season. Some of the leading hotels included the Traymore, Haddon Hall, Galen Hall, the Brighton, the Dennis, and the St. Charles, many of which survived into the 1970s.

April was a month for outdoor sports, and golfers enthusiastically took to the links. On April 15, duffer W. C. Fowlnes won the Atlantic City Cup, the top prize in a tournament held at the course in Northfield. Lesser prizes included the President's Cup and Northfield Cup. The tournament was hailed as one of the most successful ever. At the same time, plans for a racetrack in the Chelsea district circulated, though the future of racing would be offshore.

Visitors continued to be amazed by the advances in technology they could find at the shore. At the Hotel Rudolf, the friends of New York merchant H. B. Rosenthal figured a way that he and his wife could celebrate their anniversary even though she was at home in New York. Throwing a surprise anniversary dinner party for Rosenthal, the friends allowed his wife to be "present" by bringing a telephone to the party and making a long-distance call. This was probably not what he expected when he agreed to a night "with the boys," but it was considered enough of a novelty to make the papers.

For Easter, the staff of the Rudolf outdid themselves, and received acclaim for presenting the most lavish holiday display in the city. The lobby of the hotel was completely bedecked in flowers, including carnations, lilies, and roses. All week, dancers packed the Japanese Music Room at the Rudolf. All other hotels were filled to capacity, as that year's Easter was reportedly the most successful in years thanks to particularly favorable weather: leading up to the Boardwalk Easter pageant, the city enjoyed clear, bright 60-degree days.

The Mask and Wig Club of the University of Pennsylvania, which used to perform regularly in Atlantic City, offered another diversion with its sold-out performance of "Mr. Hamlet of Denmark" at Steeplechase Pier. Those not lucky enough to get tickets contented themselves with other amusements at the city's piers and theaters, and those with more of a taste for water indulged in yachting or bathing in the surf.

After Easter, hotels, piers, and theaters continued to welcome record numbers of visitors from New York, Philadelphia, and throughout the region. The Atlantic City Kennel Club held their annual dog show, in which winning canines from Boston, Philadelphia, Pittsburgh and elsewhere vied for best in show.

Thanks to the successful month, hotels up and down the Boardwalk began planning to expand, and Atlantic City's appeal as a truly national resort grew. In its first 50 years, the city had come a long way, but much of its history—Miss America, Sinatra at the "5," casinos—was still yet to be written.

Starting the Season

Traditionally, Atlantic City was a mostly-summer resort town. While it had attractions throughout the year and actively worked in to bring in guests during the winter, the prime season began at Memorial Day and ended at Labor Day, though thanks to the efforts of the Miss America pageant the season was extended a week or two into September. Throughout the history of Atlantic City, Memorial Day Weekend has been an important and exciting time.

Initially, the Easter Parade was the official debut of summer, even though it took place in the spring, but as years went on, Memorial Day seemed a more apt beginning. While large crowds flooded the railroads and poured into town before that date, there was something distinctly off-kilter about efforts to prematurely open the season. In 1903, for example, a solitary minister from the Wild West jumped the gun by imploring a bathhouse keeper to provide him with a bathing suit in the first week of May. Although he had never swum in the ocean, he felt he was a rugged enough man to dip into the chilly waves, and for an hour or two he amused a large crowd of spectators—none of whom followed him into the surf—before making his point and leaving the water.

By 1905, Memorial Day had become the accepted opening date for the beach and ocean. On that weekend, the Atlantic City Yacht Club officially declared the year's sailing begun with a marine parade in which boats glided through the Inlet and down the beachfront, a regatta, and a banquet. The Seaside Yacht Club and Chelsea Cricket fleet, rival nautical organizations, also sponsored races and hosted open houses, hoping to draw members away from the city's leading yacht club.

In that year, just as the future rival city of Las Vegas was being founded, Atlantic City was a well-established convention destination and health resort, and hoteliers always looked to expand on both front. Over Memorial Day weekend, the resort welcomed a special convention group: the American Laryngological Association. This group, founded in 1878, consisted of doctors and scientists who studied disorders of the larynx and upper respiratory tract. Atlantic City hoteliers were particularly eager to host the meeting because, at the time, one of the main selling points of the city was the salubrious quality of its air. But the city was not content to pitch itself as only a health resort. Over Memorial Day weekend, many hotels hosted representatives of prospective convention groups in hopes of luring their conventions to the town later that year.

Memorial Day became most famous for the ceremonial "unlocking" of the ocean by the Atlantic City Beach Patrol, and, weather and ocean temperature permitting, many visitors chose that weekend for their first dip in the sea. Before public bathing under the watchful eye of the city's Beach Patrol became the norm, about a dozen private bathhouses monopolized the safe spots for swimming. Each of them marked the opening of the season in its own way.

In 1915, the city celebrated its wildest Memorial Day yet. A daredevil named "the Human Fly" thrilled Boardwalk on-lookers by scaling the walls of one of the beachfront hotels, while at the same time actress Valeska Suratt flew overheard in a hydroplane and dropped roses on the crowd. The trolley company also chose that weekend to introduce its latest innovation: the "Tango Car," a trolley that could host any event from a card party to a formal tea and, as it was outfitted with a parquet floor, was eminently suitable for dances. Since then, with clubs like the Wave and Mixx, nightlife in Atlantic City has certainly come a long way.

Not even World War II could stop the Memorial Day festivities, though it did dim the lights for a few years. In 1944, the city marked the start of the season with a flower mart, during which gifts and foodstuffs were sold to visitors, with profits benefiting local charities. After the war, Memorial Day resumed its spirit of rollicking fun, and neighboring resorts like Ocean City joined in the good times by hosting parades, speedboat races, and other rites of summer.

Into the 1960s, Atlantic City hotels advertised specials for Memorial Day, and the pomp of the unlocking of the sea continued to officially mark the opening of the season, as locals braced themselves for the annual influx of tourists and summer visitors. But with the coming of casino gaming in 1978, Atlantic City became more of a year-round destination. While today Memorial Day still officially represents the start of summer beach-going, it is merely one long holiday weekend out of many for most visitors to the shore.

'Twas the Season

Although most of the excitement in Atlantic City happens during the summer season, the Christmas holiday has seen its share of festive mirth as well.

Today, the time between Thanksgiving and New Year's is relatively slow for the casinos in Atlantic City, and things were no different in the years before legal gaming. At present, casinos can mitigate the slump by running special promotions or other inducements to get patrons in the door. Around the turn of the century, with no legal casinos, hotels relied mostly on the resort's reputation as a healthy year-round destination.

Since Atlantic City air had both salt and a lack of pollen, those afflicted by hay fever found it to be a healthy haven. Those suffering from a variety of respiratory ailments (who could afford to do so, of course), were advised to spend the winter season in Atlantic City, where relatively warm, dry, allergen-free air would do them good.

Atlantic City developed a reputation as a winter resort for healthier folks as well. The December 12, 1903 *New York Times* reported that yuletide arrivals in Atlantic City had been higher than usual that year, owing chiefly to favorable weather. Though there were a few "invalids" going to the shore for the salubrious sea air, most of the hotel guests were visiting "sportsmen," attracted by the hunting and fishing. One group of New Yorkers returned from the mainland with forty quail and nearly as many rabbits, presumably settling the question of what was for dinner. Charter fishing boats also stood at the ready to take guests to the fishing banks, five miles from the shore.

For Christmas, each of the hotels held lavish dinners and erected Christmas trees, competing against each other for the honor of having the city's largest. Laurel ropes and sprigs of holly decorated the front parlors and smoking rooms of fashionable hotels. In 1905, local hoteliers commented on the fact that, while Philadelphians dominated the resort after Easter, Christmas and New Years were reserved for New Yorkers.

Hotel operators turned to Christmas as a way of promoting Atlantic City as a bona fide all-year resort. Originally, most hotels shut their doors in the fall and re-opened at Easter, which then marked the beginning of the season. By 1908, hotels were advertising Atlantic City as a year-round resort. The Hotel Pierrepont, for example, offered special Christmas and New Year's rates and, as an added bonus, free sea water baths.

In 1914, the Hotel Rudolf, which later became the Breakers Hotel at New Jersey Avenue and the Boardwalk, waxed poetic in an advertisement which claimed that Christmas at Atlantic City had become as popular as Easter for the "Elite and Fashion of America." With ideal weather conditions, a range of outdoor activities were possible, and the Boardwalk was thronged with revelers basking in the mild sea air. Even so, its sun parlors were "fully heated." The Rudolf advertised special holiday events in addition to its usual entertainment, which included afternoon and evening dancing.

Sometimes, Christmas cheer even extended to the animal kingdom. In 1924, Mrs. E. B. Griffith gave gifts of blankets, carrots, and apples to 25 lucky horses on her Ventnor estate. Two years later, newspapers reported record numbers, and remarked that, in imitation of Easter tradition, throngs crowded the Boardwalk dressed in the holiday finest. Yet that same year the Federal Prohibition department made wholesale arrests after discovering that merchants were selling bogus Christmas toys—trick dolls that concealed a half-pint "kicks" of liquor. This marked an unwelcome intrusion into what, Prohibition notwithstanding, was a "wet" holiday in the cabaret district.

By 1940, several holiday traditions had been established. Hotels provided individual turkeys to families, so that the head of the household could carve it, as if they were still home. The various resorts continued to vie with each other for the most immense tree, and lit up their exteriors in green and red lights. This became known as the Festival of Light, and it remained a tradition for years. It became a tourist draw, and hotels rented busses so that their guests could tour the island and observe the fantastic displays of the Festival of Light. After Christmas dinner, those wishing to exercise rode horses on the beach and bicycles on the Boardwalk, skated in Convention Hall, or bathed in indoor sea baths.

Hotels continued to advertise for the Christmas holidays through the 1960s, and the Festival of Light also continued But by 1977, a single advertisement for Christmas asked vacationers to "pamper the nostalgia" for a "final view before the Great Change" that casinos would bring.

With casinos came a shift in the city's marketing. While many casinos run special holiday promotions, they generally don't advertise for families to spend the Christmas week and bask in the mild sea air. Still, looking at casino holiday lighting displays, one can get a sense for the grandeur of the Festival of Light of Christmas past.

Spreading Enlightenment

L ike most growing cities, Atlantic City in the late 19th century needed a public library to serve its citizens. Without a place where the public could read and learn, it was feared that the city would not be considered truly first-rate. So in 1901, residents voted, by the impressive total of 6,602 to 30, to create the Atlantic City Free Public Library. Voters did not, however, fund the building of a library; the next year, a temporary facility on the third floor of City Hall began lending out books from the 1,000-volume collection of the Women's Research Club that had been generously donated to the fledgling library.

At the time, many municipalities were turning to a single benefactor to build new libraries: Andrew Carnegie, the steel baron whose "Gospel of Wealth" held that rich men, like himself, had an obligation to give back to the community.

Carnegie practiced what he preached, and then some; he personally gave over $333 million of his fortune on a variety of projects including aid to religious institutions, endowing (and in some cases founding) institutions of higher education, and supporting the arts. But he reserved most of his largesse for libraries. He sponsored his first library in his hometown of Dunfermline, Scotland in 1883, and six years later began building libraries in his adopted country, the United States. Between 1883 and 1919, Carnegie sponsored nearly 3,000 libraries worldwide, including 36 in New Jersey. It was natural, then, for Atlantic City to apply for a Carnegie grant in their search for a permanent home for their public library.

A firm believer in self-help, Carnegie had an almost mystical reverence for the power of libraries to enlighten and help people better themselves. He had the motto "Let there be light" inscribed over the first library he built, and most Carnegie libraries featured a lamp at their entrance to symbolize the enlightenment to be found within. Towns applying for a Carnegie grant generally had to meet three criteria: they had to demonstrate the need for a public library, provide the building's land, and agree to provide 10 percent of the building's construction budget for its maintenance.

The Atlantic City library's Board of Trustees acquired land at Illinois and Pacific Avenues and received $71,000 from Carnegie for the building's construction, which began in 1904. After the new library was officially dedicated on January 1, 1905, another Carnegie grant paid for the building's decoration. It had open stacks, an innovation common to Carnegie Libraries, that let patrons browse for books on their own; this was fully in step with Carnegie's self-help philosophy, and encouraged readers to pick up unfamiliar titles. The library also had a community center and auditorium, and a small exhibition space.

The library proved a popular meeting place and reading place for Atlantic City residents, and over the years its collections grew, far out-distancing the original 1,000 volumes. By the 1970s, it was clear that the original structure could no longer serve the city as its primary library, and in 1981 city authorities began planning a new library.

The new building opened in 1985 and Tennessee and Atlantic Avenues; it cost $3.8 million to build and currently houses over 140,000 books, as well as sizable holdings of magazines, newspapers, videotapes, audio tapes and recordings. Of interest to local history buffs is the Heston Collection, named for one of the library's founders, who also helped found the city's hospital (now Atlanticare Regional Medical Center). The collection includes resources that document the cultural, economic, social and historical development of the city, and is an essential source for anyone interested in conducting in-depth research into Atlantic City's past. With online catalog access (begun in 1992) and free public internet access added to its conventional holdings, the Atlantic City Free Public Library has moved into the digital age. The library continues to serve the community in ways that its original founders could not have imagined.

The future of the original library on Pacific Avenue promises to be as interesting as its past. With money from the Casino Reinvestment Development Authority and the city, the original building has been renovated and expanded. It is now occupied by Stockton College as the Carnegie Library Center, which hosts undergraduate and graduate courses and continuing education programs for area residents.

In that way, even in the 21st century the building continues to fulfill Andrew Carnegie's desire that it serve as a beacon for those seeking enlightenment.

The City's Hospital

Atlantic City's medical care facilities have had a history as long and interesting as that of the city itself. From the early days of private care to today's growing AtlantiCare, which is Atlantic County's largest non-casino employer.

In its earliest decades, Atlantic City did not have a hospital. Doctors cared for patients in their own homes or in private institutions. But since the city's population grew in the late 19th century, and millions of tourists continued to flock to the beaches each summer, local citizens began demanding that a real public health facility be built.

In the early 1890s, the closest thing to a hospital on Absecon Island was the Rockford Sanitarium, also known as the Atlantic City Sanitarium, located on Atlantic Avenue between Kentucky and Illinois Avenues. Its owner, John J. Rockford, ran it more like a hotel than as a hospital, which was fitting: before he bought it, it had been the original Surf House hotel, then the Margate Hotel. The 52-bed facility had an operating room, but was open only to paying customers.

In 1892, a fundraiser netted $1,200 towards a fund to build a hospital, but its organizers, far short of the money needed to buy property and build, simply gave the proceeds to Rockford with the proviso that he provide a bed for any sick person unable to pay for care. Two years later, the city agreed to pay Rockford one dollar a day for all of its patients, and Atlantic City now had a place where all could seek medical care.

Both Rockford and the city became disenchanted with their arrangement. In September 1897, Rockford notified the city that he was ending their contract, as he could not cope with the numbers of destitute patients the city was forcing upon him. Perhaps not coincidentally, a newly formed Atlantic City Hospital Association voted in that month to build a real hospital as soon as possible. In the interim, City Council and Rockford reached a compromise, and he agreed to continue to accept city patients.

After several rounds of fundraising, the hospital association's Board of Governors purchased a 12-room building on Ohio Avenue for $16,000, and spent another $4,000 or so renovating and furnishing it.

The Atlantic City Hospital officially opened on November 30, 1898. With more of an eye on community support than hospital hygiene, the governors invited all interested citizens to shuffle through the building on its opening day. According to its bylaws, it was to be open to all, irrespective of race, color, or creed.

On the following day, the hospital welcomed its first patient, a young boy named Gussie Johann who had broken his leg in a vehicular mishap not likely to be repeated today: he fell from a wagon after the horse pulling it had been butted by a goat. By December 2, he had company: another boy recuperating from a bullet wound, a condition unfortunately still common in Atlantic City today.

The hospital's first resident physician, Clyde Fish, started work soon after it opened, and in the following year an annex built in honor of Henry Boice provided the first brick hospital facility on the island. A residence and school for training nurses opened in 1901 (it closed in 1955).

A 100-room, 5-story structure that cost $100,000 to build opened in 1908. It was joined by a new Annex in 1928; this building contained a brand-new operating room, dispensary, X-ray, kitchen, and cafeteria. These would remain the major hospital buildings until the opening of the 8-story South Wing (1959) and East Wing (1964). These were later renamed the Frank Sinatra and James Crosby wings, respectively.

The hospital continued to grow in the 1970s. It was renamed the Atlantic City Medical Center in 1973, and opened its Mainland Division in Pomona two years later. In the 1980s construction kept the Mainland and City facilities current, with a parking garage opening in 1983 and a host of other improvements throughout the decade.

In 2005, the newly-renamed AtlantiCare Regional Medical Center's city division broke ground on a 7-story, $98-million tower that would put the rickety Rockford sanitarium to shame. As the city changes around it, the only thing certain is that Atlantic City's hospital—whatever its name—will continue to grow.

Pride of the Vikings

It's not hard to remember "the old high school" in Atlantic City—nearly everyone who was in town before the turn of the last century remembers the stately, sand-colored brick building sitting at Albany and Atlantic Avenues, its clock tower always imposing, but rarely telling the right time.

But the high school several generations of graduates knew was actually once the "new" high school, and was in fact the third high school built in the city.

The first high school building on Absecon Island was built in 1895—relatively late, considering the city was incorporated more than 40 years earlier. It stood at Illinois and Artic Avenues. The builders apparently expected schooling to be much less popular with teenagers than it was, because within six years the school had to be abandoned, as there were simply too many students for the small building.

In 1901, the high school was moved to another new building, this one at Ohio and Pacific Avenues. This building proved more congenial to education—even after it no longer housed the city's high school, it served as the Ohio Avenue School for decades. Though it has since been demolished, the neighboring administration building has been repurposed for use as an office building.

High school students bid farewell to Ohio Avenue on September 17, 1923, when the new high school opened up, across from the then-brand new memorial to those who had served in the First World War.

The school cost a total over $1.75 million, and was widely regarded as a groundbreaking institution. It opened with a 1,000 seat auditorium and a 6,000-pipe organ, and had an array of dedicated classrooms, including rooms for science, sewing, music, and mechanical drawing.

The high school opened in an optimistic time. Atlantic City was growing, and it seemed likely that it would continue to do so forever. The high school population certainly was expanding. In 1893, when high school classes lacked their own building, three teachers taught 147 students. By 1902, when the Ohio Avenue school opened, enrollment had topped 260. In 1915, enrollment passed 1,000 for the first time, and there were nearly 50 teachers on staff.

So, when the new high school opened in 1923, it was designed with further expansion in mind. Indeed, in that year enrollment passed 2,000, and continued to climb for the rest of the decade, hitting nearly 2,400 in 1930. By this time, over 100 teachers labored to instruct pupils at the school.

The school's teams, competing under the Viking nickname, were powerhouses in boys' and girls' sports from the start.

Over the years, tens of thousands of students passed through the halls of the high school, and it remained one of the area's top educational facilities. The high school became more than an institution, and became a valued part of the community.

But as the city's fortunes declined in the 1960s, it became apparent that Atlantic City High School was no longer the exemplar of secondary education it once had been. A 1967 study concluded that the building had already outlived its usefulness, and that, for the sake of students, parents, and teachers, a new building should be built.

In some communities, this would have triggered an immediate drive to build a state of the art new school building. Few Atlantic City residents—or ACHS students—would be surprised to learn that, in fact, nothing happened for nearly a quarter-century.

In 1990, residents approved the financing and construction of a new high school, which started rising on a piece of land on "Great Island," which for most residents had simply been an empty stretch of marsh between Atlantic City and Pleasantville.

After four years of construction, the new school was ready, although, characteristically, it was not done in time for the start of the school year. Finally, on November 4, 1994, the new school opened its doors. This facility cost no less than $83 million to build. Even adjusted for inflation, this was a far cry from the $30,000 spent on the original Arctic Avenue school.

Since then, Atlantic City High School has continued to welcome students in its new facility. The "old" high school building was leveled to make way for a parking lot, and has stood for the past few years as a rather unimpressive welcome to the city for travelers arriving via the Albany Avenue bridge.

Recently, a development group bought the old high school site and adjacent land, raising expectations that, in the future, the site would be home to a casino or related tourist facility. That hope has not become reality yet, but it remains possible that one day the site will be used for more than parking.

Fire Pirates

Every city relies on trained fire fighters to combat blazes. Atlantic City's fire department has a long and distinguished history, since it has had to contend with the unique challenges brought by the city's hotel and convention—and later casino—industry.

Fires were an ever-present danger in Atlantic City. Into the 20th century, even major hotels were constructed from wood. These buildings had a distressing tendency to catch on fire; many early hotels and rooming houses were rebuilt more than once over their own ashes. Yet it took, seemingly, a long, long time for the city to get serious about the fire danger.

At first, Atlantic City had no way to extinguish fires, as an 1866 *Philadelphia Inquirer* report on a blaze lamented. The policy seemed to be to let things burn and rebuild. In 1872, the city purchased several "Babcock fire extinguishers," but didn't hire professionals to deploy the early chemical fire-fighting tools.

Without a paid force, the city relied on several volunteer fire departments. Volunteer departments had a history in the U.S. going back to 1736, when Benjamin Franklin organized the nation's first in Philadelphia. Several volunteer companies sprang up in Atlantic City in the 1870s and 1880s, in response to the ever-present threat of fire in a crowded city filled with wooden structures.

The Beach Pirates were one of the more interesting volunteer fire corps. Composed mostly of Boardwalk merchants, the company had a reputation as a rich man's group: rival firefighters called the Beach Pirates "silk stockings." The shoe probably fit, because the Pirates were not the most adept firefighters on the block; in 1899, their own station burned to the ground.

In their defense, the Beach Pirates were fighting another blaze when the fire started near their Boardwalk home, but this was hardly a good advertisement for the Pirates or the volunteer fire departments. The Beach Pirates, unfazed by the loss, however, relocated to Captain John Young's hotel with what could be salvaged of their gear.

For decades, volunteers responded to calls in Atlantic City's hotels, restaurants, and private homes—they even doused a blaze that ironically consumed the city's garbage incinerator. Frequently hailed for their selflessness, the volunteers often performed acts of daring in front of large crowds—rushing into burning buildings to save those trapped inside, or fighting back a wall of flames.

As brave as the volunteer fire companies were, by the summer of 1902 citizens were demanding the creation of a full-time professional force. The catastrophic May 1902 fire that laid waste to two Boardwalk blocks spurred calls for the city to finally create a truly professional firefighting organization.

In November 1903 City Council officially created a paid department and elected Louis H. Donnelly, William H, Fowden, and Hugh Genoe as commissioners to oversee it.

But the professional force raised controversy. In 1906, the state Supreme Court ruled that the ordinances that created the paid department were illegal. Volunteer Chief Wiesenthal, who'd been fighting against the professionals since 1903, attempted to take possession of the department's headquarters, but was put off by the fire commissioners. Within the week, the city hashed out a compromise by paying Weisenthal and others back pay, and the professional force resumed its duties uncontested.

Over the ensuing decades, the Atlantic City Fire Department had its hands full with fires in the city's tourist and residential areas, though improved fire safety regulations mitigated fire damage and prevented widespread blazes like the famous April 1902 conflagration.

The department recently [in 2007] made history again when it hired the city's first professional female fire fighter, Anne Gramlich. She's not the first woman to fight fires down the shore: Adelheid von Buckow had helped a volunteer company in 1875 and eventually joined under her married name of Adelhied Specht. Adelheid was not paid, though, so Gramlich is truly making history as a professional firefighter.

With most buildings made of brick and concrete, fires are not the apocalyptic danger they once were, but the Atlantic City Fire Department continues to provide priceless protection to its citizens.

Watching the Waves

Today millions of people flock to Atlantic City for casinos and entertainment, but the city's biggest draw once was its beach. Even when bathers wore full-body complements of tops, skirts, and stockings when going in the ocean, they needed protection—and the Atlantic City Beach Patrol was there to provide it.

Drownings were an unfortunate reality in early Atlantic City. Seemingly every month, one or sometimes several bathers were dragged under the waves. Into the 1870s, Atlantic City most frequently popped up in news stories as the site of yet another tragic drowning.

Early on, city authorities realized they had a problem. The first "constable of the surf" patrolled the city's beaches in 1855. William S. Cazier was at the time a 25 year-old man who was paid $117 for his first summer's work: he was to assist any bathers in need. As the city grew more popular, the beach constables were replaced by on-duty members of the regular police department, who but on bathing suit and stood ready to jump to the rescue of any endangered swimmers—but only between the hours of 11 a.m. and 1:30 p.m.

This system left most of the beaches unprotected most of the time. For that reason, many hotels hired private lifeguards to chaperone their guests, and volunteer brigades formed as well. Though the volunteers weren't paid, they did get their share of excitement and the chance for occasional gallantry. Since they were untrained, they were not always successful at preventing swimming accidents, and drowning continued to be a major problem on Atlantic City's beaches.

In 1870, city authorities took another tack, installing "life lines" at certain beaches. These were heavy cables run from the beach out to sea, where anchors secured them. Theoretically, bathers were supposed to enjoy the surf while holding onto a nearby "life line." Not surprisingly, this system had only limited appeal, and was not effective in preventing drownings.

The city took its first steps toward creating a full-time professional beach patrol on August 21, 1891. In June of the following year the Atlantic City Beach Patrol was first deployed.

The Beach Patrol figured into the first rescue of the 1892 season, but not in the most flattering way. On June 20, a passer-by on the Boardwalk noticed 14 year-old Clarence Hopper struggling in the surf, and he notified two lifeguards, who apparently hadn't noticed the tumult. The lifeguards then struggled to pull their large boat into the ocean, and were taking so long that the lad surely would have died had not H.H. Parker, a passing swimming master, jumped into the waves (wearing a full suit of clothes) and dragged him to safety himself.

Later rescues went a bit more smoothly—for the most part—as the Beach Patrol for a time posted its guards in boats offshore, where they warned back bathers who tried to swim farther than was safe and effected quick rescues.

The Beach Patrol assumed its modern form in 1904, when Mayor Franklin Stoy appointed Dr. J.T. Beckwith as Beach Surgeon. That summer, the Beach Patrol performed 891 rescues without a single beach fatality. Beckwith was later promoted to Police and Beach Surgeon, and in 1913 his assistant, Dr. Charles Bossert, was named the head of the Patrol. By this time, 90 guards and captains patrolled the shore.

During World War II, with most able-bodied young men called to serve their country, the city faced a lifeguard shortage. As a publicity stunt, the city hired a crew of female lifeguards, who found that "drownings" increased remarkably when they were around—most of the victims were seemingly healthy men. Though the women did not last, by the 1980s women had returned to the beaches as lifeguards, and they were taken far more seriously.

The Patrol continued to grow, with over 150 members by the 1950s. Today, it continues to protect and serve swimmers and beachgoers throughout the city, and is one of the city's proudest institutions.

Ocean Marathon

August might be one of the best months to spend on Absecon Island. Visitors to Atlantic City get to enjoy cool ocean breezes and all of the excitement of the summer season. But for more adventurous—and better conditioned—visitors, August in Atlantic City means one thing: the World Championship Ocean Marathon Swim, better known as the Around-the-Island Swim. Since 1954 (not counting a brief hiatus) it's been an Atlantic City August tradition.

This world-famous ocean race started with a friendly challenge in 1953. A local entrepreneur named Jim Toomey convinced two lifeguards, Ed Solitaire and Ed "Dutch" Stetser, to swim around Absecon Island. For $100 each, they jumped into the surf. Fourteen hours later, Solitaire emerged the victor—Stetser finished an hour later.

The first Around-the-Island Swim was swum in 1954, the year that Atlantic City celebrated its Centennial. While the Centennial Train was chugging up and down the Boardwalk, an international field of swimmers—one hailed from Portugal—tested the waters and swam into racing history. Tom Park captured the $5,000 prize by finishing first. Canadian Cliff Lumdson finished second, as he did the following year, when Park won again. The Canadian finally got the better of his rival in 1955 when he beat Park by 2 seconds to capture the Around-the-Island crown. Lumdson and Park would vie for the top spot for the rest of the decade, usually finishing within a few minutes of each other. In the 1960 edition, they actually tied, both finishing in second place at exactly 10 hours, 40 minutes, and 7 seconds.

Women competed in the ocean challenge as well. Marilyn Bell, a spirited 16-year-old from Toronto, Canada, was the first woman to cross the finish line. The women's champion usually finished behind the men's winner, but in 1991 Australian Shelley Taylor-Smith beat the entire field, setting a course record of seven hours, 12 minutes, and 34 seconds; the following year she won again in just over seven hours, setting another record (which stood until 1996) and establishing herself as a true inter-gender champion.

What draws swimmers from around the world to Absecon Island? The Ocean Marathon Swim is widely considered the most difficult water race in the world. Starting in Gardner's Basin, they first swim an ocean leg parallel to the beach before rounding the island at Longport and hitting the back bay. For 22.5 miles, swimmers must battle tides, currents, wind, ocean temperatures, and even jellyfish—hazards that swimmers safe in Olympic-sized pools never contend with. Because weather and tidal conditions make such a difference, finishing times vary from year to year: in some years, not even the best challengers could break the 10-hour mark, while in others several finished in less than seven.

The early 1960s saw the race dominated by Herman Willemse of Holland: he won the race from 1960 to 1964. Though these were good years for the Dutchman, they were bad ones for Atlantic City, as tourist visitation slumped. As a result, the race was discontinued in 1964 and might have been relegated to the history books if it had not been revived in 1978, the year that casino gaming began to transform the area.

The race was relaunched in that year, but only members of local beach patrols took part. But in the following year, the marathon swim once again featured competitors from around the world. The 1980s were dominated by Paul Asmuth, who consistently won. In the 1990s, Stephane Lecat of France became the first to break the seven-hour barrier. His countryman, Stephane Gomez, set the new course record in 2004 with an incredible 6:37:09 finish; German Angela Maurer set a women's record that same year by finishing in just over seven hours.

The World Championship Ocean Marathon Swim is a unique event that residents and visitors to Atlantic City should savor, whether as hardened competitors, helpful volunteers, or cheering on-lookers. In a city often dedicated to the pursuit of pleasure, it stands as a testament to hard work, endurance, and determination.

Hitting the Boards

Professional hockey has a long history in Atlantic City, though it is, as of now, on hiatus. Most recently, from 2001 to 2005, Atlantic City was home to the Boardwalk Bullies, a hard-hitting East Coast Hockey League team. But this was not the first team to play in Boardwalk Hall. The original ice squad to call Atlantic City home thrilled fans for years and made history in crossing the color line.

From its opening in May 1929 Convention Hall, as it was then known, was capable of hosting hockey games. During the 1929-1930 season the Hall hosted four National Hockey League games: the New York Rangers took on the Ottawa Senators in December, the Pittsburgh Pirates played the Chicago Black Hawks in January, and in March the Pirates returned to face the Montreal Canadians and Ottawa suited up against the New York Americans. These were all official games that counted in the standings, and were regarded as highly significant for the city. The governor of New Jersey, Morgan Larson, dropped the puck at the first game, which New York won 3-1 in front of 10,000 spectators. Clearly, hockey might work in this new facility.

Beginning 1930, a team named the Atlantic City Seagulls started playing in the National Amateur Athletic Union, and won that league's championship, named the Boardwalk Trophy, in 1932. Perhaps the worst year of the Depression, that might have been an unlucky time to launch a new minor league hockey league, but the Tri-State Hockey League began then with four teams: the Baltimore Orioles, Philadelphia Comets, Hershey B'ars, and Atlantic City Seagulls. The next year, the league changed its name to the Eastern Amateur Hockey League and added four teams: Bronx Tigers, New

York Athletic Club, New York-Hamilton Crescents, and the St. Nicholas Hockey Club; the Comets had already gone defunct. The league's membership fluctuated greatly; over the next few years, it had as few as four teams, and new members like the Pittsburgh Yelo Jackets, Riverdale Skeeters, New York Cubs, Boston Olympics, and Washington Eagles replaced failed franchises. The Seagulls were one of only two charter franchises to remain with the league through the 1941 season. All in all, the Seagulls were a model franchise; after finishing first in points in their inaugural season, they won the league championship three times, and never finished in last place.

But world events forced an end to the Seagulls. With the coming of World War II, the United States Army requisitioned Convention Hall for use as a base headquarters. Obviously, this meant that playing hockey there was out of the question. Rather than find an alternate home, the Seagulls folded. Immediately after the war, an unexpected surge in the convention business kept the Hall booked and prevented any serious talk of the Seagulls returning to the ice.

In 1947, though, hockey came back to the boards, as the ice returned to Convention Hall and the Seagulls resumed playing in the Eastern Amateur Hockey League. In addition, figure skating Sunday mornings and Monday evenings, combined with public skating hours on nights when no hockey was scheduled, kept the zamboni machine working. Though the EAHL was inactive for the 1948-1949 season, it returned the next year, and the Seagulls remained a vital part of the league.

Perhaps the Seagulls' greatest contribution to the history of American sports came on November 15, 1950, when the team signed Art Dorrington, a Nova Scotia native, to a contract. Though three black men played in Canadian minor leagues at the time, Dorrington was the first to do so in the United States. In his first season, he led the Seagulls to the league championship, and it is likely he would have gone on to break the color barrier in the National Hockey League had he not suffered a career-ending injury.

Despite their historic role, the Seagulls did not enjoy much success after their ground-breaking 1950-51 campaign. The 1951-52 season would prove to be the Seagulls' last. The league folded the next year, and when it was revived in 1954 as the Eastern Hockey League, it did not field an Atlantic City team.

A minor league basketball team took the Seagulls name; in the 1960s, they played against the Harlem Globetrotters, suggesting that they were not frequent winners. The team was revived in 1995 as a United States Basketball League franchise, and, despite winning three straight championships, disbanded in 2001, after a winless season.

That year, the Boardwalk Bullies began playing in a renovated Boardwalk Hall. As a measure of their commitment to the city's hockey heritage, they retired the number of hockey pioneer Art Dorrington, who served as a community consultant for the team.

Though the Bullies didn't last long on the Boardwalk, there is no denying that Atlantic City has a long and noteworthy history on the ice.

The Sport of Kings

Atlantic City has always been a resort town, and for much of its history, horseracing has been a popular American diversion. It is only natural that the two should come together, and that racing should become part of the Atlantic City experience. Still, horseracing has had a checkered history in Atlantic City.

In the United States, horse racing enjoyed several periods of popularity. It was initially a favored sport of the Virginia and Maryland gentry in the colonial period, and remained widespread after the nation achieved its independence. Future president Andrew Jackson was an ardent horseman—in 1805 he bet $5,000, then a tremendous sum, on his own horse. In a widely-attended Tennessee race, Jackson's horse won.

Horse racing had a minor presence in Atlantic City from its earlier years, as amateur racing on the beach—particularly harness racing— was not unknown. But there was no real race track, or professional racing, throughout the city's first boom period.

Racing declined toward the end of the 19th century, just as Atlantic City's star was rising. The first try at bringing an enclosed race track in Atlantic County started in 1885, with the founding of the Atlantic City Turf Organization. It wasn't the best time to build a new track. Throughout the country, tracks were closing in droves in the 1880s and 1890s, as Americans were disgusted with the increasing influence of professional bookmakers, who often fixed races.

Still, the Turf Association scraped together the funds to lease a section of land on the city's north side, roughly between Maryland and Virginia Avenues at Mediterranean Avenue. It was to be a mile-long oval track. The Turf Association proceeded with construction on the track, draining and banking the course. But it ran out of funds, and after it defaulted on a load of timber which would have built the grandstand and stables, the Association fell apart. The land was auctioned off in 1888, and plans for a racetrack were abandoned.

When the state of New Jersey outlawed wagering on horse races in 1893, much of the momentum behind the drive for a racetrack was lost. But wagering on horses was re-legalized a half-century later, and, with the city still linked to gambling (albeit illegal), the quest for a course resumed.

Atlantic City—or at least Atlantic County—finally got a race track when the "Atlantic City Race Track" opened on July 22, 1946 in Hamilton Township, about 14 miles from Absecon Island. Later to be known as the "Atlantic City Race Course," the track's investors included many celebrities, Frank Sinatra, bandleader Xavier Cugat, Bob Hope, and Sammy Kaye among them. It was one member of the "Golden Triangle" of New Jersey tracks—Monmouth Park and Garden State Park were the other two.

The race course's president, John B. Kelly, Sr., was no slouch himself. An Olympic champion rower, Kelly later became a wealthy contractor, and he is memorialized in a statue on Philadelphia's Kelly Drive. He is also famous as the father of screen star Grace Kelly, who later became Princess Grace of Monaco.

Kelly helmed the race track until it was sold, in 1960, to Philadelphia dentist Dr. Leon Levy. His son, Robert, ran the track into the 1990s, and they shared a reputation as innovators who would try nearly anything to draw racing fans.

The track's signature event, the United Nations Handicap, was first run in 1953, and it became, true to its name, an internationally-heralded event. In 1990, the event's name was changed to the Caesars International, and it was last run at the ACRC in 1997. In 1999, once again under the UN moniker, it moved north to Monmouth Park, where it has remained since.

In its glory days, the race track drew crowds of over 30,000. But the coming of casino gaming, and the general decline of horse race attendance throughout the nation, spelled trouble for the Atlantic City Race Course. Though it continued to innovate—in 1983 the track broadcast the first full simulcast card ever—attendance dwindled.

The Hamilton Mall opened on part of the race course's land in 1987, and soon more people came to the area to shop than to watch races. In 1998, the course sold off the lights of its toteboard and drastically contracted its racing season, running live races only four days each year. Though the receipts from the races were paltry, the track could still continue to simulcast races.

With a current plan to build an off-track betting parlor on part of the race course's land, the end for the track seems near—the land is supposed to be developed for residential and commercial purposes. But whatever happens, the place of the Atlantic City Race Course in racing's—and the area's—history will not be forgotten.

Flight Path

Everyone who has flown in or out of the Atlantic City International Airport has seen the sign for the William J. Hughes Technical Center. The Center has been an integral part of the area for decades, and celebrated its 50th anniversary in 2008.

The Technical Center opened as the National Aviation Facilities Experimental Center in 1958 on the site of the Pomona Naval Air Station. This station, which began operating in 1942, served to train air combat groups including fighter, bomber, and torpedo squadrons. A year later, the facility's emphasis shifted and it was used only for training fighters.

After World War II ended, the Navy continued to use the station in Pomona to train fliers. In 1958, control of the site was transferred to the Airways Modernization Board, a division within Civil Aeronautics Administration that looked to coordinate civilian and military aviation research and development. By the end of that year, the CAA had become the Federal Aviation Agency (FAA), and NAFEC became the technical arm of its Bureau of Research and Development.

Just as it was opening NAFEC, the CAA was closing its Technical Development and Evaluation Center in Indianapolis. Many of the engineers, pilots, and technicians who worked at Indianapolis transferred to Pomona. Once the Center was fully staffed, it boasted over 2,000 employees.

According to a 1960 *New York Times* profile, the most important job that the experts at NAFEC worked on was cutting down on congestion near major airports. Specific projects included testing new landing strip lights, improving air and ground radar, and developing better ways to process air traffic control data.

In its early years, NAFEC was composed of 184 separate buildings, many of them dating to the war years, spread out over more than 5,000 acres. One study found that the Center was losing over 100 man-years of labor time a year because of the time workers spent trekking from one building to another. In addition, the facilities were extremely outdated and ill-suited to technical innovation. So in 1964 the Center began a three-phase building program that would significantly modernize its physical plant.

But the FAA only finished the first phase, and in 1973 FAA Administrator Alexander Butterfield proposed closing the Center entirely, moving most of its functions to the Aeronautical Center, a training facility in Oklahoma City.

In the pre-casino 1970s, NAFEC was the largest employer in Atlantic County, and shutting the Center would have disastrous financial consequences for the area. So the "Save NAFEC Committee," assisted by freshman Congressman William J. Hughes, began lobbying for a construction/lease program that let the county build new facilities for the FAA, thus keeping the Center open.

In May 1975, these efforts paid off, as Secretary of Transportation William Coleman announced that NAFEC would remain open. Three years later, construction started on a $50 million headquarters building, signaling the government's commitment.

When the new building officially opened in 1980, the FAA changed the entire facility's name to the "FAA Technical Center."

The Technical Center was extremely active in the 1980s, with over 150 separate projects running at the same time in those years. The Center was the linchpin of the FAA's efforts to modernize air traffic control. In addition, researchers expanded the scope, adding a human factors laboratory that tested operators' reactions to various situations and an Air Traffic Simulation Facility that allowed technicians to recreate the air traffic patterns of any airport in the world—an early example of virtual reality.

On May 6, 1996, in recognition of a distinguished career that included passionate advocacy for the Center, the facility was officially re-dedicated at the William J. Hughes Technical Center. Since then, the Center has weathered yet another threatened closure, and as it begins its second half-century, it continues to lead the way in research for safer, more secure, and more efficient aviation.

Hap's Highway

Having discussed the life and career of Senator Frank S. "Hap" Farley earlier, it makes sense to recall the story of how one of his greatest projects, the Atlantic City Expressway, made it from the drawing board to reality.

Since the early 20th century, a few shore visionaries had spoken of the need for a limited-access road between Philadelphia and Atlantic City. As the automobile became a more important—and more widespread—form of transportation, a quick, direct route from one of the city's biggest feeder markets became an even greater need.

As early as 1932, the Regional Planning Commission, a Philadelphia-area traffic master-planning commission proposed a series of parkways around the Delaware Valley metropolis, including one extending southward to the shore that roughly paralleled the course taken by the Expressway today.

But these plans came to naught. To get to Atlantic City, most Philadelphians relied on the Pikes—Black Horse and White Horse—neither of which was an express route. With traffic to the city declining, many skeptics wondered what the point of an expensive new highway would be.

In the late 1950s, however, prospects began to look brighter. The construction of State Route 42, better known as the North-South Freeway, provided a non-stop road between the I-76 highway adjacent to Philadelphia and Turnersville, a distance of about 11 miles.

Opening in 1959, the North-South Freeway was just the start. While many state lawmakers opposed building a high-speed route between Philadelphia and Atlantic City, Hap Farley remained a staunch supporter of the road. Those who didn't see the need for the link derided the project as "Farley's Folly," but in the end the legislative juggernaut twisted enough arms and smoothed enough feathers to get the bulldozers rolling: construction on the road began in 1962.

On July 31, 1964, Farley presided at a noon-time ceremony that officially opened the Expressway, even though the road wasn't finished. It extended only from the terminus of Route 42 in Turnersville to the Garden State Parkway. Still, the road was a success: in its first 10 days, more than 150,000 vehicles used it.

A year later, at noon on July 30, 1965, the final seven-mile leg of the Expressway was finished, and drivers finally could motor from Philadelphia to Atlantic City with only two stops: the Egg Harbor Township toll plaza, where they paid 75 cents, and the Pleasantville toll plaza, where they were charged 15 cents.

The road had cost $52 million to build, and was estimated to reduce the driving time from Philadelphia by 25 minutes. Yet some didn't see any point in paying for the privilege of driving on it; a few unmanned toll gates only accepted exact change; if a driver didn't have the change on him, he was allowed to take a courtesy envelope and mail the toll to the Expressway Authority. But only 17 percent of the drivers who took the envelopes bothered to send in the cash. The authority estimated that it was losing $1,000 every month to scofflaw drivers. So, on March 1, 1966, the honor system was abolished and motorists were required to pay the toll before leaving the road.

At the time, few could have appreciated just how important the Expressway would become to Atlantic City. Tourism was on the decline, and there were few attractions to greet visitors when they got to the island.

But the Expressway offered a new hope. Within two years of the road's opening three new hotels—the Holiday Inn, the Howard Johnson Motor Lodge, and the Four Seasons—had opened near the Expressway's terminus. In 1967, Hilton Hotels announced plans for a 20-story Statler Hilton Inn a block from Convention Hall on the Boardwalk. In unveiling the hotel, a Hilton spokesman declared the Expressway to be the "prime factor" in determining the hotel's location. Ultimately, the plans came to nothing, but the Expressway was at least getting major companies to consider investing in Atlantic City again.

And, despite the diminished appeal of Atlantic City, the road was successful. Both traffic and toll collections rose steadily throughout the late 1960s and early 1970s. During a major nor'easter in November 1968, the Expressway proved its worth. Both the Black Horse Pike and White Horse Pike were forced to close because of high tides, but the Expressway, built three feet higher than the older roads, remained open.

With the Expressway a proven winner, all that remained was to honor its benefactor. On April 12, 1977, its operating authority officially dedicated the Hammonton-adjacent rest area as the Frank S. Farley Service Plaza, a fitting tribute to the man who made the road a reality. With over six million dollars in tolls collected annually, the Expressway was doing better than even Senator Farley could have hoped.

But with the coming of casino gaming the following year, the Expressway would see record traffic, more growth, and a less happy by-product, higher tolls. Today, nearly 70 million vehicles a year drive the road, proof that Hap Farley's dream was no folly.

From the Heart

Today one of the best-established local charities in South Jersey, the Ruth Newman Shapiro Cancer and Heart Fund was created out of necessity during a time of despair. Over 50 years after its founding, it has done more to help those in need than anyone at the time could have predicted.

Ruth Newman Shapiro, the daughter of Rose Newman, was born in Atlantic City and attended Atlantic City High School, where she was a top student who was involved in many after-school activities. After attending college, she married her high school sweetheart, Matthew Shapiro.

Ruth and Matthew adopted several children and had a child of their own. A devoted mother and wife, Shapiro had a busy, productive life that was cut short when she died of cancer at the age of 32.

Her mother chose to find some meaning in her loss by doing something about the poor state of local cancer care. Together with her daughter, Doritt Linsk, and six other local women, many of them former schoolmates, she started a small group that would, she hoped, raise enough money to afford a cobalt unit. This was a piece of medical equipment, first widely used in the 1950s, that used radiation from Cobalt-60, to damage or destroy cancerous cells.

At the time, cancer patients had to drive to New York or Philadelphia to get cobalt treatments. Those who didn't have the resources or support for regular trips to these cities had no hope to fight the disease.

Rose and her compatriots started with five thousand dollars that had been given in donations after Ruth's death, organizing the Ruth Newman Shapiro Cancer Memorial Fund in 1961. They raised nearly

$20,000 from their 300 members and, within the year, gave a down payment for a cobalt machine for the Atlantic City Hospital.

When she first brought together the group, Rose thought that, with the cobalt machine paid for, the organization would disperse. But she soon found that local cancer patients still had needs that were unfulfilled, and the RNS Fund continued its work. In 1965, the Atlantic City Hospital dedicated the Ruth Newman Shapiro Cobalt Unit and, three years later, unveiled a mammography unit and a suite of diagnostic tools that the group had donated.

As the hospital grew, so did RNS. In 1988, the Fund made a million-dollar pledge to build the Ruth Newman Shapiro Regional Cancer Center at what was now called the Atlantic City Medical Center, City Division.

The fund supported treatment for cancer patients at other local institutions, including Shore Memorial Hospital, the Bacharach Institute for Rehabilitation, and the Cape Regional Medical Center.

While RNS continued to assist South Jersey cancer patients, the fund's directors (all of whom, incidentally, are volunteers) learned that there was a similar need for support of the region's cardiac care facilities. So RNS began to raise money to create better facilities for those suffering from heart disease. In 1997, the fund announced a five-year mission to upgrade cardiac care at Shore Memorial Hospital. Two years later, the new Ruth Newman Shapiro Cardiac Care Unit opened as part of the hospital's Critical Care Center. In late 2001, the fund delivered the last installment of its $750,000 gift.

In 1998, the Ruth Newman Shapiro Cardiopulmonary Rehabilitation Center opened at the Bacharach Institute Rehabilitation Center's main campus in Pomona, and in 2001 the Heart Institute-Rose Newman Pavilion at Atlantic City Medical Center's City Division began providing cardiac surgery and interventional cardiology.

In the area of cancer diagnosis and treatment, RNS was no less active, with a mobile mammography van hitting the streets in 1995, as well as on-going programs to support patient care at Atlantic City Medical Center (renamed the AtlantiCare Regional Medical Center in 2005), Shore Memorial Hospital, and Burdette Tomlin Memorial Hospital.

The Ruth Newman Shapiro Cancer and Heart Fund has been able to assemble such an impressive track record over the years because of the passion and determination of its all-volunteer staff and the success of its fundraising events. These include an annual golf tournament (started in 2002), several luncheons and events, and the Show House at the Shore, an annual summer tradition that started in 1992.

Each year, the Show House takes over an area home and turns loose an army of designers and artists, turning it into a veritable exhibition of the latest in home design and fashion.

In the summer of 2009, the Show House presented "La Dolce Vita" at one of Ventnor's most storied residences, 12 South Suffolk Avenue. The Dutch Colonial built in the 1920s was most famously the home of Paul "Skinny" D'Amato, owner of the 500 Club.

It's fitting that the Ruth Newman Shapiro Cancer and Heart Fund, which has been a stalwart charity for over a half-century, has crossed paths with another towering figure in Atlantic City history.

A Popular Pachyderm

Today Atlantic City is renowned for its towering casino resorts, but back in the 1880s few could have foreseen a boom in high rise construction on Absecon Island. When an enterprising developer built a giant wooden elephant there, he put the town of South Atlantic City—which is today called Margate—on the map and created an American icon.

At that time, Atlantic City was slowly growing, but the nearby town of South Atlantic City, cut off from the bustle by a tidal creek, had few prospects. James Vincent de Paul Lafferty, Jr., owned several lots in the town, which was little more than a collection of fishing shacks. Figuring to make his fortune in land speculation there, he enlisted Philadelphia architect William Free in what seemed a quixotic scheme—to design and build a 65-foot wooden elephant in the midst of his holdings.

The elephant, Lafferty hoped, would help to publicize South Atlantic City. While we can doubt his sales acumen (Lafferty sold off the elephant and his lands six years later with no significant profit), he had an incredible eye for promotion. In the late 19th century, elephants were exotic animals indeed.

In 1881, Lafferty hired a Philadelphia contractor to build the elephant, and it quickly rose above the sands of South Atlantic City. Lafferty installed his offices in the elephant, showing off his land to prospective buyers from the howdah, or riding carriage. It was a local curiosity at first, though word got out slowly. Laffetry designed two more giant elephants, Cape May's "Light of Asia," (which was disassembled in 1900) and Coney Island's Elephantine Colossus, which burned to the ground in 1896.

When, in 1887, Lafferty unloaded his South Atlantic City lands, Anthony Gerzen walked away from the deal with the real estate—and the elephant. The elephant would remain in his family's possession for more than eighty years. After his 1902 death, his son John acquired the property.

The elephant had previously been open to tourists: visitors paid 10 cents and were allowed to wander throughout the furnished interior and climb the stairs to the howdah. But in 1902 the elephant closed to the public for the season, as an English doctor rented it as a residence, living in the belly of the beast with his family for the summer.

The following year, a storm heavily damaged the structure, and after it was repaired, it operated as a tavern. The elephant would remain a bar, off and on, until 1920, when National Prohibition put it—and bars throughout the nation—out of business.

During John's tenure as owner, the elephant acquired the moniker "Lucy." Reportedly his wife Sophia thought up the name, though no one remembers exactly how or why. Lucy is apparently a gender-bending pachyderm; though she's usually identified as a "she," only male Asian elephants have tusks.

After John passed away in 1916, Sophia continued to operate Lucy as a tourist attraction, adding an "Elephant Hotel" across the street. Though the 1944 hurricane devastated the surrounding area (the Margate Boardwalk was never rebuilt), the elephant survived, a bit worse for wear.

Sophia presided over Lucy until her 1963 death, and while she continued to care for the pachyderm, the elephant, like Atlantic City, had declined over the years. In the late 1960s, it became clear that Lucy was becoming a hazard, and the new owners of the property would demolish the dilapidated elephant.

Unwilling to see this landmark disappear, in 1969 a group of concerned citizens formed the Margate Civic Association and began planning to "Save the Elephant." The city agreed to allow the Association to move Lucy to a piece of land two blocks south of its original location, and on July 20, 1970, the 90 year-old elephant was towed to its new home between Decatur and Washington avenues on the Margate beachfront.

Local businesses—from the Atlantic City Race Course to Skinny D'Amato's 500 Club—generously helped the cause, and by 1974, Lucy was opened once more for tours. By 1976, when the landmark was officially placed on the National Register of Historic Places, the elephant's skin had been repaired and repainted.

Lucy gained a new generation of fans when, in 1986, she appeared on a segment of Mister Rogers' Neighborhood. Rogers, in a film cutaway, took young viewers on a brief tour of the landmark.

Today, the Save Lucy Committee continues to nurture Margate's famous elephant, which is open for daily tours in the summer. Now well over 130, Lucy remains a must-see for all visitors to the Jersey shore, young and old.

The City of Ventnor City

A bsecon Island is now built up from Maine Avenue in Atlantic
City to 11th Avenue in Longport, but until the early 1900s, the
island was home to several distinct settlements. Around this time,
these areas developed their own municipal governments. Ventnor,
adjacent to Atlantic City, is decades younger than its neighbor, but it
has a history that is no less interesting.

In 1853, one year before the incorporation of Atlantic City,
Samuel R. Richards bought an enormous tract of land west of what is
now Jackson Avenue for the Camden and Atlantic Land Company.
This was the same company that developed much of Atlantic City,
including its first major resort, the United States Hotel. The company
was tied to the Camden and Atlantic Railroad, which was in the
process of linking Atlantic City to Philadelphia.

Richards' tract ran from what is now Jackson Avenue to what
is now Fredricksburg Avenue. This may seem an arbitrary division,
but it made sense at the time. Once, Jackson Avenue was a small
waterway that divided Absecon Island in two—as late as 1700, it was
still open water. Over the 18th century, the region filled in with sand,
but at the time of Richards' purchase it was still known as "Dry Inlet,"
and was a natural boundary.

The land bought by Richards would, in time, become Ventnor
City, but at the time it was wild, undeveloped sand dunes and
woodlands.

The area remained that way for decades. In the mid-1880s, plans
to lay out streets and begin development advanced a bit; in 1887, the
name "Atlantic Heights" was proposed for the future development.
Samuel Bartram Richards, son of the man who initially bought the

land and now president of the Camden and Atlantic Land Company, began grading the land.

Atlantic Heights seemed a fine enough name, but Richards' wife had other ideas. She and Samuel had just gotten back from a trip to England during which they had visited the Isle of Wight, a small island in the English Channel. The island's attractions included Ventnor, a seaside resort that recently come into prominence with the arrival of a railway. Mrs. Richards felt there was a certain parallel between this up-and-coming health resort and the town her husband was planning on a small island off the South Jersey Coast, so she recommended that it be named "Ventnor."

Richards' advice proved sound, and, in 1889, her husband's company officially adopted the name. The year before, a rail station had opened near what is now Cambridge Avenue, and plans for further development were discussed.

The first real growth came with the construction and opening of the Carisbrooke Inn in 1891. Bounded by Cambridge, Sacramento, Ocean, and Ventnor Avenues (behind the current city hall), this was the center of the town's social, economic, and political life. With 400 rooms, this was a massive hotel for the times—indeed, it was nearly as large as casino-era high-rises like the Sands and Golden Nugget. Named after a castle overlooking Ventnor, England, this hotel drew travelers looking for relaxation, as opposed to the thrill-seekers that were filling up Atlantic City hotels.

The following year, Thomas Richards built the first private residence in the growing town, which was still administratively part of Egg Harbor Township. As the area began to fill up with residents, they began to consider independence. After much debate, on March 17, 1903, the town was incorporated as Ventnor City.

The founders insisted on the grandiose (and redundant) name, "the City of Ventnor City," despite its small size. In fact, the "city" had only eight eligible voters, and more than 20 public offices to be filled. To make up for the shortfall, several Atlantic City residents officially changed their residence to Ventnor and helped out.

Within a few years, Ventnor had blossomed. The first grocery store opened at Ventnor and Little Rock Avenues, which today hosts a WaWa market. By 1907, more than 80 houses had been built, and the city's first city hall had opened.

At its incorporation, the city had a one-man police force: Benjamin F. Comley, a Civil War veteran, who patrolled the city by himself until 1906, when Harry Frings joined him. Others followed as the department grew.

The city opened its first jail in 1908, and its first occupant was no garden-variety criminal. Marceline Orbes was, at the time, the world's most famous clown, star of the New York Hipprodrome, a giant circus/theater in midtown Manhattan. Marceline was so well known that he used only his first name in his billings.

While in Ventnor, Marceline ran afoul of local animal cruelty watchdogs, who demanded that the police arrest him for mistreating his horse. With a brand new holding facility ready, Comley and Frings were only too glad to oblige. After a short time as the jail's debut act, Marceline paid a 10-dollar fine and returned to New York.

Ventnor's Fire Department also got its start in these years. In 1906, the city organized a volunteer force, which was asked to fight fires with nothing more than six fire extinguishers. Some had pressed for a professional, paid department, but the majority opinion argued that such a squadron would be too costly.

As the city became more built up, however, and insurance premiums rose, Ventnor's citizens began to see the other side of the story, and in 1910, the Ventnor City Fire Department, a group of paid professionals, was founded.

At this stage, Ventnor was still growing. Though promoters were pleased with its development since incorporation, the city's best days lay in the future.

One of the clearest signs that Ventnor had arrived as a town was that, in 1907, it attracted its own newspaper, called the *Ventnor News*. With Carl Voelker as publisher, the *Ventnor News* ran, with a few interruptions, until 1928, when it merged with the *Pleasantville Press*.

At the same time, Ventnor was being transformed into a city. In 1910, the last open woodlands in the city—a stand of cedars between Troy and Buffalo Avenues south of Atlantic Avenue—were cleared.

In the early years, the massive Carisbrooke Inn anchored Ventnor's tourist trade. This was also one of the few places were alcohol was served in the city. At the time, "dry" sentiments were on the rise: even in cosmopolitan Atlantic City, many hotels, including Haddon Hall, didn't serve intoxicating liquors. Ventnor soon came under the prohibitionist spell, and after 1909 the city council refused to issue any new licenses for saloons or taverns within city limits.

The next year, the Carisbrooke Inn closed and was torn down, marking the end of the first era of Ventnor's history. It was also the last time liquor was served publicly in Ventnor, though several liquor stores would continue to sell alcohol for home consumption. To this day, there are no bars within the limits of Ventnor City.

As it developed, Ventnor tried to find a niche as a health resort. The city's boosters adopted the slogan "If you want to live, live in Ventnor," suggesting that immortality could be had merely by crossing Jackson Avenue. The editors of the *Ventnor News*, after some quick research, learned that no one had died within the city limits of Ventnor during all of 1907, which bolstered the town's claims to healthiness.

Despite its promotion as a health resort, there wasn't much focus on Ventnor's beaches. The first beachfront house wasn't built until 1911, at Little Rock Avenue. In 1963 this historic residence was torn down to make way for the equally significant Monaco Motel, which was for many years the most glamorous and exclusive hospitality destination in town. Many tears were shed when, in the summer of 2013, the Monaco was demolished to make way for townhouses.

Ventnor followed in the footsteps of its larger neighbor. Atlantic City's first boardwalk was built in 1870, and the wooden way assumed its present shape in 1896. Ventnor opened a continuation of the boardwalk from Jackson to Frankfurt Avenues in 1905, and in 1910 succeeded in extending the boards all the way to the Margate border at Fredricksburg Avenue. The massive 1944 hurricane obliterated most of this boardwalk, and it wasn't completely rebuilt for another eight years.

During the years that the boardwalk was being completed, a bridge over the Inside Thoroughfare at Dorset Avenue was built, allowing the development of Ventnor Heights.

Dorset Avenue wasn't completely paved until 1925, but it quickly became one of the city's busiest streets. With the rise of automobile traffic, navigating the city streets was getting more hazardous by the day, and in 1926 the city installed the first traffic light—called an automatic policeman—in the middle of the intersection of Ventnor and Dorset Avenues. It was moved to a better-protected location on the adjacent sidewalk after a speeding driver struck and flattened the new signal.

Ventnor's fishing pier had its origins in this period as well. First constructed at Cambridge Avenue in 1919, it was extended in 1929. In addition to the structure jutting out into the waves, several large pavilions at the pier's base served as meeting places for Ventnor residents and, in 1927, as its first library. This building was severely damaged by a fire in 1940 but was rebuilt, and served the city until 1962, when a new, larger library opened at the corner of Newport and Atlantic Avenues.

Despite its proximity to Atlantic City, one of the most thoroughly profane resorts on the East Coast, Ventnor evolved to serve as a religious retreat of sorts. In the early years, the Baptist Missionary Society built cottages for missionaries on sabbatical at Ventnor and Portland Avenues. Later, the Medical Mission Society bought much of that block, and several properties farther north on Portland Avenue, building homes that housed missionaries on leave for furloughs as long as a year.

While relaxing after missions in parts of the developing world, missionaries could stay at the society's Ventnor houses for up to an entire school year, rent free. Longtime Ventnor residents may remember going to school with the children of these vacationing missionaries. The society still maintains a few houses on Portland Avenue, though the bulk of its holdings have since been sold and redeveloped.

Today, Ventnor is still primarily a residential community. Though it has changed a great deal from its early days as a health resort, the town is still cognizant of its history.

Two examples will suffice to prove this. First, though the original Carisbrooke Inn closed in 1910 and Ventnor's hotels and motels have, over the years, been converted to condominiums or closed, there is still a hostelry called the Carisbrooke Inn that welcomes guests. A bed and breakfast with that name on South Little Rock Avenue— just steps from the site of the city's first beachfront house—opened in 1996. It's not as big as the 400-room original, but it provides a welcome nod to Ventnor's history.

Of greater significance, in 2006, the city replaced its municipal ice rink/miniature golf complex on Atlantic Avenue at New Haven Avenue with a newer, larger library that incorporated the "original" 1962 structure. This spacious reading center has an expansive yellow stucco façade that is modeled on the pier-side library building of 1929.

Even while moving forward, Ventnor is looking back.

A tale of two campaigns: in 1974 (right), casino gambling would have been legal throuhgout the state, but in 1976, it was all about Atlantic City. *Allen "Boo" Pergament.*

Crowds lined the Boardwalk to gamble at Resorts International when it opened on May 26, 1979. *Allen "Boo" Pergament.*

Opening in a renovated Haddon Hall, Resorts International quickly became a gaming powerhouse *Resorts International.*

Caesars Boardwalk Regency, though it was a renovation of the existing Howard Johnson's, brought a new look to the Boardwalk after its 1979 opening. *Allen "Boo" Pergament.*

The Brighton, which became the Sands in 1981, was the first casino to open in an entirely new building. Here it is months before its August 1980 opening. *Allen "Boo" Pergament.*

Harrah's Marina, shortly after its November 1980 opening. *Martin Stern Collection, UNLV Special Collections.*

The gleaming pink tower at Bally's Atlantic City, opened in 1989, was a modern addition to a casino that also included the historic Dennis. *Robert Rossiello.*

Replacing Million Dollar Pier, Ocean One brought a 1980s twist on Captain Young's onetime address. *Allen "Boo" Pergament.*

Still under construction here, Steve Wynn's Golden Nugget shook things up when it opened in late 1980. *Allen "Boo" Pergament.*

Built over the skeleton of the Ambassador Hotel and opened in November 1981, the Tropicana continues to grow. *Robert Rossiello.*

The Playboy hoped to emulate European sophistication. Instead, it became the first Atlantic City casino to close permanently., though by that time it was the Trump's World Fair. *Martin Stern Collection, UNLV Special Collections.*

Built as the Hilton, opened as the Castle, operated for many years as the Marina, and now called the Golden Nugget, the casino Donald Trump opened in 1985 has had four distinct identities. *Robert Rosseillo.*

The Showboat, which opened in 1987, charted its own path to success. *Martin Stern Collection, UNLV Special Collections.*

The Taj Mahal, started by Resorts and finished by Donald Trump, the Taj Mahal was for years one of the city's most successful casinos. *Robert Rosseillo.*

In the first thirty years of casino gambling, Atlantic City's skyline was dramatically transformed. *Photograph by author.*

The Borgata quickly became the most successful casino in Atlantic City after its 2003 opening. *Boyd Gaming.*

Revel was supposed to lead a new wave of casino development. It closed after two years and five months.
Wikimedia Commons.

Steel Pier's amusement rides, sand, dunes, and a lifeguard boat. The future of Atlantic City might lie in its past. *Robert Rosseillo.*

Five

Casino Capital
of the East

A Resort Reborn

On November 1, 1976, the big red brick building at North Carolina Avenue and the Boardwalk was plain old Haddon Hall. It was one of the last remaining historic hotels in town—the biggest of the bunch—but it was still just an aging hotel in a dead-end resort. But when, on the following day, New Jersey voters approved the referendum that legalized casino gaming in Atlantic City, Haddon Hall was thrust into history: this would become the place where the East Coast tasted legal casino gambling for the first time.

It was an unlikely site, at least from the point of view of history. Haddon Hall and its sister property, the Chalfonte, were once owned by Quakers who, as a matter of policy, refused to serve alcohol to their guests. These strait-laced proprietors would have been aghast at the free-flowing booze and wild gambling action that would soon break loose within the walls of a converted Haddon Hall.

In expectation that the referendum would pass, a company named Resorts International bought the hotel, hoping to refit it as a casino. They were not disappointed, though Resorts nearly missed taking part in the gambling bonanza.

Resorts had once been called the Mary Carter Paint Company. In 1968, chairman Jim Crosby sold off the paint business and bought a Bahamas casino, renaming the company in the process. Crosby and Resorts president I.G. "Jack" Davis were bullish on Atlantic City and, after the referendum passed, raced to get Resorts International opened in the former Haddon Hall. The over-worked Division of Gaming Enforcement was unable to finish its licensure investigation in time, though, and the Casino Control Commission was forced to issue a temporary license to Resorts the night before the casino was set to open. Along the way, state regulators scrambled to formulate—and enforce—elements of the new gaming rules.

The public couldn't wait to start playing. On Friday, May 26, 1978—the start of Memorial Day weekend—lines started forming outside the casino almost before dawn. For months, city officials had been planning for the sudden influx of visitors: 150,000 cars a day were expected, and each of the city's 8,000 hotel and motel rooms was booked.

The sky was overcast, but no one minded. At 10 a.m. Governor Brendan Byrne made a short speech and cut a red ribbon strung across the casino's Boardwalk entrance. Inside, entertainer Steve Lawrence placed the first official bet—$10 on the pass line at craps. He rolled a five, then sevened out. Thousands of gamblers raced through the casino, looking for a spot at the 84 tables or 893 slot machines.

The casino's first months were almost unthinkably profitable. When state and casino officials finally counted the take, Resorts International had made more money than any casino ever. In its first year, the casino earned nearly two and a half times more than the Las Vegas Strip's biggest property, the MGM Grand. This was the kind of money that got attention: the big Las Vegas operators who hadn't already bought land in Atlantic City started wishing they had.

The casino opened each day at 10 a.m. and closed at 4 in the morning on weeknights, 6 on weekends; in its first days, there was a 15-minute wait just to get in. To start the place out right, Steve Lawrence and his wife, Eydie Gorme, headlined a show produced by Tibor Rudas in the Superstar Theater, giving the crowd a taste of Las Vegas-style entertainment, complete with showgirls, choreography, and glitz. Hungry visitors could stop at several restaurants, including Le Palais, a French eatery, and Camelot, a British-themed steakhouse.

By the end of June, Resorts had added abut 500 slot machines and 50 more table games and boasted a casino bigger than any in Las Vegas. It was, without a doubt, the most successful casino in the world.

As Atlantic City grew in the early 1980s, Resorts International continued to prosper and planned a huge second casino, the Taj Mahal, across Pennsylvania Avenue. As early as 1981, it announced its intentions to build a 38-story behemoth.

Work on the new casino progressed slowly, but Resorts was active, making plays to acquire both Trans World Airlines and Pan American Airlines in 1985. In that same year, the company ran into regulatory difficulties due to irregularities in the operation of its Bahamas casino, but retained its license.

Jim Crosby's 1986 death threw the company into turmoil, and when the dust had settled in November 1988, Donald Trump owned the Taj site and Merv Griffin had Resorts.

Griffin looked to give Resorts a Hollywood makeover but, despite his success in television, was never able to pull the casino from a mire of debt. Griffin filed for bankruptcy in 1989. Emerging from bankruptcy in 1990 under the leadership of former Trump Plaza president Jack O'Donnell, the casino posted a profit the following year.

In 1996 Sun International, owned by South African casino magnate Sol Kerzner, bought the property. Sun planned a massive rebuilding project, but made only modest improvements before selling Resorts in 2001 to Colony Capital LLC, a private equity fund headed by Thomas J. Barrack, Jr. Colony, which paid $140 million for the property, invested heavily in Resorts, adding the 459-room Rendezvous Tower in 2004, completely remodeling and expanding the casino itself, and bringing daylife brand Nikki Beach to the city.

The Colony reboot, however, didn't pan out any better than Sun International's. Nikki Beach closed after the 2005 season, never to reopen. Refinancing the casino in 2007 for $360 million to better position it for the wave of competition that seemed imminent turned out to be a bad decision. Instead of fighting for a share of a growing pie, Colony was stuck with unsustainable debt payments in a declining market. By 2009, the company could not make its loan payments.

Lenders seized Resorts from the defaulting Colony group, and for a time it looked as if the casino might close. Then the team of legendary casino regulator and executive Dennis Gomes and New York real estate developer Morris Bailey stepped in, buying the property for $31.5 million—a commentary on how far values had fallen in the city's casino market.

Gomes steered Resorts in a new direction, embracing a speakeasy theme that drew on the popular *Boardwalk Empire* series and opening the city's first gay nightclub in a casino, Prohibition. At the time of his February 2012 death, Resorts appeared to be headed in the right direction.

Indeed, that summer a partnership with Jimmy Buffet was announced that would transform part of the casino floor into a Margaritaville-themed area and add the Landshark Bar and Grill, along with other dining and drinking options. The renovation, which launched in 2013, brought much-needed energy to the property, helping it to navigate the stormy waters of post-monopoly Atlantic City.

The arrival of Parrotheads, however, was not the biggest change in Resorts. In August 2012, the Mohegan Tribal Gaming Authority announced that it had agreed to invest in and manage Resorts, folding the property into a loyalty program that included its flagship Uncasville, Connecticut Mohegan Sun casino and Pocono Downs, a Pennsylvania racino which Mohegan also operated.

The reborn (again) Resorts continues to blaze a trail in Atlantic City. Its current management is carrying the historic legacy of the resort pioneer into the future. It is fitting, perhaps, that a building constructed by Quakers, who were among the first British colonists to approach American Indians in a spirit of friendship, is now under the purview of a resurgent Indian tribe.

Hail, Caesar

Caesars is one of the best-known names in the Atlantic City casino industry. Though the casino had a rocky beginning, it has enjoyed more than 30 years in the spotlight in the center of the Boardwalk.

The origins of Caesars Atlantic City lie far away, on the Las Vegas Strip. In 1966, motel builder and dreamer Jay Sarno built Caesars Palace, which was the most luxurious casino that Las Vegas had ever seen to that point. Sarno, who had built the casino with $10 million in loans from the Teamster Union's Central States Pension Fund, quickly became disenchanted with his partners. In 1969, he sold the casino to a publicly traded Florida company named Lum's, whose principal owners were brothers Clifford and Stuart Perlman.

Lum's already owned a hot dog chain by that name, as well as a meat processing company, a chain of army-navy stores, a sit-down restaurant named SteakThing, and other businesses. Within a few years, though, the Perlmans realized that the casino business was the real money-maker; they sold off all of Lum's non-casino assets and renamed their company Caesars World.

When gaming was approved in Atlantic City, Caesars quickly began shopping for a site to build a casino. Shortly after the state of Nevada adopted a law that allowed its casinos to conduct gambling operations in other states in May 1977, Caesars executives announced that they would be building a $115-million casino on the land where the storied Traymore hotel once stood.

Meanwhile, a company named the Jemm Corporation leased the Howard Johnson's Motor Lodge at Arkansas and the Boardwalk, announcing plans to expand the 425-room hotel and add a casino. The new resort would be called the Regency. Millon-Dollar Pier, which the company also leased, was to be converted into a shopping mall that would rival San Francisco's Ghirardelli Square.

But the Jemm Corporation, in June 1978, decided to lease the property to Caesars rather than develop it itself. Caesars planned to spend $30 million to expand the hotel to 537 rooms and build a 52,000 square-foot casino, which would be cheaper and quicker than building a casino from the ground up.

Considering that Resorts International was on its way to earning $134 million in revenues in its first year of operation, this was a smart move. Caesars Regency would more than pay for itself, and help fund the Traymore-site Caesars, which was to have been named Caesars Palace.

Work on the Howard Johnson's site began immediately, and by May of the following year the hotel portion, renamed the Boardwalk Regency, had opened. The casino was finished, as well, but licensing concerns held up its opening.

New Jersey's Division of Gaming Enforcement had delayed giving the casino a temporary operating license until Caesars World chairman Clifford Perlman had stepped away from active involvement in the company. The company had been warned by the Nevada Gaming Commission to avoid future contact with Alvin Malnik, a Florida lawyer who had reputed ties to notorious underworld financier Meyer Lansky. Questions about financial dealings between Perlman, Malnik, and a Las Vegas casino manager who had been convicted of skimming millions of dollars from the Flamingo casino on behalf of Meyer Lansky continued to dog the company, even though it was one of the most widely-recognized casino operators in the world. As this drama played out, work on the casino continued.

Finally, on June 26, 1979, Caesars Boardwalk Regency opened with 95 table games and 1,431 slot machines. As with Resorts International a year earlier, prospective gamblers formed lines down the Boardwalk, waiting for hours just to get in, and within a few weeks of its opening the casino was looking to expand. In its first year, the casino made more than $91 million. Its profits of $16 million for the year were more than those of Caesars Palace and Caesars Lake Tahoe combined.

The bet on Atlantic City had paid off for the company, but there was a price. In October 1980, the Casino Control Commission ruled that, if Caesars World were to get a permanent license to run the

Boardwalk Regency, it would have to dismiss its chairman and vice chairman, Clifford and Stuart Perlman.

The Perlmans left but the company continued, and has not looked back since. Several expansions—from a 1985 project that added a 12-story hotel tower and more casino and shopping space to the transformation in 2006 of the former Million Dollar Pier/Ocean One into the Pier Shops at Caesars—have taken the casino far beyond its Howard Johnson's origin. In 1987, the property's name was officially changed to Caesars Atlantic City.

The casino has changed hands several times, as well. In early 1995, corporate giant ITT bought Caesars World. Three years later, it spun off its casino holdings, including Caesars Atlantic City to Starwood, a hotel operator. In 1999, Starwood sold all of its Caesars to Park Place Entertainment, which already operated Bally's Park Place and the Atlantic City Hilton in Atlantic City. The company briefly renamed itself Caesars Entertainment before being acquired by rival Harrah's Entertainment in 2005.

Harrah's, which changed its name to Caesars Entertainment in 2010, folded the property into its Total Rewards program. The Pier has been replaced by the Playground, which is not owned by Caesars, though they are still connected by the Boardwalk skybridge. As of this writing, Caesars seems to have fallen into a holding pattern.

From a tiny motor inn, the property came to dominate the foot of the Atlantic City Expressway. With two major parking garages across Pacific Avenue, 1,139 rooms in four hotel towers, more than 3,000 slot machines and 160 table games in a two-story casino, Caesars Atlantic City is still a force to be reckoned with.

Landing on Park Place

B ally's Atlantic City was, for many years, Atlantic City's largest casino by several measures, including total square footage and total number of slot machines. For a time, Bally's also included the Claridge property under its administrative aegis.

While both the Claridge and Dennis hotels have long and storied histories, the "new" part of casino/hotel, which opened as Bally's Park Place, is no less interesting.

For decades, the Marlborough-Blenheim had stood at Ohio Avenue and the Boardwalk. By the time casinos were legalized in 1976, however, the hotels had already seen their best days.

Reese Palley, an art gallery owner who had championed the cause of casino gaming, bought the Marlborough-Blenheim in March 1977 with other local partners, including attorney Martin Blatt. He planned to raze the Marlborough while keeping the Blenheim, whose distinctive spires had been made possible by a reinforced concrete engineered by Thomas Edison that became a major component in hotel construction after its first use in the Blenheim.

The Bally Manufacturing Corporation, one of the country's largest slot machine makers, would operate a casino that was to be built in the new 750-room hotel built on the Marlborough portion of the project. Though the company did not have any experience in operating casino in Nevada, or any other jurisdiction, it made an immediate move to cement its reputation as a gaming heavyweight with the hiring of William S. "Billy" Weinberger, president of Las Vegas' Caesars Palace casino, as the chief executive of its new Atlantic City operating unit.

In June 1977, Bally signed a long-term lease of the Marlborough-Blenheim, which gave it the right to demolish both hotels. That summer, the company bought the adjacent Dennis hotel, again reserving the right to renovate or raze and build anew. Its initial plan, however, was to retain the Marlborough-Blenheim; architects Venturi, Scott-Brown (known for their book *Learning from Las Vegas*) proposed a model for the updated structure.

By January of 1978, Bally's plans had changed. Retaining the California architectural firm Maxwell Starkman Associates, the company decided to demolish all three historic hotels and build an "exciting, prestige casino complex" that included a 39-story hotel tower.

The company modified its plans, however, keeping the 535-room Dennis and, after leveling the Marlborough and Blenheim, building a giant, featureless, concrete box of a casino that it called Bally's Park Place. Work on the $120 million project started in earnest in 1978, with fast-track construction slated to last little more than a year.

The name of the casino, Park Place, played on its prominent address: the site was adjacent to Park Place, a city street made famous by the Parker Brothers classic board game Monopoly. Park Place, at $350, was the most expensive property on the board, after the Boardwalk. Plus, it sounded better than Bally's Ohio Avenue.

Even before its opening, the casino made headlines when, in October 1979, Major League Baseball Commissioner Bowie Kuhn gave Hall of Famer Willie Mays an ultimatum: abandon his new job in community relations for Bally's, or sever all ties with professional baseball. Mays was already working for the New York Mets, but Kuhn forced him to choose between his job with the baseball team or his new position with the casino, which stood to pay double the annual salary. A resigned Mays chose Bally's, both for the security it could give his family and for the opportunity to work with Atlantic City's African-American community.

Regulatory concerns also dogged the casino. In early December, Bally Manufacturing president and chairman William O'Donnell agreed to step down from his position with the company, pending an investigations into allegations of associations with organized crime figures. But the Casino Control Commission still issued Bally's a temporary operating license, and the casino opened on December 27, 1979, though it was not yet finished.

Though Palley had originally projected that it would cost $50 million to renovate and build a casino hotel around the Blenheim, Bally's Park Place ultimately cost a reported $300 million.

More than 500 hotel rooms in the renovated Dennis hotel were ready to greet visitors, as was the 50,000 square-foot casino, with 54 gaming tables and more than 600 slot machines. But the Boardwalk entrance to the property wouldn't be finished for months. In addition, the Casino Control Commission limited the number of games in play because it said that Bally's had not hired enough personnel to oversee the casino.

A month later, the commission allowed the casino to run full bore, with nearly 100 tables and over 1,200 slots in operation. From there, Bally's posted steady increases in its revenues; by 1981, it was the highest-earning casino in town, after Caesars Boardwalk Regency.

Bally Park Place's parent company expanded, buying the MGM Grand casino hotels in Reno and Las Vegas from billionaire Kirk Kerkorian in 1986 then, the following year, Atlantic City's Golden Nugget from Steve Wynn. Bally renamed the Nugget Bally's Grand. But the casino owners did not neglect Park Place: they added its glass-enclosed, 850-room hotel tower in 1989 and, in 1991, opened Bally's Parking Place, a 1,500-space garage connected to the casino by a moving walkway.

Bally's Wild Wild West opened on the Boardwalk across Michigan Avenue from Park Place in 1997, the first—and, to date, last—outrageously themed Atlantic City casino.

Bally's Park Place seemed to be destined for better things when, in 1998, the company that now owned it (formed from a merger of Bally's with Hilton's casinos) was named Park Place Entertainment.

But two years later, in 2000, Park Place Entertainment executives made the decision to take the Park Place name off of their Atlantic City casino. The resort bounded by Park Place and Michigan Avenue was renamed Bally's Atlantic City. It absorbed the Claridge casino-hotel the following year. The company renamed itself Caesars Entertainment in 2003, shortly before being acquired by Harrah's Entertainment, which itself took the name Caesars Entertainment in 2010.

Since the post-2006 slowdown, the Atlantic City casino is no longer one of the city's top revenue-producing properties. In 2014, Caesars Entertainment sold the Claridge hotel, whittling Bally's Atlantic City back down to its core casino-hotel and the Wild Wild West.

A rose by any other name would smell just as sweet, but without the Park Place name and its link to Atlantic City's history and cultural influence, an intangible piece of the property's mystique has been lost.

Sand Blasted

During its brief history, the Sands epitomized the best—and worst—of Atlantic City's casino revival.

At one time, the Brighton Hotel, one of the city's most famous, stood at Indiana and Pacific Avenues. Though the Brighton was leveled in 1958, it remained alive in Atlantic City's memory, and when a group of local business owners planned a new casino hotel on the site, using the Brighton name seemed to augur well for its chances.

The major stockholders in Great Bay, the Brighton's parent company, Eugene V. Gatti and Arthur J. Kania, planned a small casino (at only 32,000 feet, it was about one-fifth the size of the Borgata's casino today) in a 504-room hotel with little room for expansion.

When it opened on August 13, 1980, the Brighton seemed to have a lot going for it. It was only the fourth casino to open in Atlantic City, following Resorts International, Caesars Boardwalk Regency, and Bally's Park Place.

The Brighton was also the first newly built casino hotel in Atlantic City, making good on a promise that the 1976 casino referendum would guarantee a wave of new construction. It was the first major hotel to be built in the city since the Claridge in 1930.

But there was no disputing that the casino was, even by contemporary standards, tiny; it was only half the size of Resorts' and Bally's gaming spaces.

Indeed, it had auspicious beginnings: the crowd of 1,500 waiting gamblers grew impatient at its opening ceremonies and shouted down a planned dedication speech, demanding that the officials "open the doors!"

But the gamblers apparently didn't break down the doors for long. By the fall, the casino was losing money ($15.4 million by the end of the year), and though a planned sale to Holiday Inns collapsed, by February 1981 the Brighton was sold to Inns of America, a Dallas-based Holiday Inns franchisee run by the Pratt Brothers; the casino's operating company was later re-named the Pratt Hotel Corporation.

Since the Pratts had just bought Las Vegas' Sands from the Summa Corporation (which controlled Howard Hughes' erstwhile casino empire), they chose to rename their new acquisition the Sands, hoping that a bit of the Rat Pack's magic would rub off.

The Pratts brought in Stephen Hyde and other executives from Caesars. Under the new regime the property rebounded. But as Hyde and his cohort moved on to other casinos—and as it became clear that smaller wasn't necessarily better—the casino lost traction. But the Pratt company remained bullish on Atlantic City, buying the failed Penthouse site and announcing plans for a second casino—Sands Boardwalk—in 1986.

Two years later, the project had become the Sands Hollywood, but it was challenged in the courts by Donald Trump and remained mostly speculation; it was never built.

In the early 1990s, as the second casino was tabled (it is today the site of Trump Plaza's North Tower), the possibility of the Sands itself being renamed the Hollywood was mooted. July 1996 was targeted as the date for the transition, but the closest Brighton Park got to Hollywood was the Epic Buffet; the Sands opened a new all-you-can eatery stocked with 400 original props and costumes from Roman and biblical celluloid epics like "Cleopatra," "The Ten Commandments," and "Ben Hur." The casino itself added 26,000 square feet of floor space, including a new baccarat pit, in 1994, awaiting a flood of new gamblers.

But the Sands' performance was anything but Epic. In 1996, the Hollywood Hotel Corporation spun off the unprofitable casino, which filed for bankruptcy in 1998. It found the money to expand slightly, buying the Midtown Motor Inn, knocking it down, and clearing its access to Pacific Avenue.

In 2000, billionaire Carl Icahn purchased the casino. Icahn turned around the struggling Stratosphere in Las Vegas before selling it in 2007, and it was initially hoped that he could work similar magic with the Sands.

But, under a succession of leaderships, the Sands continued to struggle until, in September 2006, Icahn sold it to Pinnacle Entertainment. Pinnacle closed the casino on November 11, 2006, ending the Brighton/Sands' 26 year run. The company planned an unnamed mega-project that would have encompassed the former Sands and Traymore sites.

The Sands went out with a bang with an October 18, 2007 implosion. Hopes were high that its replacement would help bring Atlantic City to a new level. In a sense, it did. As the seriousness of the slowdown in gaming revenues became apparent, though, Pinnacle mothballed the planned mega-resort, leaving a derelict lot where a functioning, if not always profitable, casino hotel once stood. After canceling its casino in 2010, Pinnacle held onto the land for a few years, before selling it to a group of local investors who have (as of 2015) yet to build anything on it.

The Sands is gone, with nothing having replaced it, but few who worked or played there will soon forget its momentous life as an Atlantic City casino pioneer.

Better People Place

After Nevada allowed publicly traded corporations to legally own and operate casinos, hotel companies became intrigued by the possibilities. Hilton Hotels was an early adopter, buying the Flamingo and what became the Las Vegas Hilton from Kirk Kerkorian in 1971. Another hospitality giant, Holiday Inn, originally deferred from investing in casinos. But a series of decisions would see the company buy one of the industry's most respected names, build one of Atlantic City's strongest-performing casinos, and create an international gaming empire.

Holiday decided to buy into casinos after seeing the growth of gaming in Nevada and its potential in Atlantic City. It made its first move in 1978, when the company joined with Los Angeles-based L & M Walter Enterprises, in a company known as Marina Associates to build a casino hotel, not surprisingly, on 14 acres of land Walter had acquired on the Atlantic City marina.

As work on the property—designed by acclaimed casino architect Martin Stern, Jr.—continued, Holiday acquired Harrah's Inc., the company founded by Bill Harrah in 1937. Holiday folded their gaming operations (the marina project and a partially owned Las Vegas casino) into the Harrah's organization. The under-construction marina casino became Harrah's Marina. As Resorts, Caesars Boardwalk Regency, and Bally's Park Place opened to long lines and full coffers, work continued.

Harrah's Marina opened on November 23, 1980. In addition to a 506-room hotel, the resort had 44,000 square feet of gaming space. In early 1981, the addition of the 1,000-seat Broadway by the Bay Theater allowed the company to add nearly 200 slot machines to its floor.

In keeping with Bill Harrah's management philosophy, the Atlantic City casino would cater to the broad middle class of gamblers, eschewing both high rollers and grind players. This was reflected in the property's design: From the start, it had a 2,400-space attached parking garage, something that other casinos took years to develop. Unlike other Atlantic City casinos, it did not develop a bus marketing program, but instead relied on a steady stream of longer-playing, wealthier drive-in customers. As it advertised, Harrah's was "the Better People Place," suggesting that "better" people patronized its casino. The strategy worked: Harrah's became one of the city's better-earning properties. Holiday was so confident in the Marina's ultimate success that in 1981 it bought out its partner, L & M Walter.

Harrah's Marina quickly became the most profitable casino in Harrah's system, which was at the time the country's largest gaming enterprise, generating nearly as much revenue as its three Nevada properties combined. But the company did not rest on its laurels. A 1984 expansion brought a 107-slip marina to the resort, letting would-be gamblers dock right at the casino. The following year, an $80 million expansion project added the 224-suite Atrium Tower, three new restaurants, a cabaret, and more casino space.

The casino continued to innovate, holding a three-day wine tasting—the first for city casinos—in 1984. Bally's Park Place had previously been denied permission to hold a similar event. The wine tasting only came to pass after four months of negotiations, which shows the excessive hand gaming regulators wielded at the time. In 1985, it offered the city's first smoke-free gaming tables; it also rolled out Atlantic City's first $5, $25, and $100 denomination slot machines, opening up an entirely new category of premium slot player. Those kinds of moves paid off; in 1986, the Marina was the city's third highest-grossing casino, behind only the larger Bally's Park Place and Steve Wynn's Golden Nugget.

The Marina was initially going to be only one of Harrah's Atlantic City casinos, and for a time Harrah's operated at Trump Plaza on the Boardwalk as well. But with the dissolution of that partnership in 1986 and the stabilization of the market, Harrah's accepted that the Marina was its only bet in the city. So, in 1990, keeping with a company-wide policy to name its casinos after their hometowns (Harrah's Del Rio, for example, became Harrah's Laughlin), Harrah's Marina became Harrah's Atlantic City.

In the 1990s, Harrah's Atlantic City continued to make money for its rapidly-expanding parent company, which in 1995 was spun off from Holiday successor Promus as Harrah's Entertainment. In 1996, it added more gaming space, followed by the 410-room Marina Tower. But this $81-million expansion was just the beginning. Countering perhaps the recent announcement of the Borgata, Harrah's disclosed its own plans to grow in early 2000; it added 450 rooms in the 25-story Bayview Tower, which was completed in 2002. The Bayview soared over the 16 stories of the three earlier towers, giving Harrah's a more vertical presence by the bay and more than 1,600 guest rooms.

Harrah's was expanding in other ways. In 1997, the company brought Showboat, Inc. for $519 million. The purchase gave Harrah's its own Boardwalk property at last. Also in that year, Harrah's debuted Total Rewards, a cross-property loyalty program that has been credited with spurring much of the company's subsequent growth.

The Borgata's success proved that a large casino with higher-level amenities could attract players, and Harrah's pivoted itself to follow. The most visible result of a $550 million expansion that began in 2006 was the Friedmutter and Associates-designed 44-story Waterfront Tower, which opened in 2008 with 951 guest rooms and 13 suites. This soaring tower rivaled the Borgata, as did the new amenities, designed by Paul Steelman Associates: a year-round glass-domed, 80,000-gallon swimming hole called The Pool, the Elizabeth Arden Red Door Spa, and a host of new restaurants and retail attractions, including a food court with local tastes, including Ventnor's (arguably) finest eatery, Sack'O'Subs.

The expansion came as Atlantic City was struggling, but it helped to transform Harrah's into the perennial second top-earning casino in town, trailing only the Borgata.

Harrah's did not stop there. The Waterfront Convention Center, opened in 2015, added 100,000 square feet of meeting space to the resort, creating what the company called "the largest hotel-conference center complex from Baltimore to Boston." With gaming still in decline, the new convention space seemed the best way to reliably fill Harrah's nearly 2,600 hotel rooms.

The new convention center should help to ensure that Harrah's Atlantic City is in the forefront as Atlantic City transitions into its next phase. Harrah's led Atlantic City in the Age of Slots; it is only fitting that it is staking a claim to the non-gaming future.

Touch of Gold

Casino magnate Steve Wynn is universally credited with remaking the casino resort in Las Vegas with the 1989 opening of the Mirage. But many people forget that he made a huge impact in Atlantic City with his short-lived Golden Nugget in the early 1980s. If Wynn had stayed in Atlantic City, the past 30 years might have played out quite differently.

Stephen A. Wynn's father ran a bingo hall in Maryland, and from a young age Wynn was fascinated by the business of gambling. In 1967 he moved to Las Vegas and bought a share in the Frontier, a small Strip casino, where he learned the casino business as a slot manager and assistant credit manager.

After the Frontier was sold to billionaire Howard Hughes, Wynn dabbled in a few businesses before returning to the casino industry at downtown's Golden Nugget. The casino was then a rather bland downtown gambling hall without a hotel. In 1973, after a large stock purchase, he became president and chairman of the board of the casino. Once in power, he cleaned house, firing thieving or dishonest employees, and dramatically remodeling the casino. Within a year, Wynn had quadrupled the Golden Nugget's profits. Soon, he would build several hotel towers and make the casino downtown's finest.

With the legalization of gaming in Atlantic City, Wynn set his sights on the East Coast. He first came to town in June of 1978. Wearing a Willie Nelson t-shirt and draw-string pants, he scoped out real estate incognito. Walking into the lobby of the small Strand Motel on Boston Avenue and the Boardwalk, he offered owner Manny Solomon $8.5 million for it. After Solomon made a few calls and confirmed Wynn's identity, they shook on it. Steve Wynn was now in the Atlantic City casino business.

Wynn chose to build another Golden Nugget and planned it from the ground up as a Victorian era, white-and-gold luxury hotel. Architect Joel Bergman, assisted by a young Paul Steelman, executed Wynn's ideas for the property, with Henry Conversano acting as interior designer.

When the Golden Nugget opened on December 9, 1980, it became Atlantic City's sixth casino. It had 506 rooms—just barely over the 500 mandated by the Casino Control Act—and, at 40,000 square feet, a relatively small casino. Only the Sands had fewer table games. Yet the Golden Nugget was a hit: in 1981, it ranked fourth in total revenues despite its small size, out-earning, per capita, bigger casinos like Resorts and Bally's Park Place. More than either of those, the Golden Nugget demonstrated that a smart operator could make lots of money in Atlantic City.

By 1983, the Golden Nugget became the city's top-earning casino, with over $262 million in revenues for the year. Considering that the hotel had cost $160 million to build, it is clear that Wynn had scored an unqualified success.

The Golden Nugget was such a popular stop for gamblers because of Wynn's personality: he appeared in the Nugget's television commercials (in one, he famously brought headliner Frank Sinatra extra towels) and he was a constant presence on the casino floor, greeting employees and patrons alike.

Wynn earned himself a place in the annals of Atlantic City history when, one year, he gave a car to each of his managers. This exceptional bonus spread the message that Wynn rewarded good service. With his balance sheet firmly in the black, he had good reason to be pleased.

Success at the Nugget convinced Wynn that Atlantic City was a profitable market. He began planning a larger, more elegant casino in the Marina District. But he soon became annoyed by what he regarded as cumbersome regulatory restrictions. Though he held onto his marina tract, in 1986 he reached an agreement to sell the Golden Nugget for $440 million to the Bally Manufacturing, which already owned Bally's Park Place down the Boardwalk.

It's intriguing to wonder what would have happened if Wynn had not become so disenchanted with New Jersey regulators in 1986. He went on to open The Mirage on the Las Vegas Strip in 1989, sparking a building boom that transformed Las Vegas from a polyester playground to a hip destination resort. Ten years after it opened, the Las Vegas Strip once again surpassed Atlantic City in gaming revenue, and it never looked back.

If Wynn had been given a freer hand in Atlantic City, it's a good guess that an "Atlantic City Mirage" would have triggered a similar boom by the shore. Had that happened, Atlantic City, not Las Vegas, might be the nation's leading casino destination today.

After the sale became official in 1987, Bally changed its new casino's name to Bally's Grand. Trading on the high-end gloss Wynn had brought to the property, the company planned to market the former Golden Nugget to its premium customers while concentrating its mass marketing on the gigantic Park Place. It seemed a good plan, but without the Wynn touch, the property drifted from its roots.

In 1996, Hilton Hotels bought Bally Entertainment (the company which by that time owned the Bally's casino properties) for $3 billion in what was then the largest acquisition in casino industry history. Hilton, which had been licensed in New Jersey in 1991, got the chance at last to put its name on an Atlantic City casino when it renamed The Grand, turning it into the Atlantic City Hilton, and adding a new hotel tower, perpendicular to the original. The addition brought the property's total room count to 800.

In 1998, Hilton spun off its gaming operations into a new company, Park Place Entertainment. The following year, Park Place bought three Caesars casinos, including Caesars Atlantic City, from Starwood, tying the Hilton into an even larger casino empire.

Yet there would be more consolidation. In 2005, Park Place, which had since been renamed Caesars Entertainment, announced plans to merge with Harrah's Entertainment. The Caesars/Harrah's merger would have left the resulting super-giant with five Atlantic City casinos: Harrah's, Showboat, Caesars, Bally's Park Place (with the Claridge), and the Hilton.

To mollify anti-trust concerns, Caesars sold the Hilton to Colony Capital, which had, in 2001, bought Resorts. Colony now owned properties at each end of the Boardwalk and a small network of casinos throughout the nation, including Las Vegas.

Colony combined the management of their two far-flung Atlantic City casinos under one executive umbrella, but proved unequal to the task. An ambitious billion-dollar expansion plan, announced in 2007, would have more than doubled the size of the resort's casino—by now the smallest in town—and added 1,000 hotel rooms.

The expansion was canceled the following year amidst Atlantic City's slumping gaming revenues. The Hilton was particularly hard-hit by the slowdown. By 2010, the property which, under Steve Wynn's guidance, had been the top performer in town, was trailing all other casinos in most meaningful financial metrics.

The casino's poor performance was highlighted when, in June 2011, it lost the right to call itself the Atlantic City Hilton. Hilton Hotels and Resorts terminated the licensing agreement that had allowed the casino to use the Hilton name despite no longer being owned or operated by the company or an affiliate. The de-naming seemed to catch the property's owners flat-footed; it was hastily renamed the "ACH," much like Colony's other Hilton casino, the Las Vegas Hilton, would become the LVH after its licensing agreement was canceled the following year.

The ACH, predictably, struggled, showing little attitude, charisma, or heart. In February 2012, Colony renamed the property the Atlantic Club, debuting a retro logo that, it hoped, would make a connection with local and less affluent gamblers. The casino was streamlined, table limits lowered, and restaurant prices dropped to attract more players who would make up in numbers what they lacked in individual bankrolls.

It was an inspired move that may have worked in a better economy, but it was clear early on that the Atlantic Club had little better prospects than the ACH. Colony continued to look for a buyer. Though revenues increased under the new direction the property had taken, the Atlantic Club's assorted liabilities were simply unsustainable. The Rational Group, owner of the PokerStars online gaming website, offered $15 million in the spring of 2013 for the property, but that purchase dissolved in the fall after a fair bit of acrimony. Rational was, presumably, not interested so much in the casino itself as it was in the wedge its ownership would give them to New Jersey's new online gaming market. In any event, the company never took possession of the property.

The Rational Group offer was the Atlantic Club's last chance. Colony was unable to find a buyer willing to take on the casino as a going concern and unable to continue operating the property at a loss; it announced plans to close and sell the once-promising resort to Caesars Entertainment and Tropicana Entertainment—between them owners of five Atlantic City casinos—for $23.4 million. Tropicana got the Atlantic Club's casino games and player database, while Caesars received the property itself, which it did not plan to reopen.

In May 2014, Caesars sold the Atlantic Club and its surrounding land to TJM Properties, a Florida-based company that had recently purchased the Claridge from Caesars. As with the Claridge, TJM was content to run its new possession without a casino, although, unlike the Claridge, it did not make any apparent moves toward renovating or reopening the shuttered Atlantic Club.

In December, TJM announced plans to sell the former Atlantic Club and its environs to Endeavor Property Group, a Devon, Pennsylvania-based residential and mixed-use property owner. Some speculated that Endeavour planned to turn the former casino into timeshare or senior housing, but in July 2015 the company revealed that it sought to transform the site into a hotel-theme-park-dining complex with both family-friendly and adult entertainment options.

Endeavor's plan, which as of this writing (summer 2015) has just been announced, may be the latest transformation for the property that got its start when Steve Wynn came to the Boardwalk, looking to buy in. Wynn transformed the site—and the city—for a time, and, with luck, whatever replaces his one-time casino masterwork will help to define the city's next evolution.

Boardwalk Bunny

Even before casino gaming was legalized, Hugh Hefner's Playboy had its eye on a New Jersey casino. All the way back in 1972, when legalized gambling ideas were first floated, company officials expressed interest in a casino at its existing club in McAfee, Sussex County. Since the company ran four casinos in Britain, it was thought that the company would be a natural in the American gambling arena.

After the 1976 referendum allowing casinos in Atlantic City, Playboy shifted gears. In the following year, Playboy Clubs International president Victor Lownes testified at a public hearing that his company was prepared to spend $32 million on a casino project. He further urged that the "English system" be adopted—casinos would be limited to 16 hours and barred from offering players drinks at tables. Casinos would be forbidden from offering live entertainment, and credit would be tightly restricted.

Luckily, Lownes didn't carry the day—Atlantic City's casino laws, though stricter than those of Nevada, were decidedly more liberal than Britain's. But his attitude foreshadowed future problems the Playboy casino would have.

The casino ran into obstacles before it was off the drawing board. The Federal Aviation Administration blocked Playboy from building a 33-story hotel tower on its Convention Hall-adjacent plot, claiming thatit would impede air traffic at Bader Field.

In response, the building's height was reduced to 22 stories. Las Vegas architect Martin Stern, Jr., who built the Las Vegas Hilton and MGM Grand, designed a green glass tower with a three-level casino and a Playboy Key Club, among other amenities.

As work progressed on the casino, Playboy Enterprises' fiscal health slipped. With its clubs and hotels not performing up to par, the company was counting on a tremendous boost from its Atlantic City casino. But to get the financing needed to build the now $135 million casino, it accepted the Elsinore corporation as a partner.

The Playboy was issued a temporary permit on April 4, 1981, with the proviso that several Playboy International executives remain out of operations. At the time, Playboy's London casino was at the center of a Scotland Yard investigation.

The casino officially opened on April 14, following four days of play money gambling. Though the casino showed a profit over the summer, a cloud hung over Playboy's prospects for a permanent license. The company was forced to sell its British casinos, and Casino Control Commission officials questioned both Playboy and Elsinore's "suitability" for licensing.

In the end, the CCC issued a license to Elsinore but denied one to Playboy. Playboy then agreed to sell its share in the casino to Elsinore, who re-named the resort the Atlantis—a poor choice, when one thinks about the original fate of the Lost Continent. By the summer of 1984, Playboy Bunnies were out, the giant bunny logo on the crest of the building replaced by a seashell. The age of Atlantis had begun.

Almost from the start, the casino took on water. Among the reasons cited for the property's difficulties was its three-floor casino design; although other properties, like Caesars Atlantic City, were able to make multi-level gaming floors work, Atlantis was simply on too cramped a space to run well. Absent the Playboy mystique, there was little to set the property apart. In November 1985, it filed for bankruptcy, and continued to struggle for nearly five more years.

Atlantis finally sank when, in the spring of 1989, Donald Trump bought the casino for a mere $63 million. As gaming regulations limited any one operator to three casinos, Trump closed the casino and operated the property as the hotel-only Trump Regency, using it to house overflow from the adjoining (on the other side of Boardwalk Hall) Trump Plaza. The two properties were connected by a walkway that passed through an upper level of Boardwalk Hall.

In May 1996, after a regulatory change allowed him to own four casinos, Trump reopened the property as Trump's World Fair at Trump Plaza, with the Plaza's management team running both properties.

But this world's fair was no cash cow; three years later, Trump closed the casino and hotel, citing its failure to turn a profit, and demolished it, promising to build a newer, more fantastic resort in its place, using both the World's Fair land and Boardwalk Hall's west hall. He would spend $750 million to build something that would compete with the coming wave of super-properties; Steve Wynn had announced plans to build a Las Vegas-quality megaresort in the Marina District, and this would be The Donald's response.

"A fitting tribute to the millennium," he called the planned development, and, in the end, he was right: a vacant lot replaced what had once been a working casino hotel. Already burdened with over $1 billion in debt, Trump did not secure financing to realize his ambitions; in any event, Steve Wynn, partially because of Trump's spirited opposition to his request for the Brigantine connector project, did not return to town anyway.

Trump's plans for the site—which he eventually revealed to be a 62-story, 4,600-room hotel casino—perhaps came to naught because of the bad fortunes of his other Atlantic City casinos. When, in 2005, Trump Hotels and Casino Resorts entered bankruptcy, he agreed to auction the site to satisfy THCR creditors. Trump didn't want to let the land go, however; he placed a $25 million bid.

This, however, was one deal Trump couldn't perfect. He was outbid for the site by builder Bruce Toll, who paid $25.15 million for it. Toll, whose father had owned the Howard Johnson's that eventually became Caesars Atlantic City, initially planned to build condominiums on the site but in 2011, he paid $5.5 million to lift a deed restriction that had barred the site from use as a casino hotel, fueling speculation that he would build a gaming property there. As of 2015, he had repositioned the property for a more modest use: a retail shopping complex that was well under construction by the summer.

Whatever the parcel's eventual use, the original casino occupant, the Playboy, is its own indelible chapter of Atlantic City history.

Smaller and Friendlier

The Claridge has the distinction of holding three records in Atlantic City history. Opened in 1930, it was the last major hotel built until the casino era. Until that time, it was the tallest building on the Boardwalk. And, when it reopened as a casino in 1981, it was the first (and only) classic hotel to transition into the gaming years with both its original structure and identity (mostly) intact.

The Hotel Claridge had the worst timing in Atlantic City construction history, at least until Revel. The $5 million hotel opened a year after the Great Depression started—hardly a positive beginning. It barely made it into the casino era, having been closed in 1973 and shopped unsuccessfully for several years.

The coming of casinos, of course, boosted the empty hotel's value. A group of investors led by Daniel Rizk, a New Jersey developer, and Francis D'Addario, a Connecticut industrialist, bought the Claridge in 1977 for $3.5 million. They planned to spend another $25 million updating and expanding the 400-room hotel. The latter was crucial; without at least 500 "first class" rooms, the hotel would not be licensed to conduct gambling.

By 1979, D'Addario had emerged as the leader of the Claridge. Nicknamed "Hi-Ho," D'Addario was no stranger to public attention: he slapped the "Hi-Ho" name on the buildings and trucks of his many construction-related businesses and was planning a "Hi-Ho Promenade" mall in Milford, Connecticut. By that time, D'Addario had partnered with Del Webb, operators of the Sahara, Mint, and other Nevada casinos: Del Webb would design the casino and manage it on a fee basis. Del Webb, which was also planning to build the Sahara casino near Albany Avenue and the Boardwalk, had no trouble taking on the additional work; in Las Vegas, it owned both the Mint and Sahara casino hotels, so running two operations was nothing new.

D'Addario was supremely confident that his "Hi-Ho Claridge Hotel Casino" would be Atlantic City's runaway success, though his only gambling background was a 5 percent share of a company that operated three jai alai frontons in Connecticut. "Ninety-nine percent of my businesses are successes," he told the *New York Times* in March 1979. "I'll have to stumble badly to miss in Atlantic City."

Del Webb joined D'Addario as more than a manager, taking a 50 percent stake in the project, whose costs had ballooned far in excess of the $25 million he had originally forecast. D'Addario had turned to Del Webb because of the company's expertise in casino gaming— it had been running Nevada casinos since 1962—but this history turned into a liability. Shortly before the property's scheduled July 1981 opening, the Division of Gaming Enforcement insisted that Del Webb should not be given even a temporary permit to manage the casino, citing a federal indictment for alleged kickbacks stemming from the 1975 construction of an addition to Las Vegas's Aladdin casino. Del Webb was barred from managing the casino at all.

To meet the state's requirement of 500 first-class hotel rooms, Del Webb added a (nearly) matching red brick wing to the Pacific Avenue side of the Claridge, complementing its original architecture.

The Claridge did open on July 20, 1981, but without Del Webb's guidance quickly foundered. In November 1981, Del Webb was acquitted of the federal charges, paving the way for its possible licensure. In pleading for its license, Del Webb executives asserted that they had removed executives responsible for past irregularities and that, in its absence, the Claridge was in dire straits.

Rejecting a Division of Gaming Enforcement demand that Del Webb remove former chairman Robert Johnson, the Casino Control Commission awarded the Claridge—with Del Webb as operators—a permanent license in July 1982, one year after its opening.

The Claridge, whose casino was less than 30,000 square feet big, pitched itself as "Atlantic City with style," an apparently unwelcoming approach, as it lost $30 million in 1982. Del Webb countered by expanding the casino, adding 150 slot machines and several table games, as well as a new deli and lounge. The casino also hired Yankee great Mickey Mantle as a greeter, a move not without controversy: Major League Baseball Commission Bowie Kuhn insisted Mantle resign his position with the Bronx Bombers before sullying himself in the casino business.

The expansion didn't quite turn the trick—the Claridge still lost $21 million in 1983—but Del Webb was optimistic enough about the property's chances that it bought D'Addario and his partners out, assuming full ownership of the casino. Still, the Claridge continued to lose money, and Del Webb sold the Claridge to a group of passive investors, retaining a long-term management contract..

The Claridge's struggles were not for lack of trying. It staged a series of Broadway shows in an effort to stand out from other casino's entertainment, and in early 1986 started to offer complimentary food, drinks, and entertainment to all table players, but just premium ones. This expansion of casino giveaways was an attempt to buy business, and one that helped push other casinos to match. Ultimately, giving too much away led a host of casinos into trouble.

Choosing to refocus on its core real estate business, in early 1988 Del Webb announced that it would sell its casino operations, including the Claridge.

By 1989, the Claridge was making a pitch for "pure gamblers." Other Atlantic City casinos, it told gamblers in a full-page *Win Magazine* ad, were all about "the flash, the entertainment, the shows." But not the Claridge. There, "gambling is Numero Uno. Period." No matter how big, or how small, the casino asserted, a gambler would feel home at the Claridge, where its smaller size translated into better service. "The Claridge...is more like a private club. Friendly, intimate. You can hear yourself think."

This didn't translate into higher revenues; the Claridge was for most of the 1980s the second worst-performing casino in town after the Atlantis, and it moved into the basement after the Atlantis closed in 1989. Yet the Claridge did report modest profits until 1996, when a series of unfortunate events—including the deaths of two elderly women after they drove their car through a wall in the Claridge's new self-park garage and plunged six stories—drove the casino to the brink of bankruptcy. It was considered a possible takeover target for Hilton Hotels.

The Claridge held on, but in August 1999 announced that it had missed a debt payment and would file for bankruptcy. In 2001, after besting Sands owner Carl Icahn, Bally's Atlantic City owner Park Place Entertainment bought the Claridge, folding its casino and hotel operations into those of its larger neighbor. Though its tower still stood high, the Claridge ceased to exist as an independent casino hotel.

Park Place, and later Caesars Entertainment, gradually reduced the casino footprint of the venerable hotel, eventually operating it as the non-casino "Claridge Tower" of Bally's. That changed when, in 2014, Florida-based TJM properties bought the Claridge, agreeing to operate it as a casino-less hotel.

There was one fewer casino on the Boardwalk, but the Claridge—a product of the worst years of the Depression—had a new life. It was the latest chapter for the city's smallest, and maybe pluckiest, casino.

Tropical Retreat

One of Atlantic City's biggest—and at times most controversial—casino resorts, has a history that spans the city's high and low points.

The Tropicana stands on the site of the Ambassador Hotel at Brighton Avenue and the Boardwalk. The Ambassador, which opened in 1919 with 400 rooms at a cost of $4 million, was for years the "monarch of the Boardwalk." The hotel was successful, and almost immediately added a 400-room expansion. For many years, it was the largest hotel in Atlantic City.

Fourteen stories high, the Ambassador guarded the Downbeach flank of Atlantic City's hotel corridor along with the President, which would open nearby in 1926. In the early 1920s, it was one of a chain of Ambassadors, including hotels in New York and Los Angeles.

Yet the ensuing decades were not kind to the Ambassador. In 1966, the hotel closed. In mid-1970s local hotel man Martin Ashner bought the empty Ambassador and contemplated renovating and reopening it as a casino hotel before selling it, and the nearby Deauville, to Ramada Inns for $35 million.

Ramada, a nationally-known hospitality chain that sought to dominate the mid-priced hotel market, was spurred by the legalization of casino gaming in Atlantic City to make the purchase. In late 1978 company executives announced plans for the Phoenix, a $70 million casino that would include 549 guest rooms and a 60,000 square-foot casino.

The Phoenix truly would rise from the ashes of old Atlantic City: Ramada executives planned to give the Ambassador a less-than-extreme makeover, refurbishing the 60-year-old structure. This would allow them to get the casino open—and revenue flowing—as quickly as possible. The company planned to build a second, 1,000 room "Phoenix-class" hotel next door, presumably if the first proved a success.

But the Casino Control Commission vetoed Ramada's initial design in mid-1979, arguing that the city had enough refurbished hotels: only by building a completely new structure could Ramada deliver the kind of first-class hotel that voters had been promised in 1976.

Ramada executives were predictably chagrined at being held to a different standard than the operators behind Resorts International, Caesars Boardwalk Regency, and the Claridge, all of which were in repurposed structures. A compromise, in which Ramada stripped the Ambassador down to its steel skeleton and built a modern hotel around the frame of the existing one, truly satisfied no one but allowed construction to begin at last in October 1979.

Two months later, Ramada Inns bought one of the Las Vegas Strip's most famous casinos, the Tropicana, for $70 million. Seeking to capitalize on this established brand, the company renamed its Atlantic City project the Tropicana Hotel and Casino.

The Tropicana was initially slated to open in June of 1981, but construction delays kept pushing back the opening date. Even before the dice started rolling, Ramada had difficulties with its property; as opposed to catering to the mid-market customers that its hotels did, the company insisted on chasing more affluent customers.

The casino finally opened on November 26, 1981, and struggled. With a smaller than originally projected casino, the Tropicana posted an operating loss over its first five weeks. The next year brought no improvement, as the Trop continued to struggle. In part to escape the mountain of debt the company had incurred in building the Atlantic City casino (final costs were nearly $400 million), the company began selling many of its hotels.

The Tropicana's appearance, too, left something to be desired. Tasked by the Casino Control Commission with building a modern hotel, Ramada erected something that looked like a sci-fi prison block: alternating bands of white concrete and black windows did little to add pizzazz to a squat, nearly featureless building.

Yet there was hope. A new parking garage in 1983 helped the casino revenues grow at nearly twice the rate of the market, allowing the Tropicana to post a profit for the first time in its history. The

Atlantic City property became the star of Ramada's portfolio, lifting the company itself to profitability. By 1987, it was generating the bulk of Ramada's revenues.

In the mid-1980s, executives began planning for expansion and retrenchment. In an increasingly competitive market, they needed to differentiate the Tropicana. In late 1988, Ramada unveiled a new 500-room hotel tower across Brighton Avenue, expanded casino space, and a two-acre indoor theme park named Tivoli Pier. Inexplicably, they chose to drop the storied "Tropicana" name in favor of the unappetizing "TropWorld," most likely in an attempt to trade off of the success of theme parks like Disney World.

The following year Ramada sold off its hotel division, spinning its casinos into a new entity named Aztar, a name chosen to recall the grandeur of the Aztec empire. TropWorld was the chief revenue-producing asset of the company.

But the would-be Aztec emperors of the Boardwalk had difficulty remaining focused. Underutilized capacity continued to plague the casino; though it made a greater percentage of its profit from slots than most other casinos, it had lower-than-average win-per-slot numbers. Throughout the early 1990s, TropWorld continued to chase high-end table play, instead of focusing on value-driven slot customers.

The pursuit of premium players inspired the casino's next expansion. In 1996, 600 new rooms in a tower perched on top of the parking garage opened, and each of the existing 1,000 guest rooms was renovated. A new poker room and an Asian games room, the Jade Palace, were designed to lessen the casino's dependence on slot players.

This expansion reversed the previous six years of history. The Tivoli Pier amusement area was deemed expendable and replaced with gaming space. Six luxurious high-roller suites underscored the new desire to attract high-end play. Finally, to cement the "elegant and luxurious" new image the property was to project, the casino's name was changed back to "Tropicana."

These additions gave the Tropicana the state's largest hotel (1,624 rooms) and casino and drove revenue increases across the board. But before all of the blue tape was even down, the Tropicana began acquiring land for another expansion across Pacific Avenue from the original casino building. Original plans called for a combination of more hotel rooms, a major entertainment venue, convention facilities, and new parking. Depending on how Atlantic City grew over the next decade, Aztar executives hoped to tailor a new Tropicana that would capitalize on the market's growth.

By this time, the Atlantic City Tropicana had become, without a doubt, Aztar's flagship property. Its Las Vegas property was in holding pattern, with major improvements and expansions deferred while the company considered a comprehensive redevelopment plan.

In 2000, Aztar finally announced more concrete plans for expanding the Atlantic City Tropicana. Ironically, the company looked to Las Vegas for guidance. Seeing the higher rate of non-gaming revenues Las Vegas Strip properties enjoyed compared to Atlantic City casinos, Aztar decided to attempt to penetrate the market for overnight visitors who would come for additional non-casino attractions.

The company slated the expansion's opening for 2003, which would coincide with the debut of the Borgata, the marina district resort that was, not by accident, also attempting to "grow the market" for bigger-spending customers.

While planning this more luxurious expansion, the Tropicana didn't neglect its traditional, day-tripping, slot-playing customers. A 2001 promotion, the Chicken Challenge, allowed slot club members the chance to test their mettle by playing Tic-Tac-Toe against a Leghorn hen, with $10,000 at stake. The game was incredibly popular, with lines as long as 30 minutes. Although the chicken only lost a reported five times in the three years that the promotion continued at the Trop, there was never a shortage of challengers.

Ground broke on the expansion in April 2002. Work was halted, however, by a catastrophic collapse in the under-construction parking garage that claimed the lives of four construction workers and injured 20 more. Ultimately, the casino and its construction partners were issued citations for improper working procedures, and in 2007 they agreed on a $101 million settlement with the families of those killed and injured in the mishap.

The accident slowed work on the project, and other developments proved less than favorable for the casino's prospects. The threat of Pennsylvania and Maryland legalizing slot machines cast doubts on the growth potential of Atlantic City, at a time when the Tropicana was betting $245 million on the city's future.

In November 2004, the Tropicana finally unveiled its expansion, which included a Latin-themed shopping and dining center, the

Quarter. Connected to the existing casino by a skybridge, the Quarter featured a new parking garage, nine restaurants (including Las Vegas favorites like Red Square, The Palm, and P.F. Chang's), 26 shops, and the 500-room Havana Tower. With 2,129 guest rooms, the Tropicana was once again the largest hotel in Atlantic City.

Aztar executives proclaimed the Quarter a success, but they would soon be facing a challenge more daunting than the conquistadors that had vanquished the Aztec empire: investment bankers with an appetite for mergers and acquisitions.

Throughout 2005, speculation about buyers for Aztar swirled throughout the city. In March 2006, the company entered into a merger agreement with Pinnacle Entertainment, a prominent riverboat operator. Pinnacle would acquire all Aztar stock for $38 a share. No sooner had the ink on the contract dried, however, than Colony Capital Acquisitions, a private equity firm that at one point owned the Atlantic City Hilton and Resorts, offered $41 a share.

Not to be outdone, Ameristar Casinos, another regional operator, chimed in with a $43 per share bid. By late April, Columbia Sussex, a private hospitality operator, had also entered the fray. The share price climbed to $48, and Columbia Sussex ultimately won the bidding war with a $50 per share offer.

Finally surrendering $2.75 billion for the Atlantic City and Las Vegas Tropicanas, as well as three smaller casinos, some industry analysts believed that Columbia Sussex had overpaid. Indeed, the company's subsequent administration of the Atlantic City casino was marked by cost-cutting measures that drew the ire of Local 54, a major casino union, and New Jersey regulators.

Columbia Sussex's administration of the property was questioned in the company's application for license renewal in 2007, and the company's refusal to demonstrate financial responsibility and "honesty and integrity" led the Casino Control Commission to deny the renewal, effectively taking the casino away from its owner.

In December 2007, the Commission appointed former state Supreme Court Justice Gary Stein as the property's conservator. Stein was charged with finding a buyer for the Tropicana. Originally, he hoped to receive as much as $1 billion for the casino (in fact, he rejected bids of $850 million and $950 million), but as the economic situation deteriorated in Atlantic City—and nationally—a buyer failed to materialize.

After nearly 18 months of limbo, former Sands owner Carl Icahn, in conjunction with other bondholders who together held $1.4 billion in Tropicana debt, acquired the property for a mere $200 million—$85 million less than the final cost of the Quarter expansion.

With its ownership finally stabilized, the Tropicana was at last free to look toward the future. Its new owner would be well advised to consider the casino's sometimes-profitable, sometimes-perilous, past.

Trump's Tower

Donald Trump's name today is practically synonymous with Atlantic City casinos—although his name is currently on only one of them, his larger-than-life personality has been part of the city for a generation. True to form, perhaps, "the Donald's" introduction to Atlantic City was anything but a sure thing.

In 1980, up-and-coming New York real estate developer Donald Trump began planning an Atlantic City hotel and casino. He obtained a lease on 4.5 acres next to the city's Convention Hall (today Boardwalk Hall) that year. But because of the difficulty of obtaining financing—interest rates were prohibitively high—and regulatory hurdles, the Trump organization did not start building for years.

In part, Trump was leery of building in Atlantic City because the Casino Control Commission had made casino development a gamble. Already, the gaming regulators had forced Caesars World's founders, Clifford and Stuart Perlman, to step down from their company before giving Caesars Boardwalk Regency (today Caesars Atlantic City) a license. Over the next few years, the Hilton company was denied a license after they'd built a casino (which Trump ultimately opened), and Hugh Hefner's regulatory problems torpedoed the Playboy casino; Trump was right to be wary.

Trump refused to turn so much as a shovel of dirt in Atlantic City until the Casino Control Commission voted yea or nay on his license. In March of 1982, he got his wish: in record time, the Commission voted to reserve a license for Trump. This took less than two hours; by contrast, hearings for the ill-starred Playboy dragged out for two months.

Yet Trump was still not ready to build. He didn't doubt his organization's prowess at building a top-quality hotel, but had no experience running a casino. He therefore went looking for a partner who would handle the casino end of the operation.

In the early 1980s, Holiday Inns, Inc. owned three casinos: Harrah's Marina in Atlantic City, Harrah's Reno, and Harrah's Lake Tahoe. Seeing a cost-effective way to expand in the growing Atlantic City market, the company agreed to partner with Trump.

Trump proved himself a formidable negotiator. In return for Trump supplying the land to build and his own know-how, Harrah's agreed to pay him to build the casino, give him an equal share in any profits, and not hold him liable for any possible operational losses for the property's first five years. This was just one of many negotiations that made Trump a legendary master of "the art of the deal."

In November 1982, work on the casino, now called Harrah's at Trump Plaza, started at last. Designed by architect David Jacobson, it had a narrow footprint, bringing a Manhattan flavor to the shore.

The casino—which cost $210 million to build—opened on May 14, 1984. Advertised as being 39 stories high, this was the tallest building in the city, and its 60,000 square-foot casino was then the city's largest. With 123 table games and 1,734 slot machines, it looked to be a money-making machine.

The casino's debut was not without problems. Less than an hour after opening, a smoke alarm forced the build's evacuation. In addition, flaws in the casino's slot accounting system forced the closure of several slot machines.

The opening glitches foreshadowed a troubled relationship between Trump and Harrah's factions at the new resort. The Harrah's team wanted to focus on middle-market customers, an area of the company's strength. The Trump side preferred to court high rollers, and did not build a parking garage, a necessary component of the Harrah's plan.

Yet there were some positives at the Plaza. An enclosed walkway connected the casino to Convention Hall, and a series of events there, from heavyweight boxing to professional wrestling, attracted business to the casino. Soon, some observers were wondering if Harrah's and Trump executives might be climbing into the ring themselves.

Behind the scenes, Trump and Harrah's began wrangling over the property's name; Harrah's wanted to promote it as "Harrah's," but Trump insisted on calling it the Trump casino. Trump won the argument: five months after the opening, the casino was renamed "Trump Plaza."

Tensions between the two sides reached a boiling point in April 1985 when the Trump Organization bought the Atlantic City Hilton Hotel, Harrah's marina neighbor, after Hilton was denied a gaming license. This made Trump a direct competitor to Harrah's bread-and-butter marina district casino. Three months later, Harrah's Marina launched a more aggressive advertising campaign, dropping its former slogan ("The other Atlantic City") and renaming itself "The Better Atlantic City."

In fact, Harrah's executives filed a lawsuit in federal court to have Trump's name removed from his new hotel, which he had dubbed Trump's Castle, on the grounds that a second Trump property would create confusion among customers. The suit also charged Trump with deliberately mismanaging the boardwalk property and refusing to build a parking garage in an effort to depress the casino's value.

When Donald Trump brushed off the suit as "disgraceful," Phil Satre, then president of Harrah's, claimed that Trump was attempting to engineer Harrah's into selling its share at a reduced price, or to buy Trump's share at an inflated price.

Trump charged that Harrah's was attempting the same thing, either by design or ineptitude.

"I gave them a Lamborghini," he told the New York Times, "and they didn't know how to turn on the key."

In September 1985, a federal judge sided with Trump, allowing him to keep his name on both casinos. Yet there was no reconciliation between the parties. Rumors continued to swirl that one group would buy out the other.

After months of maneuvering and speculation, in March 1986 Trump signed an agreement to buy Harrah's share in the Boardwalk casino. He immediately announced plans to spend $25 million building a parking garage and new suites at the Plaza.

With the purchase, Trump became the first organization to own more than one property outright in Atlantic City, with more than twice the casino space of his nearest rival. For the moment, he was the undisputed king of Atlantic City.

In 1997, Trump announced that he was going to sell his namesake Plaza, predicting that he would get $1 billion for the property. Unsurprisingly, no one offered him anywhere near that amount for the casino, whose performance had slid.

That sale did not go through, and Trump Plaza continued to slide as the market deteriorated. In 2013, a $20 million sale to a group that would have renovated the casino fell through. Deferred maintenance and closed restaurants did little to enhance the property's fortunes.

It wasn't surprising, then, that Trump Plaza could not adjust to the new realities of Atlantic City. Following the Atlantic Club, Showboat, and Revel, it became the fourth Atlantic City casino to close its doors on September 16, 2014.

Since then, no solid plans for the property's reuse—or even demolition—have emerged. Until someone rolls the dice again, the tower will stand as a silent testament to the city's decline.

By the Bay

The property that, in 2015, is called the Golden Nugget has perhaps the most circuitous—and most speculative—history of any Atlantic City casino, demonstrating the difficulties regulators placed before potential operators in the 1980s and the city's recent struggles.

The casino's origins date back to October 1978, when Hilton Hotels announced that it had bought an option on 22 acres of land in the Marina District, with the intention of building, with MGM Grand and Harrah's, three separately owned casino hotels. This cluster of new luxury properties would create a resort area over a mile from the Boardwalk.

Neither MGM nor Harrah's ultimately followed through with this plan, but Hilton forged ahead, announcing in 1979 a 1980 groundbreaking and 1983 opening date for the project. At the time, Hilton was a power in the gaming world: its wholly-owned Las Vegas Hilton and Flamingo Hilton casinos were consistently profitable, and it was in the midst of expanding both. Gaming accounted for over 40 percent of the company's total revenues, and opening in Atlantic City seemed like a sure way to boost the bottom line.

There were, however, complications. In early 1981, a spike in both interest rates and costs convinced Hilton to delay construction in Atlantic City indefinitely. The continuing growth of the city's casino market, though, convinced the company to move forward the following year on a 634-room hotel with a 46,500 square foot casino. With a wide selection of restaurants, a 500-seat showroom, and convention facilities, the Atlantic City Hilton was primed for future expansion—indeed, the resort's master plan called for as many as 2,000 rooms to be built in the future. Opening was scheduled for mid-1985.

The property opened on time, but Hilton was no longer its owner. In February the Casino Control Commission denied Hilton a license, accusing Hilton of links with figures associated with organized crime. With the $308 million building nearly complete, Hilton made the decision to sell the property rather than begin a protracted appeal process. Steve Wynn attempted to buy a controlling share in Hilton Hotels after Hilton turned down his bid for the Atlantic City property. Wynn's gambit failed, and Donald Trump, who had the previous year opened Harrah's Boardwalk at Trump Plaza, snapped up the Hilton for $320 million.

Trump called his new property Trump's Castle, quickly retheming the property with a generic medieval motif. Trump did try to make the most out of the Castle's proximity to the Frank S. Farley Marina, at one point stating his intention to build the world's largest gambling yacht and anchor it there.

Trump Plaza and the Taj Mahal were successful from day one, though each had persistent financial problems due to their debt. The Castle was not, and it struggled to find a place in the market.

In 1996, Trump sold the Castle to Trump Hotels and Casino Resorts for $490 million, putting Trump's four casinos (which included the Plaza and Taj Mahal as well a Gary, Indiana riverboat) under one corporate umbrella. Later that year, though, the Castle was for sale; Hard Rock International, which was in the process of building a Hard Rock Café at the Trump Taj Mahal, nearly bought the property for $325 million. Had the sale gone through, the Trump name would have come off the marquee, and the Hard Rock Atlantic City would have become a reality. Hard Rock planned to invest $50 million into an immediate refurbish that would have given the property a rock n' roll theme.

Yet the Castle continued to drag. In January 1997, Colony Capital offered to invest $125 million for a 51 percent share of the property, which Trump Hotels would continue to manage. With the money, the Castle would add 1,500 rooms, making it the city's largest casino hotel. But in March of that year the deal was canceled and Trump, chagrined at the tunnel project designed to ease access to Steve Wynn's planned Le Jardin casino resort, pulled the plug on the expansion.

Finding no suitors for the Castle, and with new competition on the horizon, Trump in 1997 gave the casino a $5 million refresh and rename (to Trump Marina), seeking to lure a younger crowd. The attempt was marginally successful, but with sliding gaming revenues and Trump's Atlantic City casinos filing bankruptcy in February 2009, the property was back on the market.

As early as 2008, New York-based Coastal Development had offered $316 million for the property, nearly matching Trump's original $320 million purchase price of 23 years earlier. Coastal hoped to re-theme the property as a Margaritaville. That deal was not consummated, and another agreement for Coastal to buy the property for $270 million collapsed in 2009. The following year, Coastal offered less than $75 million for the Marina, which by this time was the city's worst-performing casino. That deal, too, fell through.

In early 2011, though, a buyer finally emerged. In May of that year, Houston-based Landry's Restaurants, which had previously bought Golden Nugget casinos in Las Vegas and Laughlin, bought the Marina for $38 million.

For Trump, that was a less-than-artful deal: the casino, which was close to changing hands for $316 million only three years earlier, fetched only 12 percent of that price.

Landry's, led by chairman Tilman Fertitta, embarked on a $150 million renovation of the property, which brought several of the company's best-know restaurant brands, including Chart House and Vic & Anthony's Steakhouse, to the shore. The remake completely changed the look of the property's exterior and interior.

The remodel also returned the Golden Nugget name to Atlantic City, 24 years after Steve Wynn's Boardwalk casino became Bally's Grand. And, perhaps, a little of the Wynn charm rubbed off; as of 2015, the Golden Nugget was earning money like it never had before.

Started by Hilton, opened by Trump, and now returning a name from the city's glory years to the skyline, the Golden Nugget still stands tall by the bay.

Showboating by the Sea

The Showboat was an unlikely Las Vegas casino to expand beyond Nevada. Far away from the action of the Las Vegas Strip, the Showboat, opened in 1954, had long catered to two groups: Las Vegas locals and value-conscious travelers. The major attractions were bowling, inexpensive meals, and, for a time in the 1980s, tapings of the American Wrestling Association in the casino's Sports Pavilion. Yet the Showboat would eventually plant its flag as far as Australia— thanks to its success in Atlantic City.

In December 1983, Showboat announced that it had signed a 99-year lease with Resorts International on land adjacent to the Taj Mahal site, and that it would within a year, begin building a 500 to 700-room hotel, casino, and bowling alley on the site. The Showboat was part of a massive "Fantacity" complex that Resorts hoped to create: its casino, the under-construction Taj Mahal, the Showboat, and a reborn Steel Pier, linked by indoor bridges. Resorts sought to create a convention center and, eventually, add two non-casino hotels to the cluster. All of the casinos were eventually built, but they did not reach the critical mass originally intended.

From the start, the Showboat set out, nevertheless, to be something different. In a stark contrast with the under-construction Taj Mahal, which aspired to glitz and glamor even before its purchase by Donald Trump, the Showboat built its fortunes on bowling. A 60-lane, 24-hour bowling alley would, Showboat Atlantic City president Frank Modica told the *New York Times*, attract "middle America, the blue-collar workers, moms and pops and the kids." Unlike other casinos, the Showboat would not have headline entertainers, provide lavish comps for high rollers, or run an extensive bus marketing program.

It also planned a complementary child-care program, presumably so those moms and pops could bowl and gamble more freely.

The Showboat opened April 3, 1987, the 12th Atlantic City casino. Bob Hope presided over the opening ceremonies and entertained gamblers; trumpeter Al Hirt performed as well. The property's 60,000 square-foot casino, one of the city's largest, had 1,628 slot machines and 114 table games. The interior featured 40 murals painted by artist Wayne Olds and décor that provided a Victorian-era twist on New Orleans and the Mississippi.

The casino advertised eight restaurants with "prices that will remind you of the good old days," but the real attraction was bowling. Twenty local bowling leagues and both professional and amateur tournaments booked the lanes months in advance.

Showboat seemed to be doing everything wrong (few buses, no star entertainers, no lavish comps), but it did the most important thing absolutely right: it made money. After its first full month of operation, it out-earned all other casinos in slot win and was second only to Caesars in total win. Since it spent less per capita on comps and other expenses, the Showboat was more profitable than its competitors. Among those hurt most by the newcomer was Harrah's, which had built its business on the same customers that the Showboat was courting.

The Showboat didn't maintain its leadership of the market, but settled in as a comfortable middle-tier, well-managed casino. It didn't rest on its laurels, taking the first leap into operating a race book in 1993 when casino regulations were amended to allow them, and soon after beginning a major re-theming that transformed its look from Victorian to Mardi Gras.

Due in large part to its success in Atlantic City (which generated 80 percent of the company's income), Showboat, Inc. prospered in the early 1990s, making it a takeover target late in the decade. Many suitors were mentioned for the company, which was attractive chiefly because of its East Chicago riverboat and the Atlantic City Showboat. In December 1997, Harrah's Entertainment bought the company for $1.2 billion. It almost immediately sold the Las Vegas Showboat; the Atlantic City branch was the big prize.

Harrah's made changes to the Showboat's winning formula, closing its trademark bowling alley in 2000. In 2003, the property opened the 544-room Orleans Tower, which, added to the earlier Mardis Gras Tower expansion, brought the resort's room count to 1,331.

The Showboat soon looked to do more than bulk up. Like its big sister in the Marina, the Showboat tried to emulate the success of the Borgata—in this case by skewing its entertainment to a younger demographic. A partnership with House of Blues gave the Boardwalk façade a new look in 2005, but the biggest changes were inside: the $69 million project included a themed casino area and a 2,380-seat concert hall. Eminem—about as far from Bob Hope and Al Hirt as can be imagined—kicked off the new venue with a July 9, 2005 concert, signaling the new direction for the Showboat.

The floor-level changes were just the start. In 2006, 22 suites in the Orleans Tower were re-themed to match the House of Blues ambience. With perks like butler service, the suites were geared towards the younger, more affluent crowd that had made the Borgata the city's top casino.

Yet the House of Blues wasn't enough to save the Showboat. Though it remained profitable, in August 2014 Caesars Entertainment (the renamed Harrah's) closed the Showboat, hoping that its shuttering would, in the words of CEO Gary Loveman, allow it to "stabilize [its] business in Atlantic City."

After its closure, the Showboat was purchased by Stockton University, which planned to operate part as a hotel and part as an adjunct campus. The planned reuse did not come about, though, and in September 2015 Bart Blatstein, the Philadelphia developer who had already turned The Pier into The Playground, announced that he had bought the property. As of this writing, his plans for the building are unknown.

Still, the Showboat was, for many years, one of Atlantic City's most profitable properties despite doing nearly everything differently from its competitors, and its success—though it didn't last forever—is a reminder that sometimes going against the grain is the best bet possible.

The Crown Jewel

Even before Resorts International opened in a converted Haddon Hall in May 1978, its owners wanted to build something big. The previous year, they announced plans to construct a $50 million, 1,000 room hotel adjacent to Resorts between Pennsylvania and Virginia avenues. Noted architect John Portman, whose Renaissance Center (Detroit) and Peachtree Center (Atlanta) became iconic additions to their cities, was tabbed to create a modern structure that would spark further development.

This ambitious plan was not realized; four years later, Resorts International hired Wynn architects Joel Bergman and Paul Steelman to masterplan its proposed development, now called the 1500 Project. Before returning to Wynn to work on his never-built Golden Nugget Marina hotel, the pair designed a large, adaptable casino hotel.

The enormous resort—more than twice the size of the average casino—needed a theme. A Venetian motif was considered, as was a Byzantine look. Architect Francis X. Dumont finally decided to model it after a marble mausoleum built in 17th century India by Mughal emperor Shah Jahan. The Taj Mahal was a curious inspiration for a casino, but its onion domes and minarets became Dumont's design signature.

Construction began in 1985. With the Showboat under construction next door, it seemed that the balance of power might soon shift to the far end of the Boardwalk. In fact, the Taj was the centerpiece of a larger "Fantacity" master plan, which was to transform the original Resorts, the Taj, the Showboat and a rebuilt Steel Pier into the world's largest hotel and convention center.

Although connecting bridges were built between the four properties, they never became more than the sum of their parts—a disappointment, since this kind of project might have set Atlantic City down a different path.

Crosby died in 1986 but the project continued, despite bigger questions about the future of Resorts. Slowed construction pushed costs from $185 million to an estimated $525 million. In 1987, Donald Trump made a bid for Resorts, not so much for its existing casino but for the Taj.

By October, Trump had received regulatory approval to open the Taj Mahal. He projected that the casino would cost $800 million to complete. In true Trump fashion, he turned an apparent 332 percent cost over-run into another superlative, bragging that this was "the largest and most expensive single building ever built." To get around the statutory limit of three casinos per owner, Trump proposed closing Resorts, converting it into convention space and operating both buildings as a single unit—an approach he later used with the former Atlantis/Playboy and Trump Plaza.

But in April 1988, a deal was struck that enabled Trump to acquire the Taj Mahal while keeping Resorts open. TV personality and real estate developer Merv Griffin agreed to buy Trump's Resorts stock and all outstanding shares, then sell the Taj back to Trump. In another savvy transaction, Trump paid less for the Taj than Resorts had invested in it, thanks in part to his reputation as a talented builder who could finish the project and bring additional foot traffic to Resorts.

Trump picked Mark Grossinger Etess, a fourth-generation hotelier, as the casino's president. Together with Trump CEO Stephen Hyde, Etess crafted a strategy to lure enough patrons to the Taj to meet its enormous overhead. With more than $220 million in debt service and payroll each year, the casino would have to be more profitable than any other. To underscore his faith in the project, Trump dubbed it "Trump Taj Mahal," with his name in giant red letters at the top of the tower.

But Trump and Atlantic City suffered a tragic loss on October 10, 1989, when a helicopter flying Hyde, Etess and Trump Plaza executive Jonathan Benenav from New York to Atlantic City crashed near Forked River. The crash robbed Trump of three of his most capable leaders. The casino's arena was named after Etess as a tribute to his leadership.

Finally, on April 2, 1990, the casino opened. At the launch, speculation about Trump's recent split with his wife Ivana and whether reputed paramour Marla Maples would show (she didn't) overshadowed the festivities.

Crowds booed the first speaker at the opening, recently indicted Atlantic City mayor James Usry. Finally Merv Griffin introduced Trump, who told the 10,000 assembled revelers that the casino was beyond his "wildest expectations."

Inside, gamblers ogled the pink and purple décor and threw fistfuls of money into the slot machines. Locals who didn't play came to sample the restaurants, including Rock 'n Rolls, a 1950s-themed diner, and the New Delhi Deli.

The hotel's 1,250 rooms included animal-themed hospitality suites (Zebra, Tiger, Lion, Giraffe, Camel and Elephant), in what was then New Jersey's tallest building. The penthouse suites, named for great historical figures with no obvious connection (King Tut, Napoleon, Da Vinci and Cleopatra) were reserved for the highest of the high rollers, though it was said that the 4,500-square-foot Alexander the Great suite could be rented for $10,000 a night.

At the opening, Trump prophesied that the Taj would revive Atlantic City's fortunes. Less than 15 months later, the Taj landed in bankruptcy, but the casino, like its master, would continue to make history on the Boardwalk. Later additions, including the Hard Rock Café and Casbah nightclub, kept the casino relevant as the city changed around it. In August 2008, the Chairman Tower—a long-awaited addition—brought 782 new rooms to the resort.

For many years Atlantic City's most successful casino, the Taj faced difficulties in the post-monopoly era. Even before the slowdown, the Taj was struggling, entering bankruptcy protection with the rest of Trump's casinos in 2005. The opening of the Chairman Tower did not reverse its fortunes, leading to a near-terminal decline.

In 2014, the Taj came near the brink of closure, but managed to hold on. The future does not look as bright for the Boardwalk's Mughal palace as it once did, but in a building named for one of the world's architectural marvels, anything is possible.

Happy Place

For more than a decade, The Borgata has been the top casino in Atlantic City by virtually any measure. While it, like other casinos, has struggled to adjust to the new realities of post-monopoly gaming, the Borgata has consistently led the market since its 2003 opening.

The Borgata started as part of Steve Wynn's vision for the H-Tract in the Marina District, which he conceived in 1995. Wynn intended to partner with Circus Circus Enterprises and Boyd Gaming to build three connected casinos although opposition to a $330 million highway connector to the development spearheaded by Donald Trump kept the project from proceeding for years. In 1997, an agreement was finally inked to move forward with the tunnel connector project which, Wynn insisted, was a precondition for breaking ground.

In 1998, though, Wynn dissolved the partnership with Circus and Boyd, opting to go it alone, before taking Boyd back as a partner. On July 14 of that year, Mirage and Boyd entered into a partnership that would see Boyd Gaming develop and operate The Borgata, which would be owned by Boyd and Mirage.

Atlantic City's Planning Board approved both The Borgata and the planned Mirage Resorts casino next door in March 2000. Steve Wynn, however, would no longer be building it; Mirage had been bought by MGM Grand, which ultimately decided to hold off on building, although it maintained its half-share of the Boyd project, on which ground was broken in September 2000. What had originally been a $750 million, 1,400 room hotel was now a $1 billion, 2,000 room resort.

Construction on the gold tower proceeded, and on July 3, 2003 The Borgata was ready to open. Actor Stephen Dorff threw the first roll at a craps table, officially opening the city's first new resort in 13 years.

Finished at a cost of $1.1 billion, the resort was a statement of new life for Atlantic City, which marked a quarter-century of legal casino gambling in 2003. Having survived waves of competition from Connecticut, Delaware, and further afield, Atlantic City was reinventing itself. The city had become a regional gambling center; but could it survive the loss of its monopoly? Something different was needed.

The Borgata was profoundly different. Its hotel tower—which was lit purple at night—stood 43 stories high, high above its rivals, though Harrah's would soon raise its own skyscraper addition. The hotel opened to some controversy; bucking a century of tradition, it did not stock Gideon Bibles in its guestroom nightstands, instead maintaining copies of the Bible and other religious scriptures in a lobby library.

With its 3,650 slots and 135 table games, The Borgata's casino had plenty to offer traditional gamblers. But the casino's architects wanted to push the envelope, drawing the younger, cooler crowd that had reinvigorated Las Vegas.

The new focus included both nightclubs (Mixx) and younger-skewing entertainment. Where other casinos were featuring Aretha Franklin, and Fabian, The Borgata offered Dave Chapelle, Sting, Pearl Jam, and Lenny Kravitz, among others. Its eleven restaurants (including a branch of New York's Old Homestead steakhouse and eateries from chefs Luke Palladino and Susanna Foo), Toccare spa, and 70,000 feet of convention space rounded out the resort. Even its cocktail waitresses were part of the act—named "Borgata babes," they wore mini-dress uniforms created by acclaimed designer Zac Posen.

From the start, The Borgata was an impressive earner; "go to your happy place," its advertisements said, and plenty of people did. In 2005, it became the top revenue-producing casino in Atlantic City, and it has remained there since. The newcomer also spurred a wave of expansion and reinvestment that included not only two new Harrah's towers but the Tropicana's 1,600-room Quarter addition, the Pier at Caesars, and, eventually, a tower expansion at the Trump Taj Mahal.

Nor was The Borgata standing pat. In 2004, it began a two-phase expansion. First, in 2006 it would add three high-end restaurants: Michael Mina's SEABLUE, Wolfgang Puck's American Grille, and Bobby Flay Steak, as well as a 36,120 square foot expansion of the casino floor. The casino addition made the Borgata a positive behemoth, with 4,100 slot machines, 200 table games, and an 85-table poker room.

The second phase was more ambitious, adding The Water Club, an 800-room "boutique-lifestyle hotel" connected to the Borgata's main building. The $400 million Water Club had, in addition to its rooms and suites, five heated pools (both indoor and outdoor) and the two-story Immersion spa, a complement to the existing Spa Toccare. It was a leap into an upscale future that the Borgata's first years indicated was coming.

The Water Club opened, after a small delay caused by a fire during construction, in June 2008. By that time, the optimism of The Borgata's initial success had faded; that fall, a slew of new projects would be delayed indefinitely or canceled, as new competition and the recession eroded both bottom lines and confidence. By 2009, the Water Club tower was closing its rooms during the middle of the week.

The Borgata, though, has been resilient, maintaining its place on top of the market through the continuing slowdown. The Atlantic City of 2015 isn't one that anyone would have envied in 2003, but without The Borgata, it would be an even less happy place.

Revel's False Dawn

The Borgata's opening brought new optimism to Atlantic City, and a steady increase in gaming revenues in the following years convinced several developers that the city's was primed for another wave of investment.

By 2009, three of the planned new resorts—MGM Grand, Pinnacle, and Atlantic Beach—had been canceled. One project soldiered on, however, its developers hopeful that a major investment—even in the midst of a decline—would spur new business. Revel fell far short of that goal, becoming a poster child for the post-monopoly struggles of Atlantic City.

Revel got its start in 2006 when Morgan Stanley, noting the rise in gaming revenue that followed The Borgata's opening, decided to dip its toe into Atlantic City by buying a large plot of land next to the Showboat. By the next year, it had formed the Revel Entertainment Group to develop and run the project. Led by former Trump executive Kevin DeSanctis, Revel aimed to out-Borgata The Borgata. To that end, the company chose Arquitectonica, a Miami-based firm, as architect for the ambitious project. Architectonica also designed the Cosmopolitan of Las Vegas, which opened in 2010 and, like Revel, based much of its appeal on non-gaming attractions.

In September 2007, Revel announced that its resort would feature two 1,900-room hotel towers standing 47 stories high—at 710 feet, the tallest buildings in Atlantic City, looking down on Harrah's Waterfront Tower and the Trump Taj Mahal's Chairman Tower, both still under construction. It was scheduled for opening in 2010.

Work on Revel began in earnest in early 2008, though Morgan Stanley had not lined up all of its financing. Confident that markets, then in the early stages of the credit crunch, would ease up, Revel continued construction, though in the summer of 2008 it announced that it would open with only a single 1,900-room tower.

Yet money proved hard to come by, and in January 2009 Revel laid off 400 construction workers, halting interior construction. The company hoped that, moving slowly, the casino would bide its time until markets eased sufficiently to allow it to get completely financed. Later in the year, it negotiated with the Export-Import Bank of China, even moving to bring aboard a Chinese government-owned construction company as a contractor. The loan did not happen, though, and through the winter of 2009 construction on the exterior continued.

By April 2010, Morgan Stanley was looking to cut its losses, writing off the $1.2 billion it had already invested in Revel and halting construction again. The resort still needed at least $1 billion more in investment. Strident opposition from union Unite Here over proposed tax breaks for the project did not help its chances of securing new funding. Morgan Stanley announced plans to sell Revel to anyone willing to take on the project.

It wasn't until February 2011 that Revel got a reprieve: Investment firm J.P. Morgan Chase lined up $1.1 billion in loans that, together with state tax rebates, would get construction completed and the casino open at last. Work on the interior of the property resumed, and a 2012 opening appeared within sight. Kevin DeSanctis remained the head of the group, steering the project he started toward completion.

At last, on April 2, 2012, Revel opened its doors. Its mirrored glass exterior, topped by a gigantic white ball, was a distinctive addition to the skyline. Revel had at its opening 1,898 guest rooms and a casino spanning 130,000 square feet with 2,439 slot machines and 97 table games. This gave it one of the city's larger floors. Breaking with the conventional casino wisdom, Revel's gaming floor was entirely smoke-free—a bold experiment in an industry where smoking and gambling typically go hand in hand. Revel executives hoped that the resort's ample non-gaming attractions—including the HQ nightclub, a burlesque club, and 12 restaurants—would make up for the lack of smoking, which was expected to keep many "serious" gamblers away. It didn't have a buffet, either.

A month later, Revel officially opened, with three performances by Beyoncé in its 5,000-seat Ovation Hall. With the HQ nightclub packed, the vision of Revel as Atlantic City's younger, hipper future seemed almost within reach. But the casino struggled, trailing most of the market. Superstorm Sandy's October trail of destruction did not help.

A series of new loans kept the casino afloat, but it was clear that it was nowhere near profitability. The other shoe dropped in March 2013, when DeSanctis resigned and Revel filed for bankruptcy protection. Former Mohegan Sun executive Jeffery Hartmann stepped in as CEO. Revel emerged from bankruptcy two months later. The casino earned a bit of notoriety in February 2014, when NFL player Ray Rice was captured on video knocking his girlfriend unconscious in a Revel elevator.

That was not a good omen for the property, which filed for bankruptcy again in June 2014. Unable to find a buyer, on September 2, 2014, Revel closed its doors.

Built at a cost of $2.4 billion and hung with the hopes of Atlantic City's reinvention, Revel lasted only 883 days. Potential buyers continued to surface after the closure—at one point, Brookfield Property Partners, owners of Las Vegas's Hard Rock Hotel and Casino, agreed to pay $110 million for the closed casino. That plan, however, fell apart because of concerns over contracts with Revel's energy provider, ACR Energy Partners.

After months of legal wrangling, Revel found a new owner: Florida developer Glenn Straub's Polo North. Straub announced plans to spend a half-billion dollars on other acquisitions in the city, promising to transform it into a family-friendly destination. He also promised a university for "geniuses" at Revel. The students, whom Straub told Reuters would ideally be "free, white, and over 21," would "cure the world of its hiccups."

As dealings between Polo North, Revel's tenants, and its energy provider collapsed into litigation, it appeared that a quick rebirth for the trouble property in any capacity was not likely. As of the summer of 2015, it is difficult to say exactly what will rise from the ruins of Revel. It remains one of Atlantic City's most tantalizing failures.

Roads Not Taken

With the legalization of casino gaming in November 1976, the floodgates of new development sent a deluge of planned new casino hotels over Absecon Island. Many of these proposed developments happened, and over the next 10 years a building boom brought investment and jobs to Atlantic City. But the projects that weren't built point the way towards a fascinating alternate future.

In 1979, it seemed like the marina might be the real future of Atlantic City casinos. Holiday Inn had already started work on a casino there, and Harrah's, MGM Grand, and Hilton proposed a nearby complex of three casinos. Harrah's pledged to build the world's largest casino, with 120,000 square feet of floor space, on a 10-acre bay-front plot. The resort would have featured 100 cars from Bill Harrah's immense automobile collection.

This would have put four casinos in the marina area, with three more projected in the near future. There was talk of a Boardwalk-Marina rivalry. The companies involved promised a "joint effort," capped by a section of boardwalk linking the marina casinos that would eclipse the century-old wooden way by the beach.

But this cluster was not to be. After the death of Bill Harrah, Holiday Inn acquired his Nevada casinos, stuck his name on its own under-construction marina casino, and tabled its other projects, which included the second marina casino. Though Harrah's would briefly stake a claim on the Boardwalk at Trump Plaza, the company never built anything of its own on the boards, though it ultimately acquired the Showboat, Bally's, and Caesars.

After Holiday Inn canceled the Harrah's casino, MGM and Hilton announced their plans to continue. The MGM Grand Atlantic City would have been a 2,100-room, 385-foot hotel tower next to the Hilton with its primary frontage on Absecon Inlet. Had it been built, it would have been the city's largest casino until the opening of Revel.

But that incarnation of the MGM Grand did not happen. Hilton pushed back the construction of their hotel, which they finally completed but, because of difficulties in getting a casino license, was sold to Donald Trump, becoming Trump's Castle.

Other projects also changed their names. Ramada planned to build a casino called the Phoenix, possibly in tribute to the city of their corporate headquarters, but settled on the Tropicana. Penthouse bought the Boardwalk Holiday Inn and the Four Seasons, which was located on Pacific Avenue, and erected the framework for a casino that would connect the two towers. Longtime residents might remember the hulking girders that, for years, were a reminder of the casino's failure. Eventually, the site was purchased by the adjacent Trump Plaza, who developed part of it as its East Tower.

The Penthouse wasn't the only notable failure. The owner of Las Vegas's Dunes planned a seaside version, but it was never built, though for years its incomplete skeleton was a constant reminder of a future that failed to materialize. After the Dunes' financing fell through, the property was sold at auction (Golden Nugget purchased it), and is now a parking lot.

Near the Dunes, Del Webb planned an East Coast version of its Las Vegas Sahara casino. It demolished the President Hotel, but never built anything, though the company retained architect Martin Stern, Jr. to design a casino for the site. After Del Webb sold the land to Golden Nugget in 1982, Stern apparently felt free to shop the design around. The Showboat looks remarkably like Stern's original Sahara design. If things had gone differently, the familiar stepped-back tower would have been found at the west, not east end of the Boardwalk.

Another Showboat curiosity: the casino's original name was "Ocean Showboat," which would have made the idea of a Mississippi River vessel in Atlantic City a little less confusing. Instead, the Showboat became "the Mardi Gras casino," although in its latter years its New Orleans theme became less prominent.

There were countless other projects: the Hi-Hotel would have replaced the Claridge completely, while the Benihana would have incorporated the Shelburne. Neither project came to pass: the Benihana was canceled, and Del Webb merely called the casino in the Claridge hotel, which was retained and slightly expanded, the Hi-Ho casino for a time.

Steve Wynn is responsible for two Atlantic City projects that remained on the drawing board. In the early 1983, he purchased 15 acres in the Marina District, on which he planned to build a larger, higher-end complement to his thriving Golden Nugget at Boston Avenue and the Boardwalk. In 1987, though, he cashed in his chips, selling the Golden Nugget after a series of frustrations with New Jersey gaming regulators. He retained the land near the marina, however, and eight years later announced his intentions to return to the island. He would build a megaresort, with the grand opening slated for 1998.

By 1997, Wynn's resort had emerged as Le Jardin, a $750 million splash of color in the grey Northeast. With enclosed gardens, high-end restaurants, and more than 2,000 hotel rooms, this would be an East Coast version of the ground-breaking Mirage. Legal opposition to infrastructure improvements and other issues eventually led Wynn to table Le Jardin, though the project ultimately yielded The Borgata.

When Atlantic City's fortunes appeared to be improving after the opening of The Borgata, a slew of new construction was announced, all of which, with the exception of the ill-fated Revel, came to nothing.

In 2006, Pinnacle Entertainment, a regional casino operator, purchased the Sands casino and surrounding properties, including the Madison House hotel and the former Traymore site. The company announced plans to build a $1.5 billion megaresort on the 18-acre plot. The casino, which Pinnacle intended to market to gamblers from Boston to Washington, DC, would be the company's flagship.

As the Atlantic City casino market deteriorated, Pinnacle slowed its development work. In October 2008, it indefinitely suspended the project. The land remained in limbo until, five years later, Pinnacle sold it for approximately $30 million to Boardwalk Piers, an investment group that promised to bring a family-friendly development to the site. As of summer 2015, nothing has materialized.

A company that had come close to building during Atlantic City's first casino boom also had grand plans. MGM Resorts announced that it would build a wholly owned $5 billion casino resort next to The Borgata. The complex would feature more than 3,000 guestrooms in three soaring hotel towers, the city's largest gaming floor (5,000 slot machines and 200 gaming tables, about double the average), a convention center, and 500,000 square feet of shopping. This was a true Vegas-sized development, larger than anything that even Steve Wynn had planned for the area.

Late in 2008, however, MGM announced that, in light of the dramatic slowdown of the Atlantic City market and the burgeoning recession, it was tabling its development plans. What would have been a true standout was never built.

Gateway LLC, a partnership between Curtis Bashaw and Wallace Barr, jumped into the fray as well. In 2007, it announced that it would build its own new resort on land it had assembled near Albany Avenue and the Boardwalk, including the former Sahara and Dunes sites and the land that once housed Atlantic City High School.

Construction on the project, which was to be named the Atlantic Beach Resort, was set to begin in 2009. At 832 feet, its 2000-room hotel tower would be the city's tallest structure by far. With a 200,000 square-foot casino, convention space, dining, and shopping, this was another Strip-sized proposal. It isn't surprising that the weakening economy put Atlantic Beach on ice in 2009.

These certainly aren't the only built gems in Atlantic City history—stretching back to the 1850s, there have always been developers whose reach exceeded their grasp—but they are a few of the more fanciful and influential. We will never know what might have been had they been realized. Would the Dunes, Sahara, Benihana, MGM Grand, and Penthouse have given Atlantic City a greater critical mass in the 1980s and propelled an earlier evolution away from strictly gaming, or would they have just crowded out other projects? If Steve Wynn had built his Marina megaresort in 1985, would the development that happened in Las Vegas in the 1990s been siphoned to the shore? If he had returned in 1998, would Le Jardin have left the city better prepared to deal with new competition?

The greatest what-if, though, might be the 2007 wave that fizzled. We now know that the Atlantic City casino market collapsed by nearly half in the years after four ambitious new resorts were announced. The one that made it to opening, Revel, did not help and may have hurt other casinos. But if the other three projects, representing perhaps $10 billion in new investment, had also gone forward, could that decline have been stemmed?

We'll never know, but we can always imagine.

Another Ebb Tide

The closing in September 2014 of three Atlantic City casinos—Revel, Showboat and Trump Plaza—was yet another reminder that nothing should be taken for granted in the casino business.

New Jersey voted in 1976 to permit casino gaming in Atlantic City on the assumption that it would become like Las Vegas, only better. The ways Garden State lawmakers sought to make good on that promise say a great deal about how elected officials approach life. Given a chance to create an industry from scratch, New Jersey chose to make it more strictly controlled, to prevent even a hint of organized crime influence. This meant not only an unprecedented role for state inspectors in daily operations, but statutory and regulatory mandates that constricted the city's casinos. In hindsight, none of this seems to have been good policy, and it should provide a cautionary tale.

Guidelines on how casinos handle cash are reasonable. Telling them what percentages of floor space can be allocated to slot machines versus table games, or what table limits must be offered, less so. Specifying that casinos must avoid large "Las Vegas-style" neon signage is, most would argue, going a bit overboard. It's amazing that casinos in Atlantic City ever did as well as they once did, given the massive overregulation they faced.

Atlantic City casinos prospered in those years because they were the only game not just in town, but in the entire eastern half of the country. Within five years of New Jersey voters approving gaming, nine hotel-casinos were in operation, drawing 19 million visitors to the formerly moribund seaside resort, employing 30,000 people, and pulling in more than $1 billion a year.

New development, new jobs and new money: That equals success, by any standard. But even as the happy days returned, Atlantic City's monopoly had an expiration date. Before the first Jersey casino opened its doors, Florida was considering entering the game. It ended up punting, but by 1990 Iowa, Illinois, South Dakota and Colorado had approved casino gaming, and tribal governments across the country were signing compacts governing the operation of casinos.

The start of tribal gaming in Connecticut in the early 1990s was the first harbinger of eventual ruin. It triggered a modest bout of regulatory reform for New Jersey: Casinos were permitted to remain open 24 hours a day, and allowed to offer poker, keno, race simulcasting and other "new" games. But efforts to legalize sports betting prior to the Professional and Amateur Sports Protection Act's 1992 passage failed, and Atlantic City lost what could have been a monopoly to this day: the right to offer straight-up legal sports wagering outside of Nevada.

Meanwhile, it was clear that states nearby weren't going to let New Jersey keep its casino bounty to itself. Predictably, the proliferation python circled tighter: Delaware, 1995; New York, 2004; and, the killing blow, Pennsylvania, 2006.

From the start, civic and business leaders had emphasized the importance of expanding "beyond just gambling" to keep Atlantic City viable as a tourist destination. But when billions of dollars were flowing through the city's slot machines each year, there was usually a more pressing need than costly reinvestments that might not pay off. Why add new attractions when slots were a sure route to riches? So, despite investments by some, Atlantic City's Boardwalk never got the total overhaul it needed.

It was a different story out west. Las Vegas and Atlantic City have had a curious history, sometimes touching but never quite in sync. Atlantic City was an established resort—the self-styled "Queen of the Coast"—that had just celebrated its semi-centennial when Las Vegas was founded by the Salt Lake, Los Angeles, and San Pedro Railroad in 1905. Fifty years after that, with air travel becoming more accessible and the lure of legal casino gambling more potent, Las Vegas helped to push Atlantic City from its pedestal as the World's Playground. It wasn't a main factor—South Florida and the Caribbean have that honor—but it certainly contributed.

By the 1970s, Atlantic City was looking enviously at Las Vegas. Legalizing casinos seemed to be the best way to spark new development. Las Vegas, for its part, looked askance at the newcomer. When it became clear that legalization would become a reality, Silver State casino owners, regulators, and politicians warned that casino gaming was a dangerous business that probably couldn't be successful elsewhere. Mockery turned to scorn which, for a while, turned to a real fear that Atlantic City would dethrone Las Vegas as the nation's gambling capital.

And you could argue that it did. In the early years, Atlantic City casinos were able to overcome a variety of administrative shackles to outshine the neon metropolis, and, outside of the Abscam investigation (which, in any event, centered on politicians rather than casino operators) had no major organized crime scandals. In 1982, four years after its first casino opened, Atlantic City surpassed the Las Vegas Strip when it came to gaming revenue. It would continue to do so until 1999, after 10 years of post-Mirage investment totaling several billion dollars. Las Vegas needed a great deal of help to wrest its crown back from Atlantic City.

Looking back, Atlantic City seems to have been doomed by its own success. The biggest constraints weren't limits set by the market, but undue regulatory meddling. And the most serious rivals weren't across the country or overseas—they were down the Boardwalk. With that mindset predominating, it isn't surprising that Atlantic City's casino industry grew and fell the way it did. A series of entirely logical decisions led, inexorably it seems, to decay.

How has Las Vegas avoided a similar fate? Two reasons: It has aggressively marketed itself, never letting the media or anyone else define its image; and its operators have consistently reinvested. This explains why the explosion of tribal gaming in California has not hurt the Strip: While you can gamble in Riverside County, there are still plenty of things to do in Las Vegas that you can't do there. Atlantic City's fate bears out the wisdom of both policies. Tourists and gamblers aren't sentimental, and they won't keep coming if there's nothing new to interest them.

Las Vegas isn't successful because it hit on that one hidden trick to popular appeal; it's popular because it's never stopped reinventing itself, hence the current shift to eating, drinking, and entertainment on the Strip.

Atlantic City, in its long history, has had many highs and lows. The city can reverse the current ebb tide by trying to renew itself again... and again.

Coming Back Again

S and in your shoes.
    That's a South Jerseyism for someone who has become or remained a local. There's no equivalent expression for a local who' has moved away, because, presumably, the attractions of the shore are such that, no matter how hard you hose down your feet, you never quite wash that fine silicate out. I've just arrived in Atlantic City after nearly two years without a visit. It's the longest I've ever been away from my hometown.

The Las Vegas I moved to in 2001 took pride in booming population figures, soaring gaming revenues and the onward-pushing growth of the 215 Beltway. The frontier was creeping up on the Spring Mountains. It might end, some thought, with a metropolis stretching from Primm to Pahrump. The city refused to look back. Sure, there was some nostalgia about the Rat Pack days, but that was more marketing than regret. The future wasn't a dream or a scheme; it was really happening to us. This is where the smart money played.

The Atlantic City I departed was on the other side of history: a city left for dead, one that maybe, someday, might come back. Like Las Vegas, it blew up its past; some of my earliest memories were the implosions of the grand Boardwalk hotels. But this wasn't replacing the Dunes with Bellagio. Old Atlantic City—the Traymore, the Marlborough-Blenheim, Million Dollar Pier—hadn't been improved upon; gold had been replaced with concrete and red neon, when anything was built at all. Unlike Las Vegas, you never could shake the sense that you were one or two generations from the golden age.

For me it's biography, not history. My grandfather was a metal worker who'd helped build Convention (now Boardwalk) Hall and smaller motels around the city. Not the big hotels; they'd all gone up before he'd gotten his union card in the 1930s. By the time I got to know him he'd retired, but I heard the stories about how, in the late 1960s, he'd leave the house at 3 a.m. to be at a jobsite in Delaware by 7. The local work was gone.

When I was too young to know any better, my father, a local journalist, was helping rebuild the city. An early proponent of casino legalization, he'd been active in putting together the coalition that won the second gaming referendum in 1976. Casinos delivered the jobs and money promised, but it wasn't enough.

So where does that leave me, coming back to the city I've never fully left? After 11 years, I'm a Vegas guy: This is where I've made a name for myself; this is where I'm raising my kids. But there's something in the cries of the seagulls, the smell of the salt air, that says this is still home.

It's a city that's on the ropes, but that's nothing new. It was on the ropes when my grandfather first started working, even if nobody admitted it. By the time the city hosted the 1964 Democratic National Convention, no one could deny it. My father's generation thought they'd bought the future with a few casino markers; a generation later, we're still waiting. Stretches of the city that were leveled for urban redevelopment before I was born still await construction (let that sink in for a minute); beachfront buildings remain boarded up. Four casinos have closed, and plenty of analysts think that there will be more. A better future seems like the longest of long shots.

The recession knocked Las Vegas to the canvas. The city took a knee while it struggled through a brief existential crisis, but a flood of money from Asia and hordes of new visitors from around the globe helped it move into the next phase of its appeal with few lasting scars. There's new confidence, but let's not delude ourselves: the bad times will be back at some point. Just because it's not part of the narrative that's currently popular doesn't mean that the cycle is broken. Is another decline as severe as the one Southern Nevada just weathered inevitable, if not in the near future than further out? Not necessarily, but it's the worst kind of hubris to assume that it's not possible. In fact, some kind of dip—even if it's not a disaster—is likely. Anyone who has watched a roulette wheel can tell you that.

The recent unpleasantness may have been bad for Las Vegas, but the same years knocked Atlantic City, it seems, out of the ring. It's still fighting, of course, but the odds are almost comically against it.

But the sand in our shoes tells us that nearly a decade of declining revenues and growing casino competition from Maine to DC doesn't mean the end. We might be on the ropes again, but this time we're going to come back. It's only a summer away, maybe two at most. After a while, you get used to taking more punches than you land. Just answering the bell becomes a little victory.

I've used to think that Atlantic City needed to learn more from Vegas, but now I see that Las Vegas can learn something from Atlantic City: the art of living on the ropes.

Note on Sources

Over the eight years that I originally wrote the articles that form the basis of this book (and over the past few weeks as I have revised them for publication and written new ones), I have used a great many sources.

Paramount among them are the Atlantic City Heritage Collections at the Atlantic City Public Library, which is an indispensable resource for anyone who wants to do serious historical research on Atlantic City. Among the collections I used were the: Atlantic City High School Collection; Atlantic City Free Public Library Oral History Project, "30 Years, 30 Voices"; Atlantic City Aero Club Scrapbook Collection, 1910-1912; Atlantic City Beach Patrol Collection; Atlantic City Centennial Celebration Scrapbook; Club Harlem Collection; Alfred M. Heston Papers; Dr. James R. Karmel Atlantic City Project Oral History Interviews, 2002-2006; Pop Lloyd Collection; Miss America Collection; Morris Guards Collection; and the Atlantic City Free Public Library Living History Project.

I also used a number of electronic resources at UNLV's Lied Library. Of particular use were several ProQuest databases, including: National Newspapers Expanded, ProQuest Historical Newspapers: Chicago Tribune; ProQuest Historical Newspapers: The Christian Science Monitor; ProQuest Historical Newspapers: Los Angeles Times; ProQuest Historical Newspapers: The New York Times; ProQuest Historical Newspapers: New York Tribune.

Sources for the development of the city's casinos include the above as well as: monthly and annual reports issued by the Casino Control Commission and Division of Gaming Enforcement of New Jersey; annual reports and SEC filings of publicly-traded companies that operate casinos in Atlantic City; several periodicals, including *Casino Journal, International Gaming and Wagering Business, Atlantic City Action, Win, Global Gaming Business,* and *Casino Connection*; and promotional and publicity materials for the casinos and their parent companies. In some cases, I supplemented available material by interviewing those who participated in or had personal knowledge of the events and topics I wrote about.

Many great books have been written about Atlantic City's history, and I used these as well; the following bibliography provides a list of the books that I consulted in researching and writing the material in this book.

Bibliography

Alcamo, John. *Atlantic City: Behind the Tables.* Grand Rapids, Michigan: Gollehon, 1991.

Brian Burrough. *Public Enemies: America's Greatest Crime Wave and the Birth of the FBI, 1933-34.* New York: Penguin Books, 2004.

Davis, Ed. *Atlantic City Diary: A Century of Memories, 1880-1985.* McKee City, New Jersey: Atlantic Sunrise Publishing Company, 1980.

Funnell, Charles E. *By the Beautiful Sea: The Rise and High Times of That Great American Resort, Atlantic City.* New York: Alfred A. Knopf, 1975.

Heston, Alfred M. Absegami: *Annals of Eyren Haven and Atlantic City, 1609-1904.* Volume 2. Camden: By the Author, 1904.

Johnson, Nelson. *Boardwalk Empire: The Birth, High Times and the Corruption of Atlantic City.* Medford, New Jersey: Plexus Publishing, 2002.

Karmel, James. *Gambling on the American Dream: Atlantic City and the Casino Era.* London: Pickering and Chatto, 2008.

Kent, Bill. *Atlantic City: America's Playground.* Encinitas, CA: Heritage Media Group, 1998.

LeVan, Russell George. *A History of the Morris Guards, Atlantic City, New Jersey.* Baltimore: Gateway Press, 1992.

Levi, Vicki Gold and Lee Eisenberg. *Atlantic City: 125 Years of Ocean Madness.* New York: Clarkson Potter, 1979.

Liebowitz, Steve. *Steel Pier, Atlantic City: Showplace of the Nation.* West Creek, New Jersey: Down the Shore Publishing, 2009.

McMahon, William *So Young...So Gay.* Atlantic City: Atlantic City Press, 1970.

Riverol, Armando. *Live from Atlantic City: The History of the Miss America Pageant Before, After, and in Spite of Television.* Bowling Green, Ohio: Bowling Green State University Popular Press, 1992.

Simon, Bryant. *Boardwalk of Dreams: Atlantic City and the Fate of Urban America.* New York: Oxford University Press, 2004.

Sternlieb, George. *The Atlantic City Gamble.* Cambridge, Massachusetts: Harvard University Press, 1983.

Van Meter, Jonathan. *The Last Good Time: Skinny D'Amato, the Notorious 500 Club, and the Rise and Fall of Atlantic City.* New York: Crown Publishers, 2003.

Index

Also by David G. Schwartz

Grandissimo
The First Emperor of Las Vegas

Roll the Bones
The History of Gambling | Casino Edition

Roll the Bones
The History of Gambling

Cutting the Wire
Gambling Prohibition and the Internet

Suburban Xanadu
The Casino Resort on the Las Vegas Strip and Beyond

As edtior

Frontiers in Chance
Gaming Research Across the Discipline

Gambling, Space and Time
Shifting Boundaries and Cultures
(with Pauliina Raento)

www.dgschwartz.com

About the Author

Dr. David G. Schwartz directs the Center for Gaming Research at the University of Nevada, Las Vegas, writes about gaming and hospitality for *Vegas Seven* magazine, and only occasionally pines for his days as Mr. Peanut on the Atlantic City Boardwalk.

An Atlantic City native and former casino employee, Schwartz has written books about the development of casinos (*Suburban Xanadu*), the Wire Act and Internet gaming (*Cutting the Wire*), gambling history (*Roll the Bones*), Las Vegas casino builder Jay Sarno (Grandissimo), and Atlantic City (*Boardwalk Playground*). His writing has won multiple Nevada Press Association awards. Schwartz was named the 2014 Trippies Las Vegas Person of the Year in recognition of his contributions to the study of gambling and Las Vegas—and perhaps his tasty artisanal nut butters. In his neighborhood, he is more widely appreciated for his macaroons.

Schwartz received his bachelor's and master's degrees (anthropology and history) from the University of Pennsylvania and his Ph.D. in United States History from the University of California, Los Angeles. In addition to his work at the Center for Gaming Research, he also teaches history at UNLV. He lives in Las Vegas with his wife Suni and their two kids, who prefer his homemade pizza.

Visit him online at: www.dgschwartz.com.

CPSIA information can be obtained
at www.ICGtesting.com
Printed in the USA
BVHW042148080519
547798BV00014B/192/P

9 780990 00162